Sandra Krapf
Public Childcare Provision and Fertility
Behavior

Sandra Krapf

Public Childcare Provision and Fertility Behavior
A Comparison of Sweden and Germany

Budrich UniPress Ltd.
Opladen • Berlin • Toronto 2014

A CIP catalogue record for this book is available from
Die Deutsche Bibliothek (The German Library)

© 2014 by Budrich UniPress Ltd. Opladen, Berlin & Toronto
www.budrich-unipress.eu
ISBN   978-3-86388-059-0

Die Deutsche Bibliothek – CIP-Einheitsaufnahme
Ein Titeldatensatz für die Publikation ist bei Der Deutschen Bibliothek erhältlich.

Gleichzeitig Dissertation an der Universität Rostock

Budrich UniPress Ltd.
Stauffenbergstr. 7. D-51379 Leverkusen Opladen, Germany

86 Delma Drive. Toronto, ON M8W 4P6 Canada
www.budrich-unipress.eu

Jacket illustration by Bettina Lehfeldt, Kleinmachnow – www.lehfeldtgraphic.de
Editing: Ulrike Weingärtner, Gründau, Germany
Typographical editing: Judith Henning, Hamburg, Germany,
www.buchfinken.com
Printed in Europe on acid-free paper by paper&tinta, Warsaw, Poland

Table of Contents

Acknowledgements

This research was the product of my work at the Max Planck Institute for Demographic Research (MPIDR). I am very much indebted to the MPIDR for a scholarship as a doctoral student. In particular, I would like to thank Professor Dr. Michaela Kreyenfeld for her constructive advice and supervision. Moreover, I am deeply grateful for the positive support of Professor Dr. Heike Trappe. In addition, I received many comments on my work in the doctoral colloquium of the Max Planck Institute, the lab meetings of the Laboratory of Population and Policy and the Laboratory of Economic and Social Demography. Further, I thank Dr. Sebastian Klüsener, Dr. Gerda Neyer, Dr. Ann-Zofie Duvander and Professor Dr. Peter Berger for helpful advice.

My years as doctoral student were very intensive – both concerning studying but also in terms of friendship. I thank Sabine Zinn for being there in good and bad times. She was always available for discussing both scientific and non-scientific issues. I thank Marie Carnein that she never got tired to support and motivate me especially during the last months before finishing my PhD. For scientific exchange and recreational activities, I am indebted to Alyson van Raalte, Tobias Vogt, Fanny Kluge, Silvia Rizzi, Francois Peglow, Giancarlo Camarda, Falk Ebinger, Anne-Kristin Kuhnt, Harald Wilkoszewski, und Kai Willführ. My special thanks go to my family, Ruben Apitz, Jamila Reichenberger and her kids who patiently accompanied me across the years – despite the large geographical distance.

1 Introduction

The social status of women has changed radically in recent decades, and this shift is sometimes referred to as a revolution (Gerson 1985; Goldin 2006; Esping-Andersen 2009). An important aspect of this phenomenon is the rise in female educational levels. An ever-growing number of women attain higher education, and in western countries today, more females than males earn a university degree (OECD 2011a). Along with this educational advancement, the share of women in paid employment has increased considerably. While the average female labor force participation rate in the EU 12 countries[1] was under 40 percent[2] in 1975, this share had increased to 65 percent by 1989 (Bernhardt 1993: 26). By 2012, these countries had an average female labor force participation among women between 25 and 49 years of more than 80 percent (Eurostat 2013a). The share of employed mothers has also risen over time in many European countries (Thévenon and Horko 2009), and this trend has affected women's work-life arrangements.

As time resources are limited, women have to balance the number of hours they devote to paid employment and the time they spend on other activities, such as household work or childcare. Traditionally, the care of children was a female responsibility. For many women, this meant that having a career and children were mutually exclusive, or that they had to sequence phases of work and care responsibilities over their life course (Goldin 1997). Women who want (or have) to work might postpone (or even forego) their entry into motherhood. However, in recent decades many advanced countries have developed institutions that make it easier for parents to combine childrearing and paid work. These work-family policies include measures related to maternal and parental leave, public childcare, and the workplace (Gornick and Meyers 2003; OECD 2007).

Several comparative analyses have found that the public provision of childcare for children under age three is the policy that has the greatest effect on mothers' labor force participation (Pettit and Hook 2005; De

---

1   EU12 countries include 12 countries that were members of the European Union in the period between 1986-1994, including Belgium, France, Italy, Luxemburg, the Netherlands, Germany, Denmark, Ireland, the UK, Greece, Portugal, and Spain.
2   Author's own calculation on the basis of the numbers provided by Bernhardt (1993). Numbers for West Germany only; Luxemburg not included.

Henau et al. 2010). The positive effect of public childcare availability on women's employment was also established in single-country studies based on regional variations in childcare provision (see, e.g., Gustafsson and Stafford 1992; Kreyenfeld and Hank 2000; Del Boca and Vuri 2007; Kornstad and Thoresen 2007).[3]

In recent decades, most western European welfare states have intensified their provision of public (or publicly subsidized) childcare. As part of the European Employment Strategy[4], non-family care has also appeared on the political agenda of the European Union (EU). In the Barcelona targets from 2002, it was explicitly stated that, by 2010, 90 percent of children between age three and the age of school entry, and one-third of children under age three, should be provided with childcare (European Council 2002). Moreover, a recent EU resolution recommends universal childcare provision in the member states (European Parliament 2011). Government initiatives to increase childcare provision are usually justified by two arguments (European Commission's Expert Group on Gender and Employment 2009). First, it is assumed that public childcare provision makes it easier to combine work and family, and thus supports mothers' employment.[5] Second, it is asserted that childcare is the first stage of public education, and that providing access to this form of preschool education reduces the social inequalities between children.

While it is not always explicitly formulated as a policy goal, childcare is sometimes seen by governments as a means of promoting fertility. This is based on the assumption that women take their prospects for remaining employed into account when deciding whether to have children. Publicly provided or subsidized childcare offers women the opportunity to combine work and raising children, as the care duties of mothers can be dele-

---

3   From a historic perspective, the direction of causality between public childcare provision and labor force participation is less clear. It was pointed out that in Norway, for instance, "the expansion of childcare services was much more a consequence of than a prerequisite for mothers' employment growth" (Ellingsæter and Gulbrandsen 2007: 658). This was also stated for other countries (Gerhard et al. 2003).
4   For a description of the European Employment Strategy, see Eurofound (2010).
5   This is of specific importance for single parents. Growing up in a single-parent family increases the risk of child poverty (OECD 2011b). The provision of affordable public childcare might enable single parents to work, and thus ensures a decent family income.

gated to non-family carers. By offering affordable and flexible childcare services, governments support working women. A woman might prefer to take only a short break from work after having a baby, either out of economic necessity or for career reasons. Thus, providing women with the option of returning to work soon after childbirth might reduce the anticipated negative effects of having a child on a woman's career. Based on this line of argumentation, researchers would expect to find that childcare services have a positive effect on childbearing (Rindfuss and Brewster 1996). On the contrary, the empirical results on the effects of childcare provision on fertility behavior are inconsistent. Some studies have shown that there is a positive effect (e.g., Rindfuss et al. 2007), others did not find a statistically significant relationship (e.g., Lappegård 2010), and still others even found a negative relationship (Ronsen 2004). In the literature, several methodological shortcomings, such as measurement problems, were identified that might produce incommensurable results (Gauthier 2007; Baizán 2009). However, there might also be some theoretical arguments that account for these differences.

In this study, the main research question is how childcare policies shape first birth decisions. Two intervening factors might interact with the effect of public childcare for very young children (i.e., children under age three). On the one hand, the overall institutional setting is relevant. A range of policies in addition to those directly related to childcare (e.g., labor market policies and public support for homemaking parents) shape behavior. On the other hand, it is important to consider whether women have positive attitudes toward external childcare and working mothers.

The institutional argument concerns the coherence of family policies; i.e., to what extent the policy package supports a single family arrangement (Neyer and Andersson 2008). Childcare provision for children under age three mainly targets dual-earner parents (Korpi 2000). But not all labor market or family policy measures in a country necessarily support families with two working parents, as some policies might favor families with a male breadwinner[6] and a female homemaker. This provides an alternative to the dual-earner family model, and some mothers might prefer to take advantage of the policy that offers them the opportunity to take care of their children at home. In an institutional context with mixed policies, there are also incentives for the non-use of childcare. Thus, the

6   For a discussion of the possible historical origins of the male breadwinner family, see Creighton (1996).

13

expected positive effect of childcare policies on fertility decisions might be reduced.

The attitudinal argument focuses on personal opinions concerning childcare and family arrangements. Some parents might have objections to using public childcare, especially for young children. Women may, for example, belief that care is best provided by mothers. Concerning child-care services, however, it is important that (potential) parents have a positive view of non-family childcare. If people think that public child-care for children under age three has negative effects on a child's development, they are unlikely to perceive the availability of non-family child-care as an incentive for childbearing.

The aim of this study

This research aims at analyzing the conditions under which the availability of public childcare affects the transition to a first birth. One question I seek to address is whether women who live in regions with higher levels of childcare provision are more likely to have a first child than those who live in regions with lower levels of childcare provision. Moreover, I am interested in the differing effects childcare might have according to a woman's socioeconomic status and her attitudes toward external child-care. In order to identify country-specific effects, I compare Germany and Sweden.

As a theoretical foundation for understanding the decision-making process of individuals who are thinking about having a first child, I employ the "Theory of Planned Behavior" (Fishbein and Ajzen 1975; Ajzen 1991). In this framework, human behavior is preceded by an individual's reasoned considerations of the effects expected from this behavior. The decision about whether to have a first child is based in part on a woman's positive or negative attitudes regarding entry into motherhood. The woman's attitudes might change over her life course, as the expected consequences of having a child will depend on her situation, including her partnership status, education, and level of career advancement. At the same time, contextual factors which may constrain or enable childbearing plans, such as the availability of public childcare, are also relevant for the childbearing decision.

In this study, I focus on the effects of childcare provision on the entry into motherhood. In the literature, it has been argued that childcare services might be of specific interest for women who already have children. In contrast to childless women, mothers already have experience with the double burden of family and work, and they know the childcare situation in their area (Andersson et al. 2004: 408; van Bavel and Rózanska-Putek 2010: 111). The availability of childcare services might therefore be more important for mothers who are considering having another child than for women who are thinking about starting a family. However, there are several reasons for focusing on first births. Having a first child changes a woman's life more dramatically than a higher-order birth (Hobcraft and Kiernan 1995). Given the sharp increase in work-family conflicts following a first birth, the postponement of the first birth is closely related to the trade-off between family and occupational career (Mills et al. 2011). Thus, the availability of public childcare, which can help new parents combine work and family, might be of specific interest for childless adults who are of childbearing age. This is also mirrored in the share of childless survey respondents that attach relevance to childcare policies for their childbearing decision (cf. Section 6.2.6).

Why focus on public childcare for children under three?

In this study, non-family childcare refers to public care arrangements provided for children under three years of age. This includes both public institutions and publicly financed care arrangements (including subsidized family daycare). The central feature of these arrangements is that parents have to pay a fee that amounts to only a small share of family income. Children in the under-three age group are of special interest. First, caring for young children is more demanding and more time-intensive than caring of older children (Ruhm 2011). Accordingly, incompatibility issues are most pressing for working parents with young children. Second, in many countries we observe an age-grading in policies and in social practices (Saraceno 1984). For example, in many European countries, care policies divide children into the age brackets "under one year", "one to two years", and "three years to school entry". While in most western European countries at least 80 percent of children between the age of three and the age of school entry are enrolled in some form of childcare, the enrollment rates of children under age three are usually considerably lower, with substantial national variations (see the data provided by Multilinks 2011). Obviously, providing care for children over age three is accepted as a state responsibility. In contrast, for children under age three, in many countries care is traditionally regarded as a family responsibility often provided by the mother. Accordingly, mothers are more likely to stay out of the labor market when their children are under age three (Matysiak and Steinmetz 2008; Thévenon and Horko 2009). Extensive leaves can, however, negatively affect career prospects (Aisenbrey et al. 2009), a problem that is often reflected in reduced wages among mothers (Budig and England 2001). The negative effects of childbearing on a woman's career are strongest in the early years of motherhood, when childcare is particularly intensive and is often provided by the mother herself.

The focus on public childcare neglects the potential importance of informal childcare provided by grandparents, other kin, friends, or neighbors. The availability of grandparental care in particular can support childbearing (Hank and Kreyenfeld 2003). Informal care is beyond the scope of this study, as I focus on publicly provided (or subsidized) childcare and attitudes toward this type of care.

Comparing Germany and Sweden

Scholars have increasingly attributed the national differences in individual behaviors to differences in institutions (Ellingsæter and Ronsen 1996; Brewster and Rindfuss 2000; Hoem 2008). For example, one strand of research that seeks to explain variations in fertility dynamics assumes that fertility is related to economic factors, such as female labor force participation (e.g., Ahn and Mira 2002; Budig 2003) or economic uncertainties (Adserà 2004; Kreyenfeld 2010). Institutional aspects, including family and employment policies, can condition these factors, and thus mitigate (or reinforce) perceived obstacles to having children (Castles 2003; Rindfuss et al. 2003; McDonald 2006; Neyer 2006). The empirical evidence on the relationship between institutional settings and childbearing is, however, ambiguous (Gauthier and Philipov 2008). One reason for the inconsistent findings might be that the studies focused on single policies. It might be more promising to investigate policy effects in light of the broader institutional context (McDonald 2002; Neyer 2003b; Neyer 2006; Hoem 2008). But the focus on a single country reduces the opportunities to find variations in institutional settings. Comparing policies and outcomes across countries offers the opportunity to identify national differences in policy effectiveness, providing valuable information for political actors. In this study, I compare Germany and Sweden.

Germany is a country with low fertility (TFR of 1.36 in 2011; Eurostat 2013b). Since World War II, governments in West Germany have largely supported male-breadwinner/female-homemaker families. But in recent years, providing childcare for children under age three has become a political priority. In 2007, a parental leave system similar to that of Sweden was introduced. Parents can take leave for 12 to 14 months with an earnings replacement of 65 to 67 percent. In the 1990s, a legal entitlement to childcare was granted to children ages three to six years. Since the mid-2000s, the childcare provision for children under age three has expanded considerably, and, since August 2013, children ages one year and older are legally entitled to childcare. As a result of these developments, Germany's family policy today offers a mix of dual-earner and male breadwinner support.

Compared to Germany, Sweden has a high fertility level: in 2011, the country had a TFR of 1.9 (Eurostat 2013b). Family policies mainly support dual-earner families. A main characteristic of Swedish family policies is the generous parental leave system (approximately 13 months with an earnings replacement of 80 to 90 percent). Moreover, childcare from ages one to 12 is universally provided; i.e., all children can use childcare services upon the request of their parents. The majority (71 percent in 2012) of children in the age group one to two years are enrolled in public childcare (SCB 2013). For the reforms in Germany, Sweden was explicitly cited as best practice example (Erler 2009; Ostner 2010). However, it is unclear whether transferring Swedish policies to Germany will encourage German women to have children.

Given the institutional differences between the two countries, investigating the effects of public childcare on fertility in Sweden and Germany might yield some insights into national differences in the opportunity structures of parents. Germany will serve as an example of a country with policies that target two family models, while Sweden will be representative of countries with policies that for years focused on the dual-earner model (Ferrarini and Duvander 2010: 2). Admittedly, the data used in the country comparison are insufficient to control for relevant confounding factors.[7] Nation-states differ not only in terms of their family policies, but also in other respects; for example, there might be normative differences that lead to varying fertility responses to childcare services across

---

7   See, e.g., Cook and Campbell (1979: 59ff.) for a general discussion of confounding factors and possible effects on causal inference.

countries. Because of the difficulties involved in ruling out such confounding factors, I refrain from drawing final conclusions about the causal relationship between institutional factors, normative aspects, and behavior.

Outline of this book

This study is structured as follows. The subsequent Chapter 2 is devoted to the theoretical framework on which the study is based. In a first step, I discuss welfare regime typologies and how they can serve as a starting point for investigating how childcare policies shape fertility. In a second step, I present economic and sociological arguments to explain how the availability of public childcare might affect individuals' childbearing behavior. In the third part of the theoretical chapter, I present a model of human action based on the Theory of Planned Behavior (Ajzen 1991). According to this theory, attitudes are a central factor in explanations of individual behavior. The theory also takes into account institutional factors. From this model, I derive a set of testable hypotheses.

Chapter 3 presents prior research results that are relevant for my research questions. The first part looks at the results of studies that investigated the relationship between childcare and fertility behavior. The second part discusses evidence on the varying effects of childcare provision in different countries. As there are only a few studies on childcare policies, I also present results from studies investigating the selective uptake of other policies as well. Part three summarizes findings from studies on the effect of attitudes on fertility.

In Chapter 4, I present the fertility development and institutional settings in Sweden and Germany. These countries follow different family policy strategies. Swedish policies mainly favor dual-earner families, with a parental leave and childcare system that strongly supports working parents. Germany, by contrast, has long been a conservative welfare state that supported male breadwinner families, although it is lately adding policy measures that favor dual-earners.

The next two chapters are devoted to empirical analyses. Chapter 5 presents an excursus on the questions of who makes use of childcare for two-year-old children, and of how usage patterns vary across countries. Using the harmonized European Union Survey on Income and Living Conditions (EU-SILC), I compare determinants of childcare usage for two-year-old children in Sweden and western Germany. This provides an insight into the social groups to whom childcare services are an attractive option after a child is born.

In Chapter 6, I compare the effect of regional childcare availability on individual fertility behavior in Germany and Sweden. Using separate datasets for each country, I also consider whether individual attitudes toward the family affect the transition to first motherhood. Based on multi-level methods, I analyze a German (*pairfam*) and a Swedish panel dataset (YAPS).

Chapter 7 presents the central findings and concludes.

2 Theoretical considerations

This chapter is devoted to discussing different theoretical mechanisms explaining how childcare might affect fertility. Central to all of the presented approaches is the prominent role played by female labor force participation: public childcare reduces the conflict between work (or education) and motherhood, and thus encourages women to have a(nother) child.

In Section 2.1, I discuss the approach that takes a macro-level perspective of the welfare state. In this research tradition, it is assumed that welfare policies offer specific opportunities that shape the behavior of individuals. Advocates of this perspective note that social policies support different family models, such as the dual-earner family or the male breadwinner family, and that public childcare services in particular support dual-earner families by enabling both mothers and fathers to participate in the labor market. With a focus on the macro-level, this approach does not include a behavioral model that explains individuals' childbearing decisions. In Section 2.2, some of these micro-level models are presented. The economic approach argues that affordable public childcare reduces the opportunity costs of childbearing (Section 2.2.1). Viewed from a sociological perspective (Section 2.2.2), childcare reduces an individual's role conflicts and gender inequality, and could thus stimulate fertility behavior. However, these approaches do not explicitly take into account the broader institutional context and the individual's attitudes when considering childcare effects.

Employing the Theory of Planned Behavior in Section 2.3, I suggest the integration of the arguments discussed above into a single framework. This allows me to take into consideration the interaction effect of public childcare provision with (a) attitudes toward career and lifestyle; and (b) context factors, such as other welfare state policies.

2.1 Welfare regimes, childcare, and fertility

Research on welfare regimes assumes that institutional factors shape female employment and fertility behavior (e.g., Sainsbury 1994; Esping-Andersen 2000; Neyer 2003a; Meulders and O'Dorchai 2007). Differences in both female labor force participation and fertility across countries is caused by varying opportunities and constraints set by national policies.

Working women who plan to have children usually face some degree of incompatibility between work and family life (Brewster and Rindfuss 2000). Since the start of industrialization, female labor force participation has increased considerably in many western countries (Jaumotte 2004). Despite this, childcare tasks have continued to be primarily the responsibility of women (Craig and Mullan 2010). But as most jobs do not allow parents to bring children to the work place, caring for children and working for pay compete for women's time (Moen 2003). This incompatibility might lead mothers to either exit the labor market (at least for the time when their children are young) or work reduced hours. Childless women might anticipate problems balancing work and family, and may therefore postpone childbearing.

According to Arts and Gelissen (2002), the identification of ideal types can serve as a first step to learning something about policy strategies. These so-called welfare regimes are identified on the basis of empirical phenotypes. Esping-Andersen's (1990) "Three Worlds of Welfare Capitalism" fueled a scientific debate resulting in a number of typologies to capture different dimensions of the welfare state. However, it was also criticized for misclassifying countries and for neglecting the gender dimension of welfare states. After discussing Esping-Andersen's model, I present a number of welfare regime typologies that consider the gender dimensions.

2.1.1 Esping-Andersen's three worlds of welfare capitalism

One important typology to categorize welfare states was suggested by Esping-Andersen. Emphasizing the degree to which a state protects individuals against social risks, Esping-Andersen (1990) identified three welfare regimes: liberal, social democratic, and the conservative regime. One major factor for the regime categorization is the social stratification observable in a state. The second central concept is de-commodification, which "occurs when a service is rendered as a matter of right, and when a person can maintain a livelihood without reliance on the market" (Esping-Andersen 1990: 21f.). In other words, de-commodification is the degree to which a person is independent of the labor market. It is high when the state offers a generous social insurance system, such as unemployment benefits, sickness insurance, and pensions. Countries with a low degree of de-commodification follow market principles and have only a marginal social net of benefits; social protection is tied to an individual's employment. In the typology, states that belong to the liberal welfare regime have only a residual welfare state; dependence on the market is strong and the degree of de-commodification is low. In the conservative model, in which the level of de-commodification is medium, social insurance mitigates social risks, but it is based on market work. In the social democratic regime, which has universalist benefits irrespective of prior earnings, the de-commodification level is highest (cf. Table 1).

A number of authors have argued that the categorization has to be revised, either because there were not enough categories to capture all of the welfare regimes, or because there were some countries that did not fit into any of the ideal types (see Arts and Gelissen 2002 for a review). With a focus on the standard male worker, the three regime types were criticized because of the neglect of gender differences and of the family within the welfare state (Lewis 1992; O'Connor 1993; Orloff 1993; Sainsbury 1996).

Esping-Andersen replied to the criticism of his welfare regimes by adding the family (or the household) to the state-market nexus. He incorporated the concept of de-familialization and familism, as was suggested by Orloff (1993) and McLaughlin and Glendinning (1994). De-familialization refers to the degree to which a welfare state provides policies "that lessen individuals' reliance on the family; that maximize individuals' command of economic resources independently of familial or conjugal reciprocities" (Esping-Andersen 2000: 45). At the other end of the spectrum, a familistic welfare state assigns the responsibility for the welfare of individuals to the family. The childcare system plays an important role in this context because it either binds care obligations to the family, or it supports households in "outsourcing" childcare to either market or state providers.

After taking into account de-familialization and familism in his analysis of welfare regimes, Esping-Andersen continued to defend his three regime types (ibid.: 85ff.). In the countries that have a conservative regime, families play a central role, as they are – according to the subsidiarity principle – the dominant locus of solidarity; the level of familism is therefore high. Although both the liberal and social democratic countries are categorized as non-familialist, the de-familialization mechanisms differ: in a liberal regime, individuals have to rely on the market as the welfare provision by the state is marginal. In a social democratic regime, the state provides welfare in a universalistic manner, i.e., childcare is available to all children starting at a specific age (see Table 1).

Table 1:   Welfare regimes based on Esping-Andersen's classification.

	Nordic countries	Continental Europe	Anglo-Saxon countries
type	Social democratic	Conservative	Liberal
country examples (Esping-Andersen 2000)	Sweden, Norway, Denmark, Fin-land	Germany, Italy, France, Austria, Belgium, Spain, Netherlands	USA; United Kingdom, Cana-da
de-commodification	high	medium	low
de-familialization	high	low	high
female labor force participation	high	low	medium
care provider	state	family	market
fertility	high	low	high

Source: author's summary based on Esping-Andersen (1990; 2000).

On the issue of fertility, Esping-Andersen pointed to the incompatibility of work and family for women, implying that a high degree of de-familialization lightens mothers' caregiving burdens (ibid.: 67ff.). This is the case in the social democratic and the liberal countries, where we also observe relatively high fertility levels. Accordingly, Esping-Andersen found low fertility levels in countries with strong familism; i.e., in the conservative countries. It is important to note, however, that the country categorization was debated. Especially in regard to public childcare pro-vision for young children, certain countries with traditionally medium to high enrollment rates and higher levels of fertility – e.g., France, Belgium, and the Netherlands – differ considerably from other countries with conservative welfare regimes (Bettio and Plantenga 2004).

2.1.2 Gendered welfare regimes

Esping-Andersen's concept of de-familialization focuses on the question of whether care provision is provided by the state, the family, or the market (Esping-Andersen 2000). In this context, each family was considered as a single entity, or one household. He disregarded differences in the roles women and men play within the family, thereby neglecting the possible gendered division of paid and unpaid labor in a couple. The reference to a male earner family is obsolete, he argued, as today this family type is no longer dominant, and is even "close to extinction" in some countries (ibid.: 51).

In contrast, the concept of the male breadwinner model has been used to capture the degree to which women, and especially mothers, are affected differently than men by welfare state policies (Meulders and O'Dorchai 2007). Based on the concept of the male breadwinner family – in which housework and care tasks are usually the responsibility of the woman while the man provides for the family – makes it possible to capture explicitly the importance of the gendered nature of family tasks in welfare state typologies. In this context, the provision of care services for children is an important aspect of welfare state institutions. In the following section, I review the welfare regime literature that focused on gendered family roles.

Family arrangements i.e., who participates in the labor market and who does care work in a family – have varied over time, and across countries and regions. The starting point for categorizing these arrangements is the "ideal of the bourgeois family form" (Lewis and Ostner 1994): the husband provides for the family income while the wife is responsible for household chores and childcare. This gendered division of labor used to start either after marriage, or, at the latest, after the first child was born. In the literature, this family arrangement was subsumed under different terms: e.g., the male breadwinner[8] model (Lewis 1992) or the family wage model (Fraser 1994).

Given the social developments in recent decades, particularly the strong increase in female labor force participation, the family system based on the male breadwinner model seems obsolete. Women have caught up to men in terms of their educational attainment, and now have

---

8   Creighton (1996) provides an extensive discussion of the possible historical origins of the male breadwinner model.

similar university enrollment rates (OECD 2011a). However, the degree to which the position of women in the family and in society has changed differs across countries, in terms of both cultural ideals and social policies (Pfau-Effinger 1999). To account for policy differences, Lewis and Ostner (1994) identified three ideal types: the strong, the moderate, and the weak male breadwinner state. According to this categorization, strong male breadwinner states, such as Great Britain and West Germany[9,] tend to assign legal entitlements to married women who are largely dependent on their husbands. Moderate male breadwinner states, such as France, have recognized that women have roles as wives, mothers, and workers. In weak male breadwinner states, such as Sweden, women are regarded predominantly as workers. In weak (and moderate) male breadwinner states, both female labor force participation and public childcare provision are widespread.

Other gendered welfare categorizations focus on different aspects of the position of women, such as gender equality or the penalty associated with motherhood and caregiving in general. Focusing on gender equality, Fraser (1994) developed the universal caregiver model, a theoretical ideal in which men and women have the opportunity to divide paid work and care work in an egalitarian way. Similarly, Sainsbury (1996) compared male breadwinner policies with policies supporting individuals. Yet another categorization was developed by Gornick and colleagues (1997). They generated an index based on observed differences in 14 countries, with an emphasis on the degree to which each state facilitated the participation of mothers in the labor market. Some authors attached importance to the question of who has the responsibility to care for children (and the elderly): the state, the family, or the market (e.g., Anttonen and Sipilä 1996; Haas 2003; Bettio and Plantenga 2004; De Henau et al. 2006; Misra et al. 2007).

McDonald (2000a) focused on gender equity, suggesting that countries vary in their fertility levels because they have different degrees of equality between the sexes. He argued that most developed countries have reached high levels of gender equity in non-familial institutions, including in the educational system and the labor market. But there are considerable differences in the level of gender equity within the family sphere. The occurrence of very low fertility is related to the increasing

---

9   Note that Lewis and Ostner (1994) referred to West German policies at the late 1980s and early 1990s.

gender equality in these non-familial institutions, but a lack of progress in achieving gender equality in the family sphere. Women in (post-) industrialized societies can participate in the labor market to the same extent as their male counterparts, but as soon as they have a child, this equality often comes to an end because care duties are still mainly assigned to women. After childbirth, women usually reduce their working hours (or stop working) in order to fulfill the family role. If a woman has a strong career orientation, she might forgo childbearing or have fewer children than she had originally intended because she is unwilling to cut back in her career. Policies that increase gender equality within the family should therefore have a positive effect on fertility (McDonald 2002: 441). Such policies reduce the work load of women within the family and encourage them to continue their participation in the labor market or in education. As having access to childcare enables both fathers and mothers to participate in the labor market, the provision of childcare services might have a positive effect on fertility. This is the case, for instance, in Sweden.

Figure 1:   Dimensions and family policy models.

		Dual-earner support	
		low	high
General family support	low	Market-oriented family policy model, e.g., UK	Dual-earner family policy model, e.g., Sweden
	high	Single breadwinner family policy model, e.g., WestGermany	Pluralistic family policy model, e.g., Finland

Source: adapted from Korpi (2000) and Ferrarini (2006).

A categorization that takes into consideration two dimensions of family policies was presented by Korpi (2000). He argued that family policies have class and gender specific effects. Two criteria of analysis are in the focus (Korpi 2000: 143 ff.): (a) general family support and (b) dual-earner support. General family support favors families with a single breadwinner and a female homemaker. In his study, the author specified three indicators that offer general family support: cash child allowances, family tax benefits, and public daycare services for somewhat older children, i.e., over age three. The higher the level of dual-earner support, the higher the degree to which women are able to shift care work to the paid sector and to participate in the labor market. The family policy dimensions that are related to dual-earner support are public daycare services for the youngest children (i.e., ages 0 to two), paid maternity leave, paid paternity leave, and public home help for the elderly. Korpi created a ranking of 18 countries that distinguishes between three ideal typical models of family policies: general family support (i.e., single breadwinner) policies, dual-earner support policies, and market-oriented policies. This typology was expanded by a fourth group offering "contradictory" (Ferrarini 2006) or "pluralistic" (Mischke 2011) family support; i.e., high levels of support for both single breadwinner and dual-earner families. The typology is schematically depicted in Figure 1. In countries scoring high in the dual-earner support dimension, childcare is usually available and affordable.

2.1.3   Coherent family policies

It has been argued in the literature (Hantrais 1994; Neyer 2003a; Thévenon 2011) that the coherence of family policies plays a crucial role when assessing their effects. In this context, policies are deemed coherent if they follow the same set of ideas or serve the same purpose (May et al. 2006). Family policies are coherent if they support a single family model (Neyer and Andersson 2008). In order to evaluate the degree of policy coherence, Korpi's categorization offers a valuable framework. As discussed above, the author distinguished two main family policy strategies: (a) general family support (which focuses on single breadwinner families) and (b) dual-earner support (with a focus on working parents). Countries differ in how far they coherently support strategy (a) or strategy (b).

In countries with coherent dual-earner support, women are encouraged to participate in the labor market[10], even when their children are young. A policy approach that offers public childcare services in conjunction with short periods of parental leave with high levels of earnings substitution favors dual-earner families, as this combination of incentives

10   Moreover, dual-earner policies encourage men to participate in childcare. But even in a country like Sweden, men still do less housework than women (Evertsson and Nermo 2007), and fathers take only a small share of parental leave compared to mothers (Duvander et al. 2010).

encourages mothers to re-enter the labor force soon after childbirth (Lewis 2001). After the parental leave period, homemakers receive only a small flat-rate benefit or no benefit at all. Another policy that favors dual earners is a system of equal taxation, in which a person's earnings are considered individually. This increases the independence of each partner and also encourages female labor force participation (Dingeldey 2001). With a generous public (or publicly subsidized) childcare system for children under age three, the difficulties women face in balancing family and work responsibilities are minor. Moreover, in an ideal dual-earner society, parents receive no benefits to reduce the (direct) costs of having children (Kaufmann 2002: 449), as such policies could be perceived as supporting homemakers, and would thus interfere with the aim of supporting working parents.

In contrast, countries that coherently support male breadwinner families offer incentives for women to stay out of the job market after childbirth. Mothers are encouraged to take long (unpaid or flat-rate) parental leave (Gornick et al. 1997). Moreover, the joint taxation of spouses favors a single (usually male) earner (Gustafsson and Bruyn-Hundt 1991; Dingeldey 2001). In male breadwinner societies, only a limited number of places in public childcare for children under age three are offered. Thus, rates of employment among mothers are lower than in dual-earner societies, especially when children are young.

The dual-earner and the male breadwinner models are two ideal types. However, in some countries, family policies do not primarily support one of the two family models, but have some elements that favor both. This "pluralistic" family support (Mischke 2011) may result in diverse family arrangements. Sometimes policies compete with each other; e.g., in some countries parents receive a home care allowance only if they do not use public childcare. In other words, parents have to choose which type of policy they want to take advantage of. Some scholars have argued that it is difficult to identify the effect of family policies when the overall policy approach is incoherent (Lewis 2001; Neyer 2003a; Thévenon 2011). For example, if a country offers two policies designed to encourage fertility, one aimed at dual-earner and the other at male breadwinner families, the effects of the two measures will interfere with each other. In such a setting, it is difficult to disentangle the individual effects of each policy.

2.1.4 The opportunities and the limits of welfare regime typologies as analytical tools

Institutions play a central role in demographic behavior (Blossfeld 1995; de Bruijn 1999; Liefbroer and Corijn 1999; Meulders and O'Dorchai 2007). Welfare regime typologies are an important heuristic that helps us understand how policies shape behavior. It is usually difficult to compare the effects of many institutional characteristics in only a limited number of countries. In this context, typologies offer a description of policy systems and make it possible to control for a range of explanatory factors (Ferrarini 2006): instead of controlling for child benefits, parental leave regulations, and childcare services; the family policy package is subsumed in a policy regime. In this reductionist approach, ideal types of welfare regimes can serve as tools for analyzing both policies and family arrangements in a society.

Welfare regimes do not necessarily focus on the explanation of fertility differences between countries. However, they allow for a formulation of hypotheses on the relationship between welfare state characteristics and family behavior. Both Esping-Andersen (2000: 67-70) and McDonald (2000a; 2000b) observed that fertility is low when women find it difficult to balance their responsibilities at home with the demands of work. Similarly, gendered welfare regimes suggest that, in advanced countries in which women's labor force participation is the norm, policies that enable women to combine having a job and a family encourage women to have children. As public childcare for children under age three supports working mothers, it may be anticipated that childcare services are positively related to fertility in a country.

The regime approach and its analytical value have been criticized. Using typologies to understand causal relationships often means explaining the constituent parts of a phenomenon on the basis of the phenomenon itself (Ferrarini 2006). To give an example based on Esping-Andersen's (2000) typology, it seems unpromising to try to explain a high level of female labor force participation by citing the institutional aspects of a social democratic regime, since a high level of female labor force participation is an intrinsic feature of social democratic welfare states.

A major limitation of the regime approach is related to the assumption that societal phenomena are based on the actions of individuals (Coleman 1986), as welfare regime typologies do not include an explicit model to explain individuals' behavior. Despite the macro-level hypotheses based on welfare regimes, it remains unclear how different family policies account for childbearing behavior on the micro level. The regime approach largely ignores personal situations, characteristics, and decision-making processes. Thus, the idea that the behavior of individuals is determined primarily by welfare regimes seems unconvincing (Huinink and Konietzka 2007: 123).

2.2 Childcare services and fertility behavior on the micro level

The use of welfare state typologies makes it possible to compare countries' fertility levels, childcare provision rates, and labor market policies supporting working mothers. However, one shortcoming of the regime perspective is that it does not offer a theoretical framework for explaining individual action. The remainder of this chapter is dedicated to the discussion of theoretical arguments on the micro level. First, I present the economic view on fertility and how reproductive decisions could be affected by public childcare provision. Second, I discuss sociological arguments to explain childcare effects on fertility behavior. Finally, I look at the Theory of Planned Behavior, focusing on the extent to which (a) other institutions and (b) the attitudes of potential mothers affect the relationship between public childcare and entry into motherhood.

2.2.1 The economic view: direct and indirect costs of children

The neo-classical economic view on fertility was established in the "New Home Economics" developed by Becker (e.g., 1965; 1981) and Mincer (e.g., 1962) in the 1960s (for a review see Grossbard-Shechtman 2001). This school of thought transferred the microeconomic theory originally applied to the business context to the sphere of behavior within families. The main assumptions of this theory are that individuals act rationally and that preferences are stable and homogenous. The basic rationale for decision-making concerning childbearing is utility maximization for the household. In the following, I describe the simple economic model of the family. I then discuss the model extension that explicitly accounts for purchased childcare.

The neo-classical economic model of the family

According to the neo-classical model (Becker 1981), family arrangements in which the wife specializes in homemaking (home production) and the husband specializes in paid work (market production) often have the highest welfare returns. This claim is based on the assumption that women's wages are lower than men's. As childcare is seen as a purely female task, men's labor force participation is not the focus. Paid childcare services are not explicitly considered in this model, thus the labor force participation of women and having a young child are seen as mutually exclusive. Accordingly, the increasing labor force participation of married women is related to a decline in fertility (Becker 1981: 237ff.).

In the microeconomic framework, children are regarded as consumer goods; the demand for children thus depends on the household income and the parents' preferences. On the one hand, children produce direct costs. On the other hand, these costs depend on the quality of children, which refers to the resources parents are willing to invest in each child (Willis 1973). It has been argued that, as their income increases, parents invest more in their children's quality: i.e., education, health, etc. As this increases the price of each child, the quantity of children decreases.

Moreover, because female labor force participation has risen substantially, women also incur *indirect* (or *opportunity*) *costs* when they have children. These costs are the time parents devote to childrearing that they could have otherwise used for paid work or other activities (Mincer 1963). Opportunity costs arise from forgone earnings (Joshi 1998) and lower future wages (Budig and England 2001). The higher a woman's wages, the higher the forgone actual and future earnings. Thus, having high earnings is related to increased opportunity costs of providing childcare and thus lower fertility (known as the *substitution effect*; see Blau et al. (2002: 97ff.)). Since more highly educated women generally have higher wages, they usually face higher opportunity costs than women with lower levels of education (Schultz 1969). Anticipating career interruptions, women might select themselves into jobs in which taking breaks would have less effect on their human capital (Polachek 1981). Those who are planning to have several children might choose a job requiring a low skill level, which would result in lower opportunity costs of having children. If this is the case, then women's fertility is negatively related to women's labor force participation, wages, and education.

These considerations refer to the relationship between childcare services and the number of children. The economic theory also allows us to take a life course perspective. Individuals' situations concerning income, prices, and preferences might change with age, affecting the timing of fertility demand (without necessarily changing lifetime fertility; Hotz et al. 1997: 309). Highly educated and career-oriented women in particular postpone first births (Gustafsson 2001). Attaining a higher level of education takes longer than completing a lower level of education. Thus, highly educated women enter the labor market later. Because a woman's income is usually limited while she is enrolled in education, she may postpone having children to later ages for financial reasons. However, it can also be argued that a career-oriented woman may postpone motherhood to a point in time when she feels more established in a career path, and when taking a baby break may be less harmful to her career (Kreyenfeld 2000). Therefore, it is profitable for the woman to remain in the labor market for some time after finishing her education, which leads to a postponement of having a first child.

Purchased childcare and fertility

The basic neo-classical model does not explicitly account for the option to reduce opportunity costs by shifting maternal childcare duties to a third person. Several authors have incorporated non-maternal childcare into a formal model of labor force participation (Heckman 1974; Blau and Robins 1988; Connelly 1992; Gustafsson and Stafford 1992; Leibowitz 1994; Blau 2001).

This model suggests that mothers with young children decide whether to participate in the labor market depending on their potential wages and childcare costs.[11] In contrast to the basic economic model, which as-

---

11 Beyond childcare prices, the quality of childcare might affect a woman's decision to use it. This is based on the assumption that mothers prefer high-quality childcare to lower-quality childcare (Blau 2001: 50). The higher the quality, the more mothers make use of purchased childcare, the model predicts. Empirically, however, the effects of childcare quality on childcare usage and maternal labor force participation are difficult to detect (see Breunig et al. 2011 for a review). Governments can improve quality by introducing minimum standards concerning group size, child-staff ratios, and educational requirements for carers. This view neglects the possibility that mothers may feel strong moral obligations to care for their children themselves; i.e., that paid care may be seen as an unacceptable substitute for maternal care, regardless of the quality of non-family childcare.

sumes that all mothers stop working after childbirth, non-maternal child-care options offer women the possibility of participating in the labor market while still having a family. An increase in the household income might also increase the demand for children (*income effect*; cf. Blau et al. (2002: 100ff.)). Mothers allocate their time to either work, childcare, or leisure. In the model, each hour in the labor market requires an hour of external childcare (Blau 2001). Childcare might be provided at different cost levels, as family members or friends might take care of the child for free, while formal providers usually charge fees.

Similarly, Ermisch (1989; 2003) explicitly included childcare costs in a model of fertility. This model considers only paid forms of childcare. Childcare fees can be conceptualized as a reduction of maternal wages because working women have to pay for childcare (*negative wage effect of childcare*). However, the model does not offer clear hypotheses concerning childbearing behavior (Blau and Robins 1989). On the one hand, child-care enables women to participate in the labor market, thereby reducing the anticipated opportunity costs of having children. This would imply that there is a positive relationship between external childcare and childbearing. On the other hand, childcare fees can be regarded as additional cost of having children, and would therefore be negatively related to childbearing.

This means that women may base their decision about whether to have a child on childcare fees and her hourly wages (Ermisch 1989). If the childcare costs are high, women with low wages would not purchase childcare. In this situation, an increase in wages would encourage women to work and reduce their family size. In contrast, a woman in a higher income group might be able to afford care services. Reducing opportunity costs, this might have a positive effect on fertility. Low childcare fees might also have a stimulating effect on childbearing.

In countries where childcare is either a publicly provided or a subsidized service, parents pay reduced prices. Depending on the legal context, childcare fees may amount only to a small share of household income, or the services might even be provided for free. In this setting, the negative wage effect of childcare costs is less relevant, while the opportunity costs of having children decrease. Women who use public child-care and return to their job (or education, or job search) soon after childbirth face only minor reductions in lifetime earnings. In this situation, the availability of childcare institutions is expected to be unambiguously positive. Childcare might also reduce the postponement of the first birth. As childcare services enable a woman to return to her job or education soon after childbirth, her career break can be short (Kravdal 1996). This might encourage childbearing at younger ages, possibly even before a woman has completed her education.

2.2.2 The sociological view: role compatibility and gender equality

The economic view offers a theory for understanding fertility decisions based on the assumption that potential parents rationally evaluate the financial aspects of childbearing. However, some scholars have argued that family behavior is a multi-dimensional decision affected by cultural factors, as well as by an individual's preferences and socialization (Rindfuss and Brewster 1996; Letablier et al. 2009). Identifying two mechanisms, I explore the sociological perspective in the following sub-sections. First, I argue that childcare could positively affect individual childbearing behavior by reducing work-family conflicts. A second mechanism is related to the reduction of gender inequality.

Reduction of role incompatibility

Public childcare provision might reduce work-family conflict. Based on role theory (for reviews, see, e.g., Biddle 1986; and Turner 2003), an adult individual has various social roles in specific contexts, such as work, parenthood, and partnership. Within each context, a person has a specific status – e.g., as a manager, a parent, or a spouse – and each status defines a set of rights and duties (Linton 1936). The activities through which these rights and duties come into effect constitute the specific role. Roles are dynamic and are the result of negotiations between each individual and those with whom she interacts (Goffman 1959). The expectation that the individual will fulfill the obligations of a given role or set of roles can be a normative requirement in society, and non-conformity may result in sanctions (Moscovici 1985). Today, most individuals have to fulfill the demands of multiple social roles. As these roles are bargained in social interactions, they can vary over time, societies, and social groups.

Since the social behaviors of men and women differ, an individual's gender is a relevant factor that determines a person's roles (Eagly and Wood 1999). Within the family, mothers and wives have traditionally been responsible for household chores and caregiving, while fathers and husbands have been responsible for providing the family income (Parsons 1959). It was argued in the past that this gender-segregated division of labor is essential to the functioning of the family (Parsons 1959: 261). In contrast, in recent decades, (post-)industrial societies have changed: for example, in the OECD countries the employment rates of men and women have converged (Jaumotte 2004). Gender role attitudes have also become less traditional in many societies (Scott 2006). At the same time, childcare has remained a predominantly female task (Craig and Mullan 2010).

Individuals strive to meet the expectations associated with their various roles imposed by themselves and others. However, meeting expectations in one domain may collide with the role requirements in a second domain, causing role strain. Role nonconformity may have negative effects on the individual's physical and mental health (Frone et al. 1997; Grzywacz and Bass 2003; Kotowska et al. 2010). In the context of families, working women may face strain because they have to fill the competing role obligations of being a mother and an employee (Greenhaus and Beutell 1985).

In his Theory of Role Strain, Goode (1960) identified various options for how a person can reduce role strain. A radical reaction is the elimination of a role; i.e., a person withdraws from the position that causes strain. In the context of fertility, a woman facing a situation of heavy role strain could, for example, exit the labor market in order to fully commit herself to the maternal role. Another option is to escape (anticipated) role strain by not having children. Another option is to organize roles into a hierarchy, neglecting those obligations that are considered to be less relevant. Yet another option is to delegate the tasks that produce role strain.

According to Goode's role strain theory, childcare services offer women[12] the opportunity to delegate their childcare duties. Before starting a family, working women anticipate the role strain they will face after childbirth. Having a (first) child means that women have to also fulfill the demands of the mother role. As most jobs do not allow employees to simultaneously work and take care of children, women think about how

---

12 Men can also face conflicts between their worker role and father role. This usually concerns the societal acceptance of caring fathers. As public childcare services do not directly affect fathering norms, the role conflict among men is less important when seeking to understand the effects of childcare on the childbearing decisions of potential parents.

they will reduce future difficulties after the baby is born. Role elimination reduces role conflict, and could mean either (a) exiting (at least temporarily) the labor market to fill the maternal role, or (b) reduced childbearing in order to better meet the demands of the job. When the goal is to combine family and work roles, delegating childcare duties reduces role overload, as a mother "gains" free time to dedicate to work (or other activities). If a woman is unable or unwilling to stop working, she may decide not to have a child, or the availability of non-maternal childcare could offer her a solution to this anticipated role incompatibility. In this situation, public childcare services may have a positive effect on a woman's fertility decision.

Reduction of gender inequality

Related to role incompatibility, although less explicitly discussed in the literature, is the question of whether childcare might positively affect fertility by reducing gender inequality. While the argument of role incompatibility identified a structural problem of childrearing, childcare services could also support an ideological change of gender roles.

Childbirth usually affects mothers' and fathers' lives in different ways. On the one hand, the time men devote to childcare and housework has increased over recent years (Sayer 2005; Hook 2006). On the other hand, women still commit more time to household duties and have less leisure time than men (Cooke 2006). This has been referred to as the "second shift" (Hochschild 1989). Especially after childbirth, the time use of parents diverges (Sanchez and Thomson 1997; Baxter et al. 2008). Women often exit the labor market or reduce their working hours in order to care for their child for at least some period of time (Hynes and Clarkberg 2005).

There might be several reasons why the anticipated gendered division between paid and unpaid work after childbirth might hamper fertility plans. On the one hand, individuals who exit the labor market are disadvantaged compared to those who work, as they give up their economic autonomy, and their entitlement to social insurance, which is usually tied to labor force participation, is reduced (Korpi 2000). The parent who stops working after childbirth – usually the mother – has to be willing to accept these disadvantages. Second, in addition to these negative economic consequences of homemaking, childcare and housework are socially less rewarded than paid work (Folbre 1997). From a functionalist perspective, the economic provision of the family by the male breadwinner is traditionally rated as more important than childrearing (ibid.: 649). Anticipating this unequal and gendered division of labor, women might be unwilling to reduce their personal and economic independence in order to have a child. This concern might be stronger among highly educated women, as their gender role attitudes are more egalitarian than those of women with lower levels of education (Alwin et al. 1992; McDonald 2000a; Corrigall and Konrad 2007).

Different policies might reduce gender inequality, and thus stimulate fertility (Neyer and Rieck 2009). Governments can ease the unequal strain on mothers by providing childcare. Although the provision of these services does not necessarily affect the division of childcare and household chores within a couple, it lessens women's childcare burdens. The "gained" hours might help to bring into balance the number of hours the parents spend caring for the child and the number of hours they spend in paid work. From this perspective, childcare services support a work arrangement that is likely to be preferred by women with egalitarian attitudes. For this group, the availability of childcare might stimulate childbearing.

2.2.3 The opportunities and the limits of micro-level approaches

According to the micro-level theories discussed above, childcare provision has a positive effect on childbearing. In contrast to the welfare regime perspective (see Chapter 2.1), both the economic and the sociological approaches consider the childbearing decision on the individual level. The availability of public childcare can affect an individual's situation, and might thus influence individual childbearing. However, both theories leave some room for criticism and alternative explanations.

The economic theory of fertility has been criticized in the literature (see de Bruijn 1999: 56ff. for a review). Overall, the assumption that people engage in a rational cost-benefit analysis when deciding whether to have children seems to be too simplistic to explain the decision-making process of childbearing, which also involves emotional, social, and cultural considerations (Burkart 1994: 73ff.). Thus, the assumption that a potential parent is a rational, utility-maximizing actor was criticized. Some scholars argued that it is unrealistic to assume that actors have access to all of the information necessary to make a perfect choice.

In order to account for the imperfect information on which individuals base their decisions, the concept of bounded rationality was introduced (Pollak and Watkins 1993: 476). Moreover, economic theory assumes that preferences, which are the basis of utilities, are stable over the life course and are homogenous across social groups. This seems to be inappropriate, as preferences change with all kinds of socio-demographic characteristics, such as age, parity, career stage, norms, institutional factors, and tastes (Bagozzi and van Loom 1978; Blossfeld 1996; Matysiak 2011: 55ff.).

The sociological approach of role conflict assumes that roles may change over time and may differ across social groups. It further posits that women not only try to meet their own expectations, but also act as part of society, taking into consideration the expectations of their partner, their parents, and their peers. Greenhaus and Beutell (1985: 82ff.) argued that there are some shortcomings in the role conflict approach. They suggested that the degree to which a person experiences strain from conflicting work and family roles depends on several factors. For example, individuals may differ in the salience they attach to each role; i.e., in their attitudes toward the work sphere and the family sphere. In addition, the person's career stage can determine the perceived role strain. Greenhaus and Beutell (1985) observed that work role requirements might be more demanding at the beginning of a woman's career, and the (anticipated) strain might therefore be greater. Moreover, within the framework of role strain theory, childcare can help to reduce structural strain arising from limited resources, such as time. However, the woman might also experience a conflict in terms of her role obligations (cf. Goode 1960: 485). For example, a "good employee" may be required to work long hours, while a "good mother" spends as much time as possible with her child. In this normative setting, childcare services help to increase the working hours. On the other side, the use of childcare reduces the amount of time the woman spends with her child, and may lower her perceived performance as a mother because she spends less time on maternal care. The role requirements can be determined by social norms, but also by personal attitudes. If the role obligation for mothers is perceived to be strong, public childcare might have a limited effect on childbearing.

Both the economic and the sociological perspectives on the relationship between fertility and maternal employment allow for the incorporation of the influence of childcare. However, they do not explicitly take into account circumstances in which potential mothers might ignore the option of using childcare services in their childbearing decisions. For example, other institutional factors might change the opportunity structure for parents by creating incentives for homemaking. Such policy alternatives might be relevant when the goal is to determine the effects of public childcare on fertility behavior (Neyer and Andersson 2008).

2.3 Integrating fertility determinants and childcare policies: the Theory of Planned Behavior

The welfare state approach and the economic and sociological perspectives discussed in Sections 2.1 and 2.2 led to the formulation of the hypothesis that affordable public childcare provision positively affects fertility behavior. However, the effect of childcare policies on fertility may depend on a number of intervening factors. In this study, I argue that two factors are of particular interest: (1) the belief among individuals that public childcare for very young children is appropriate care, and (2) other welfare state policies that support male breadwinner families.

Individuals might differ in terms of their "ideals of care", i.e., in terms of the forms of care they consider to be acceptable for very young children (Kremer 2007: 21). The level of acceptance of public childcare refers to the degree to which a person considers public childcare to be appropriate for very young children. This might vary over generations and social groups. Particularly in countries where childcare for children under age three does not have a long tradition, potential parents might have the attitude that maternal childcare is better for the development of the child. For them, using formal childcare is not an option, and thus the childbearing decision remains unaffected.

Policy coherence addresses the extent to which childcare policies fit with other family policy instruments (Neyer and Andersson 2008: 702). Other policies might interact with childcare policies. When other instruments pursue different goals, they interfere with the possible effects of childcare on fertility. Policies that support male breadwinner families may therefore conflict with policies that support working parents, such as childcare provision. For example, joint taxation might create incentives for mothers to stay home and refrain from using childcare services. This could undermine the positive effect of childcare provision on fertility.

In order to comprehensively explore childcare effects, it is necessary to integrate attitudes and institutional aspects into a model of the individual-level fertility behavior of women. A number of social psychological theoretical frameworks pay special attention to attitudinal aspects. The approach offered by Miller and Pasta (1993; 1994; 1995) focuses on childbearing motivations, attitudes, and beliefs; and on their effects on childbearing intentions. In the current study, I am interested in childbearing behavior rather than in intentions. Hakim's "Preference Theory" (Hakim 2000; Hakim 2003) focuses on the central role played by personal preferences concerning family and working life in explaining fertility behavior. Within Preference Theory the institutional context is relevant only for the formation of preferences – not for behavior (Hakim 2000: 168ff.). In contrast, I argue that public childcare institutions are crucial, as they might constrain women in realizing their fertility plans, or enable them to do so.[13] Thus, I employ the Theory of Planned Behavior (TPB) (Fishbein and Ajzen 1975; Ajzen 1991; Ajzen and Fishbein 2005). A number of studies have shown that this model is able to adequately explain family behavior in European countries (Philipov 2009). The TPB recognizes the relevance of external constraints for human action, which allows for the integration of policy factors in a model of fertility behavior (Dommermuth et al. 2011; Klobas 2011).

In the following, I present the TPB in its general form (Section 2.3.1). The theory offers a "content-free model of human social behavior" (Ajzen 2011: 64); i.e., it is not targeted at fertility, but it offers a framework for explaining different kinds of actions. For the application of the model to childbearing behavior, I integrate different theoretical approaches from fertility research into the TPB. In a second step, I use the TPB to explain how childcare affects childbearing. Section 2.3.3 is dedicated to the interaction of childcare provision with institutions and attitudes. The last section of this chapter summarizes the theoretical approach of this study, and explicates the research hypotheses for the empirical analyses.

13 Another approach that explicitly emphasizes the relationship between intentions and behavior is the "Theory of Conjunctural Action" (Johnson-Hanks et al. 2011; see also Morgan and Bachrach 2011) In this theory, institutional aspects are captured in the concept of materials (Johnson-Hanks et al. 2011: 8ff.). There were two reasons why I chose to use the TPB instead. First, the Theory of Conjunctural Action does not provide a ready-to-use theory of action. Second, a multitude of studies have shown that the TPB offers a concise explanation for fertility behavior, while the Theory of Conjunctural Action is a new approach that has not reached its full theoretical maturity (Huinink 2012).

2.3.1   The Theory of Planned Behavior

The TPB was developed by social psychologist Icek Ajzen (1991). It evolved from the Theory of Reasoned Action (Fishbein and Ajzen 1975), and was subject to several extensions and adjustments (Barber 2001; Ajzen and Fishbein 2005; Fishbein and Ajzen 2010). According to the model, before a person acts in a specific way, she forms the intention to do so. Three main aspects are crucial to understanding the cognitive processes preceding intentions: personal attitudes toward the behavior, the (dis)agreement of significant others with the behavior, and the perceived control to perform the behavior. Constraints (e.g., structural constraints) could hinder a person in realizing the intended behavior, while enablers might offer support in doing so (cf. Figure 2).

The process represents a "reasoned action" because the final behavior is led by the reasonable evaluation of the three factors. This evaluation is based on a person's beliefs. Beliefs are the sum of the information a person has about the consequences of the behavior (Ajzen 1991: 191). In the case of childbearing, such beliefs might involve, for example, the financial costs of children, the time demands of childcare, the expected emotional returns of having children, and the effects of having children on a person's standing in society.

Attitudes are fed by the beliefs about the effects of the behavior on a person's life. Perceived norms are based on beliefs about whether relevant others think the behavior is desirable. Behavioral control is a product of a person's beliefs about her ability to perform the behavior. A negative evaluation of one of the three factors might prevent a person from taking the action. The beliefs about the situation that feed the decision-making process are not necessarily objective, as they are based on a person's perceptions. They might therefore be based on wrong information or misinterpretations, and may even be irrational (Ajzen and Fishbein 2005: 193). Beliefs are the product of a multitude of background factors, such as the institutional context, religion, the economic conditions, and socialization; as well as personal characteristics, such as age and gender. Moreover, the level of access to relevant information on attitudes, norms, and resources might also differ among individuals and account for varying beliefs.

Figure 2:   The Theory of Planned Behavior.

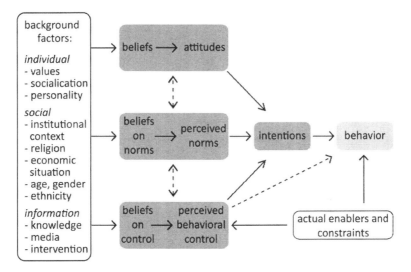

Source: adapted from Ajzen and Fishbein (2005: 194).

The TPB has been employed in numerous studies (Morgan and Bachrach 2011: 11), and has been found to be the most frequently used behavioral model in social psychology (Armitage and Conner 2001). Although it has not explicitly been designed to study fertility behavior, the model has been applied to the question of why women have children (Ajzen and Klobas 2013; see Philipov 2009 for a review). In the following, I present the central concepts of the TPB that guide my study on childbearing behavior.

The behavior of interest: entry into motherhood

In this study, the "behavior" of interest is the entry into motherhood; i.e., a woman giving birth to her first child. Indeed, within the framework of the TPB childbearing is not, strictly speaking, the behavior that directly follows from a positive childbearing intention. Rather, the behavior that immediately follows the decision to have a child is stopping the use of contraceptive methods and engaging in sexual intercourse (Billari et al.

43

2009).[14] However, for demographers concerned with fertility behaviors, childbirth is the outcome of interest (Philipov 2011). From a theoretical point of view, childbirth is the attainment of the goal underlying the actual behavior; e.g., consciously stopping contraception. Thus, fertility outcomes can be conceptualized as the result of targeted behaviors (Ajzen 2011).

As I mentioned in the introduction, I focus on the transition to first births for several reasons. For example, those who already have children might be a selective group. Kreyenfeld (2002) suggested that mothers might differ significantly from their childless counterparts in their degree of "family proneness" (ibid.: 39). Family-prone women might have a strong desire to have additional children, regardless of the structural factors. Thus, they are less affected by work-family policies, and the availability of public childcare might be less relevant for their further childbearing behavior. Moreover, a focus on first births reduces the problem of reverse causality. An increase in fertility on the macro level might also have effects on the provision of childcare. It is, for example, possible that the more children that are born, the fewer childcare spots are available because the demand has increased. Focusing on first-time mothers allows us to consider the timing of cause and effect. Women who are thinking about having a first child have to rely on information on childcare access at the time they are making their decision, as they do not have information about childcare availability in the future. Taking into account this sequence of timing avoids the problem of reverse causality, as individuals who are having a first child can hardly affect childcare availability in the past.

Within the framework of the TPB, the behavior under investigation is analyzed for a single person only. As pregnancy and childbirth is a female issue and childcare is primarily provided by mothers, the focus of the model is on women. This individual perspective neglects the assumption that childbearing in advanced societies is a dyadic decision made within a couple (Thomson 1997; Thomson and Hoem 1998; Jansen and Liefbroer 2006; Rosina and Testa 2009). With the TPB element "subjective norms"

---

14 The TPB also explains why a person refrains from performing a behavior. For childbearing, this is the case if a person intentionally avoids having a child. The requirement for a sexually active person to not have a child is access to contraceptive methods. This is usually a given in the Western world.

male partners' influence on the childbearing decision can be taken into account (see below).

Intentions to have a first child

Having a first birth is preceded by the intention to do so.[15] Intentions indicate the will of a person to perform the behavior of interest. The stronger the intention, the more likely is its realization (Ajzen 1991: 181). Fertility intentions have to be distinguished from fertility desires: desires are ideal and unconstrained, while intentions refer to the actual childbearing plans given a person's situation (Miller et al. 2004: 194). Another important feature of intentions is their (in)stability over time. Within the framework of the TPB, intentions are the product of attitudes, subjective norms, and perceived behavioral control. These factors might differ for a multitude of reasons, ranging from socialization, education, personal experiences, to decisions in domains other than the family. For childbearing, this implies that intentions might change with a woman's situation, or as she acquires new information (Iacovou and Tavares 2011). Ajzen (2005) contended that the longer the time interval between the measurement of intention and the observation of the associated behavior, the higher the probability that unforeseen events will have occurred. This means that a long pause between observing the same individual might underestimate the expected relationship between intentions and behavior.

Fertility intentions have different dimensions. They can refer to the number of children or the timing of childbirth (Miller and Pasta 1994). These different dimensions are interrelated. In the current study, I focus on the intention of first birth timing.

Attitudes toward childbearing and first births

An important prerequisite of behavior is a person's positive attitude toward that behavior (Ajzen 1991). Although the definition of attitudes varies across theoretical approaches, the central and common element

---

15   It should be noted that the TPB excludes inadvertent behaviors; as intentions are a core concept in the model, the phenomenon of unintended pregnancies is ignored here.

appears to be the evaluation of the attitude object (Petty et al. 1997: 611). This evaluation ranges from positive to negative (ibid.). In the case of childbirth, attitudes are the result of a person's evaluation of the effects of having a child. If the anticipated overall rewards exceed the emotional and financial costs, attitudes toward childbearing are positive. If, however, the expected unfavorable consequences of having a child outweigh the expected advantages, attitudes toward childbearing are negative. According to the TPB, ceteris paribus, a positive attitude toward having a child strengthens the intention to have a child, while a negative attitude reduces an individual's childbearing intention.

A theoretical approach which investigates attitudinal aspects in order to explain childbearing decisions was suggested by Hoffman and Hoffman (1973). According to their "Values of Children" approach, the "value of children refers to the functions they serve or the needs they fulfill for parents" (ibid.: 20). The authors listed a number of positive consequences of having children for parents' lives (ibid.: 46ff.). These empirical dimensions can be categorized into three conceptual components: an economic-utilitarian, a social-normative, and a psychological component (Nauck 1989; Nauck 2001). An economically positive aspect of having children is, for example, the anticipated help they will be for their parents in old age. A socio-cultural value of children might be the change of a person's standing in society through parenthood. Having children might, for example, be regarded as a final step in reaching adulthood. From a psychological perspective, individuals expect emotional returns from having children and see them as a source of happiness.

In addition to looking at the benefits of parenthood, other authors have noted the possible negative consequences of having children. Childbearing could interfere with parents' personal freedom and leisure time preferences (Bulatao 1981). The financial burden associated with childrearing can be perceived as negative (Miller and Pasta 1993).

Moreover, attitudes toward "competing behaviors" (Barber 2001: 101; Barber and Axinn 2005: 61) might be of interest in explaining the process of deciding whether to have a child. Competing behaviors are related to the other life domains affected by having children, such as career- and education-related goals, and account for the life course situations of an individual. When it comes to deciding whether to start a family, the importance a woman places on alternative life domains is crucial. The central issue is the reality that an individual's time resources are limited. Childcare is a time-consuming activity that reduces the time available for other activities, such as education, work, or leisure. As discussed above, this creates opportunity costs and role strain (cf. Section 2.2). In the family formation decision-making process, women take into consideration their career-related goals. They anticipate the gendered changes to their work and family lives, as well as the role strain and the opportunity costs associated with having children. The anticipated amount of time spent caring for children would mean "sacrificing" time that could otherwise be devoted to school or the job. The stronger the woman's career aspirations, the more "costly" this sacrifice is. Women with a strong attachment to work might feel that having a child reduces their career prospects. Because the work-family conflict is particularly strong for these women, they tend to have negative attitudes toward childbearing. In contrast, women who attach great importance to the family and children might plan to stop work, and thus do not expect to experience conflicts between work and family life. They have more positive attitudes toward childbearing.

Attitudes are shaped by a number of background factors (Ajzen and Fishbein 2005). First, a woman's socialization might feed her attitudinal beliefs. It has been shown that mothers transmit their views on family and work life arrangements to their daughters (Moen et al. 1997). Second, social factors – e.g., education, age, gender, income, and religion – shape a woman's evaluation of having children. For example, a study on the acceptance of childlessness showed that highly educated, non-traditional women with low levels of attachment to religion were more tolerant toward voluntary childlessness (Merz and Liefbroer 2012). Third, new background information might affect behavioral beliefs, and thus attitudes. Fourth, life course decisions or events and attitudes form a reciprocal relationship (Lesthaeghe 2002; Moors 2003). On the one hand, value orientations are responsible for a selection into a specific life course trajectory. Women who attach great importance to a successful career might invest their energy and time into their job, for instance. On the other hand, life course decisions, such as starting a high profile job, might lead to an adaptation of values. This implies that attitudes can vary over time.

Subjective norms, the social environment, and first births

In addition to attitudes, a second factor that influences a person's childbearing plans in the TPB framework are perceived norms; i.e., the assessment a person has of others' expectations. In the context considered here, the subjective norms are related to the social pressure a person feels to have – or to avoid having – a child. Social influence can be exerted by a "world of others" (Bernardi 2003: 528), both kin and non-kin.

A woman might perceive that her social environment – e.g., parents, relatives, friends, and colleagues – have strong opinions about whether she should have a child. Depending on the strength of her own desires, she might prefer to adapt her behavior to the expectations she perceives. The basic argument is that groups tend to dislike and reject people who deviate from what is considered to be the norm, while the group members themselves seek to avoid conflicts with the majority (Moscovici 1985: 349, 354). There are different mechanisms through which individuals feel pressure from their social group(s), usually based on a system of sanctions and gratifications. As social individuals usually avoid being sanctioned (Erickson 1988), a potential mother will be concerned about the expectations of the people in her social environment. Thus, all other things being equal, individuals will have increased fertility intentions if they believe that other people who are important to them expect them to have a child. If, by contrast, a person perceives social pressure to not have a child, it is likely that she will decide to forego or postpone childbearing.

The person with the most influence on a woman's decision about whether to have children is generally her partner. Although it is considered less frequently, research has shown that the potential father's opinion about having children is related to actual childbearing (Jansen and Liefbroer 2006). A woman is likely to place considerable weight on her partner's attitude toward fatherhood and family arrangements after childbirth when deciding whether to have a child. As cohabiting partners usually continuously exchange their views on life domains, they usually form a consensus on childbearing intentions (Miller and Pasta 1995). If a couple's childbearing intentions diverge, the influence exerted by each of the partners is related to several factors, such as the bargaining position of the woman (Rosina and Testa 2009) and the quality of the partnership (Hillmann and Kuhnt 2011).

Despite the integration of a partner's influence on the intention to have a child, within the TPB childbearing is conceptualized as an individual's decision, not a couple's decision.

Behavioral control and first births

The concept of behavioral control refers to the resources and opportunities a person believes are necessary to perform a certain action.[16] A woman's assessment of her ability to realize her childbearing plans might change her childbearing intentions, or her actual childbearing behavior, or both. Among the examples of this type of control are the availability of a partner and the physical ability to conceive. Information about childcare affect a woman's perceived behavioral control through her beliefs concerning the availability of (affordable) childcare. Let us consider a woman who plans to rely on public childcare while she works after having a child (cf. solid arrow connecting behavioral control and intentions in Figure 2). After talking to a neighbor with young children, the woman might have the impression that it will be difficult to find a place in childcare for the (unborn) child in the future. Taking this new situation into consideration, she decides to postpone having a first child (indicated by the dashed arrow connecting behavioral control and behavior in Figure 2).

A woman's perception of her level of control is *subjective*, and might be at odds with the actual situation. The degree of deviation between the subjective and the actual extent of her control depends on the accuracy of her perception. A multitude of factors might cause a woman to have inaccurate beliefs about her level of control, such as limited information about the behavior, changes in the necessary resources, and changes in the woman's circumstances or in her environment (Ajzen 1991: 185).

Actual enablers and constraints

While behavioral control is based on a person's perceptions regarding her resources, there may also be *actual* enablers of and constraints on childbearing. These include all of the external conditions that either prevent a person from having a child or support her in doing so (Ajzen and

---

16   Fishbein and Ajzen's "Theory of Reasoned Action" (Fishbein and Ajzen 1975), which was the predecessor of the TPB, was criticized for its focus on attitudes and norms, while neglecting the importance of structural constraints that might hinder the realization of intentions (Sheppard et al. 1988). In order to account for such constraints, Ajzen (1991) suggested that, in addition to attitudes and norms, perceived behavioral control also affects intentions and behavior.

Fishbein 2005). The actual enablers and constraints are the *objective* effects of personal and contextual dispositions, and they have an impact on the realization of the childbearing intention. Examples of actual enablers and constraints are the woman's actual fecundity, the actual partner's willingness to have a child, and the availability of sufficient financial means to support a child. As a feedback element, actual constraints also inform the woman's beliefs regarding behavioral control.

As an illustration, let us consider the woman from the example above. The woman had formed the intention to have a child based on the assumption that she could rely on institutional care (perceived behavioral control is high). After obtaining the information that care services are scarce (actual constraint is high), the woman adapted her beliefs about her ability to perform the behavior (perceived behavioral control is low), which may have reduced her fertility intentions. This shows how feedback mechanisms may change the perception of the individual depending on her circumstances.

In the context of childbearing and institutions, family-friendly policies are generally seen as enabling factors (Philipov et al. 2009; Liefbroer 2011). Family policies are often cited as a means of helping potential parents realize their childbearing desires and intentions (Chesnais 2000; see Philipov and Bernardi 2011 for a review). It has been argued that governments should support young adults in having the number of children they want to have. In societies with increasing levels of female labor force participation, policies that help to reduce the conflicts between family and work are expected to support women in realizing their fertility intentions. Accordingly, in advanced societies the provision of public childcare is expected to support childbearing (Rindfuss et al. 2003).

2.3.2 A model of childcare, attitudes, and childbearing

The TPB provides a framework that offers researchers the opportunity to theoretically embed the decision to have a child in an institutional context that includes childcare services and other family policies (Klobas 2011; Liefbroer 2011). At the same time, the TPB accounts for the importance of attitudes toward competing life goals, such as career plans (Barber 2001). In the following, I discuss how public childcare might affect childbearing behavior by shaping perceived behavioral control, subjective norms, and attitudes (Klobas 2011; Liefbroer 2011). The complete model is shown in Figure 3.

Figure 3:   Integrating childcare and fertility behavior into the Theory of Planned Behavior.

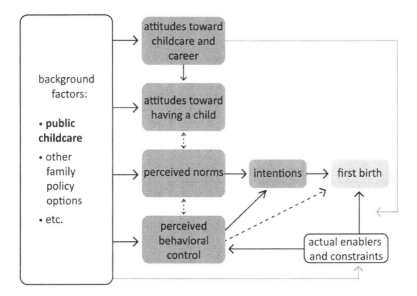

Source: adapted from Ajzen and Fishbein (2005: 194), Barber (2001: 103) and Klobas (2011:52).

Assuming that women know that childcare services are available, this knowledge affects their attitudes, norms, and behavioral control in the following ways. First, as mentioned above, changes in the provision of childcare services might influence a person's level of perceived behavioral control. Women who receive information (from, for example, neighbors or friends) that childcare is available for very young children might change their perceptions about the resources they would need to combine family and work. Affordable childcare services enable mothers to reduce the amount of time they need to take off from work after giving birth. This reduces the opportunity costs of having children, increases the income available for raising children, and allows women to balance their roles at work and at home. Thus, the availability of childcare services encourages women to have children. If childcare services are limited, women who want to stay in the labor market might have less posi-

51

tive childbearing intentions. Let us consider, for example, a career-oriented woman who has the impression (e.g., based on the reports of friends, kin, neighbors, or the media) that it is difficult to get a place in a childcare center. She might anticipate that she would need to either pay high fees for private childcare or to interrupt her employment for a longer period of time to care for the child herself. This situation might reduce her intention to have a first child or lead her to postpone starting a family.

Second, the promotion of public childcare as a political goal might affect public opinion about childcare institutions. This shift in opinion might also be reflected in changes in a woman's perceptions of the norms concerning childcare use. Institutions shape opinions and norms via two channels (cf. Sjöberg 2004). On the one hand, family policies show approval for family arrangements through a top-down mechanism. They influence the norms related to women's roles in society. Based on the categorization of Korpi (2000, cf. Section 2.1.2), we can see that childcare provision supports dual-earner families, and thus promotes ideas like non-family childcare, the employment of mothers, and a more egalitarian division of labor.[17] On the other hand, ideas about combining family and work might spread via a bottom-up mechanism: the more mothers work, the more dual-earner families will be perceived as being normal. Within the TPB framework, societal norms about the acceptance or non-acceptance of non-family childcare and working mothers might be mirrored in a person's perceptions of norms. In other words, the important people in a woman's life might approve of the dominant family model in the society, and, depending on the woman's intentions, approve or disapprove of her childbearing plans. The underlying mechanisms are complex, as new policies may result in societal transformation, but it is also possible that normative changes led to these political initiatives (see de Bruijn 1999). Moreover, because norms and values evolve over time, there might be a gap between cultural and political change (Liefbroer and · Corijn 1999: 52; McDonald et al. 2005: 38; Sjöberg 2010: 34).

Third and most importantly, the provision of childcare might modify a woman's attitudes toward having a first child, as the availability of public childcare could reduce the negative effects she associates with having

17 Following this logic, policies in line with the male breadwinner family – e.g., a cash-for-care program – would support the ideal of female homemaking and maternal re.

a child. Potential mothers might have different reasons for wanting to return to work quickly. Some might plan to advance in their careers, while others may face financial pressure to contribute to the household income (Gerson 1985; Doorewaard et al. 2004). Both situations lead to a preference for a short break, and, if informal childcare is unavailable, to a demand for childcare. Let us consider a woman who does not want to take a long break from work after having a baby. Anticipating a conflict between her job and having a child, she believes that starting a family would have negative consequences for her life. She then receives new information that public childcare is easily available at low prices. Based on the economic arguments discussed above, having access to affordable childcare reduces opportunity costs and would thus encourage the woman to have a child. Based on the sociological arguments, having access to childcare would lead the woman to assume that she would be able to balance her roles as a mother and as an employee, which would reduce the anticipated role strain and increase her feelings of gender equality. Thus, the woman should view the prospect of having children more positively.

2.3.3 How childcare interacts with attitudinal and institutional aspects

The discussed mechanisms imply that childcare provision has a positive effect on having a first child. However, I argue that the effect depends on the level of a potential parent's acceptance of non-family childcare of very young children, and the willingness to use care services after a child is born. Individuals who do not want to use public childcare might disregard the provision of public care in their childbearing decision. In such a case, the availability of childcare is less relevant. If potential mothers do not want to use public childcare, the provision of services would neither stimulate their childbearing intentions nor their childbearing behavior. In the following, I explore how the effect of childcare provision on fertility might interact with (a) other policy options in a society, and (b) attitudes toward non-family childcare. A schematic presentation of the theoretical model is shown in Figure 4.

Figure 4:   Schematic presentation of the impact of childcare services on childbearing, and the interaction effects with childcare ideals and competing family policy options.

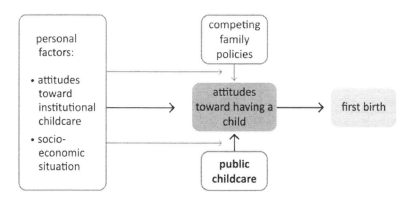

Source: author's own illustration.

Importance of other family policies

Within the TPB framework, childcare services are only one aspect of the societal context that influences the childbearing decision. Other policies also create incentives that might compete with the goals of childcare policies. It has been argued in the literature (Lewis 2001; Neyer 2003a; Thévenon 2011) that the coherence of family policies plays a crucial role in their effectiveness. As I noted in Section 2.1.3, a coherent set of family policies would support the same family model. While full-time childcare services enable both parents to work, a coherent family policy package would also offer other policies that support the dual-earner model, such as a short and generous parental leave. Conversely, some countries offer incentives for mothers to stay at home, e.g., in form of a generous home care allowance paid for several years. An allowance of this kind creates an alternative opportunity structure, and some women might prefer to take advantage of policies that support caring for children at home. Accordingly, such pluralistic policy measures are often promoted as providing a "free choice" (Eydal and Rostgaard 2011), i.e. parents can decide whether they want to use public childcare services or take care of their children at

54

home. But the options chosen by parents are not necessarily independent of their socioeconomic backgrounds (Morgan and Zippel 2003; Salmi 2006; Aassve and Lappegård 2009).

Based on the general economic theory, Gauthier and Hatzius (1997: 296) suggested that family policy measures affect different population groups to varying degrees. The authors focused their theoretical considerations on the effects of child benefits and maternity leave policies on different socioeconomic groups (ibid.). However, the general idea can be transferred to other policies as well.

When we extend the economic view on childcare policies to all family policies, we observe that most state interventions are designed to lower the costs of raising children. While some policy instruments, such as childcare, focus on indirect costs; others, such as child benefits and home care allowances, are intended to lower the direct costs of having children. The central feature of interest in this context seems to be the interaction between the relative amount a policy contributes to the household income and the absolute reduction of the cost of raising children. Lump sum payments, or a fixed monthly benefit for each child, might be seen as more attractive by families with lower incomes. The lower a mother's wages, the more relevant even a modest contribution to the household income is. For women with high earnings, such a payment is less attractive, as it amounts to a relatively small share of the household income. Similarly, a flat rate benefit paid to women who care for their young children at home represents a relatively greater financial contribution for families with lower incomes.

In contrast, policies that are proportionally related to women's incomes are especially attractive for women with high earnings. Regarding childcare services, a woman who has relatively high wages before she starts a family faces greater opportunity costs of childrearing. The availability of affordable childcare reduces these costs because the woman has the option of returning to work soon after childbirth. Women with low wages, by contrast, face lower opportunity costs, as their foregone earnings are smaller. That means that the absolute cost reduction through childcare provision increases with a woman's income, and is thus most profitable for a woman with a high income.

The mode of payment is of specific interest in countries with pluralistic (or incoherent) family policies; i.e., in an institutional setting that offers support for both dual-earner and male breadwinner families. Let us consider a country with a coherent package of family policies. Although benefits might vary for each family according to income level, number of children, etc.; the distribution of transfers or services follow the same rules. The tax benefits in a country with policies that mainly support male breadwinner families are, for example, available to all families with children (although the amount of the benefits might vary by family). In countries with policies that mainly support dual-earner families, universal childcare is offered to all families. The situation is more complex in countries that offer a range of policy types. For example, if the government has implemented instruments that support single breadwinner families, some families – those with low socio-economic status in particular – might take advantage of these policies. In this situation, the positive effect of childcare policies on childbearing does not reach all population groups.

Interaction with attitudes toward non-family childcare

In addition to interacting with institutional incentives, the effect of public childcare provision might also interact with a potential mother's attitude toward family arrangements (Fagnani 2002; Rossier et al. 2011). The use of non-family care for young children is not only based on practical or economic considerations. If, for instance, a woman believes that non-maternal childcare harms children, the availability of childcare services is not an incentive to have children. I assume that childcare provision has a positive effect primarily among mothers who have a favorable (or at least neutral) attitude toward working mothers and non-family care. As decisions about a woman's job have strong implications for family life (and vice versa), a woman is likely to anticipate how she would organize her future working life and care for her child after she becomes a mother. Whether she plans to use public childcare is not only a question of availability, but also of her personal beliefs about the effects care provided outside of the home has on the child's social and cognitive development. Assuming that she wants the best for her child, she will not see inappropriate care as an option when anticipating future care arrangements. If the woman believes that good mothers care for their children at home, the mere availability of childcare will hardly affect her childbearing decision.

Childcare is an important topic with a strong moral component for potential parents. Potential mothers form beliefs about the type of childcare that is appropriate (Hochschild 1995). As mothers are expected to act in the interests of their children, they will use only forms of care they think are acceptable. Care ideals refer to the person who is taking care of the child. Kremer (2007: 71ff.) identified five ideals of care. "Full-time mother care" refers to the idea that bonding between a mother and her child is central for the child's development; thus, the mother is seen as the preferable care provider. This ideal came into vogue after the Second World War. In some of the Nordic countries, the full-time care model was outdated by the 1950s and 1960s; while other countries did not change their care ideals until later (ibid.: 73). The ideals of "parental sharing" and "intergenerational care" both emphasize that care is located within the home and the family. In contrast, "professional care" is provided by trained carers who work in an institution like a crèche or a kindergarten. On the one hand, some parents might think that this form of care has a pedagogical value and is supportive of children's social and cognitive development (Johansen et al. 1996). On the other hand, others might be worried that in a formal care setting a very young child would not receive the warmth and attention a mother would give (Kremer 2007: 75). For this latter group, "surrogate mothers" might provide adequate care, as such care is located in a home and is provided by a woman who has children herself. Another feature is that a surrogate mother has only a small number of additional children to look after.

Parental attitudes regarding appropriate childcare depend on a number of factors. However, due to data limitations, most studies focus on attitudes toward maternal or non-family childcare. Ellingsæter and Gulbrandsen (2007: 664f.), for example, found different levels of acceptance of working and non-working mothers according to cohort and sex. Moreover, the socioeconomic status of parents seems to be relevant in assessments of whether maternal care is preferable to non-maternal care (Duncan and Irwin 2004; Stefansen and Farstad 2010). Another factor is gender role ideology: the more traditional a person is, the more likely s/he will be to see maternal care as ideal (Mason and Kuhlthau 1989). Childhood experiences also seem to be relevant. For example, during socialist times, childcare services for very young children was widely spread in the GDR. Accordingly, people who were socialized in the former GDR tend to be more accepting non-family childcare than people who were socialized in West Germany (Goerres and Tepe 2012). In general, national norms are related to childcare attitudes. In West Germany, for example, maternal care is the norm, which is reflected in the attitudes expressed by potential mothers (Rossier et al. 2011). By contrast, in France, where crèches are widely used, women have a positive attitude toward non-maternal care options (ibid.). In addition, childcare ideals vary depending on children's ages (Saraceno 1984). Such age-grading differs across countries, but in general it is assumed that the younger a child, the more preferable family care is.

When we are looking at the effects of childcare services on fertility decisions, it is important to determine whether the (potential) parents have a positive opinion of non-family childcare. Women who believe that a child suffers in public childcare might also think that it is a mother's duty to remain outside of the labor market (at least for the first few years) after childbirth. Such women are unlikely to perceive the availability of public childcare as an incentive for childbearing. In other words, if a person prefers maternal to non-family care, the provision of public childcare does not change her childbearing intentions. By contrast, if a woman wants to combine family and work, and believes this arrangement is good (or at least not harmful) for the child and for the parents, the availability of public childcare might help her to decide to have a child. Because she anticipates a potential conflict between family and career, she might view having access to childcare services as reducing the negative consequences of starting a family. For a woman in this group, the provision of childcare might positively affect her decision to have a first birth.

A factor that might interfere with public childcare provision is informal care. This is often provided by grandparents (Wheelock and Jones 2002). Women might have negative attitudes toward non-family care but approve of care provided by grandparents. Informal childcare thus provides a means of outsourcing care without using non-family care, which these mothers believe could be harmful for the child. Such an arrangement enables women to participate in the labor market without having to rely on public childcare services (Davis and Connelly 2005). As it reduces the anticipated work-family conflict, grandparental care diminishes the work-related negative effects of having children. Accordingly, the potential help of grandparents has been shown to be positively related to first birth risks (Hank and Kreyenfeld 2003). If a woman is planning to return to her job and to use informal care after childbirth, her first birth intentions will remain unaffected by the availability of public childcare services.

2.3.4 Summary and research hypotheses

The aim of this study is to explain how public (or publicly subsidized) childcare provision affects first birth timing in a society. From both a welfare state and a micro-level perspective, the availability of childcare services has a positive effect on fertility. The main argument of this study is that two intervening factors might play crucial roles in this relationship: (a) the coherence of the family policy package and (b) the attitudes toward public (or publicly subsidized) childcare. Using the theoretical framework of the Theory of Planned Behavior allowed me to include childcare and intervening factors into a model of individual childbearing decision-making. In the following, I summarize my line of argumentation and formulate testable hypotheses.

Within the TPB, women have some beliefs about the effects of having a first child on their lives. As today most women in advanced societies work, the question of whether having a child entails a long career break is important. In the early years of a child's life, childcare is very intensive and parents have to decide who will care for the child: the mother, another family member, and/or an external childcare provider. This is relevant, as the choice of maternal care implies that the mother's labor force participation is reduced. If, however, a potential mother believes that public childcare is available – by, for example, observing friends with children – she might expect that it is possible to reconcile her work and family goals. This might encourage her childbearing behavior. Childcare can be seen as an enabler of fertility intentions: women who live in communities with sufficient daycare provision will see their chances of obtaining a place for their child in the future as relatively good. Access to childcare offers mothers the opportunity to return to their jobs soon after childbirth, thereby reducing the anticipated negative consequences of having children. Thus, women who believe that levels of public childcare services for young children are adequate are more likely to have a first child than women who believe that childcare availability is low (hypothesis 1).

An intervening factor that might reduce the positive effect of childcare services on first births is a country's family policy strategy beyond childcare services. Care policies for children under age three are usually seen as supporting dual-earner families. Alternative policies, such as a home care allowance, might provide incentives for single-earner families. In such a situation, it is possible that potential parents will ignore public childcare options, preferring instead to take advantage of other policy measures. The childbearing decisions of young adults who plan to make no use of childcare, but who intend to make use of other policies, will remain unaffected by the availability of childcare. In contrast, in countries with coherent family policies, the majority of instruments target either dual-earner or male breadwinner families. Thus, the majority of potential parents will follow (or will plan to follow) the supported family arrangement. In countries with a coherent set of dual-earner support policies, women will expect to use childcare regardless of their socioeconomic status. In this setting, childcare might have a positive effect on childbearing. In contrast, in countries where governments also have policies in place that support male breadwinners, only specific groups of women will demand childcare, e.g., those with high levels of education. Women take their future family arrangements into consideration before childbirth. From an economic perspective, female labor force participation is more relevant for women with high socio-economic status because they have higher opportunity costs. In contrast, the forgone earnings of full-time mothers are smaller the lower their income is; thus, a flat rate home care allowance is an attractive option for women with lower socioeconomic status. Accordingly, the higher a woman's income and education, the greater her incentives to keep the length of her leave following the birth of a baby to a minimum, and the more important the availability of childcare services will be in her decision about whether to have a child (hypothesis 2).

A second intervening factor might be the attitudes women have concerning childcare ideals. The availability of public childcare might have less of an effect on the behavior of potential mothers who have negative attitudes toward non-family childcare for very young children. For mothers who believe that infants and toddlers should be cared for by their mothers, institutional childcare is not an option. In their view, "good mothers" exit the labor market, as maternal care is best for the child's development during the early years. Depending on their attitudes toward career-related goals, this is either the duty or the joy of motherhood, which should not be delegated to anyone other than the mother. Therefore, the availability of childcare services will have a reduced effect on fertility if a woman has traditional beliefs about family arrangements (hypothesis 3). In contrast, the availability of public childcare will stimulate first births among women who believe that non-family childcare is acceptable.

3 Previous research on childcare, coherent policies, attitudes, and fertility behavior

In Chapter 2, I discussed the theoretical effects that are expected from childcare provision on individual fertility behavior. I elaborated a model on childcare effects that makes it possible to consider intervening factors, especially attitudes and institutional effects. Many studies have been done to investigate related research questions. Before presenting my own empirical analyses, I summarize the results of prior research.

In the following, I review studies on the effect of family policies on childbearing that focused public childcare provision (Section 3.1). A distinction is made between studies that analyzed aggregate measures of fertility and individual-level fertility. As informal childcare might be a complement to public childcare, I also review studies on the effect of, for example, grandparental childcare. In the second section (Section 3.2), the findings of studies on the effect of coherent family policies on fertility behavior are discussed. In Section 3.3, I summarize the results of studies on how attitudes shape fertility decisions.

3.1 Empirical evidence: childcare and fertility

Family policies (and other policies affecting families) shape the lives of parents and children (Hantrais 2004). Child allowances and maternity leave benefits, for instance, affect the economic situations of families. Fertility might also be influenced by policies. The general argument is that policies reduce the costs of childbearing and thus stimulate fertility (Gauthier 2007). First, policies that financially support parents, such as family allowances, reduce the direct costs of childbearing and rearing. Second, policies that support parents returning to the labor market (e.g., childcare provision) reduce the opportunity costs of having children. A multitude of studies investigated the effects of (family) policies on fertility. Yet the empirical evidence remains ambiguous, as some studies have found a relationship between policies and fertility, while others have not shown such a relationship (see, e.g., Neyer 2003a; Sleebos 2003; Gauthier 2007 for reviews).

The effect of public childcare on fertility has also frequently been investigated. Researchers generally expect to find that childcare provision positively affects childbearing (cf. Chapter 2 for theoretical mechanisms). In fact, a study on fertility intentions in the U.S. showed that women feeling constrained by low childcare availability had a lower expected number of children (Presser and Baldwin 1980). However, data on a person's perception of childcare availability is usually unavailable. Instead, researchers use objective measures of childcare services provided in a geographical area (e.g., nation states, provinces, districts, municipalities). A distinction can be made between childcare provision and enrollment rates. Provision rates refer to the share of children in a specific age group for whom a childcare slot would be available. Meanwhile, enrollment rates reflect the share of children in a specific age group who are actually enrolled in childcare. The research hypothesis usually states that in a country (or region) with high childcare availability, fertility will be higher than in a country (or region) with low childcare availability.

In the following, I discuss studies that have focused on country-level fertility rates, and those that have analyzed measures of individual childbearing. In many countries, childcare data have not been collected systematically and in a comparable way until recent years (Plantenga et al. 2008). Accordingly, the studies reviewed investigate childcare effects in the 1990s and 2000s.

3.1.1   Country level studies

Macro-level analyses focus on the effect of national childcare levels on an aggregate measure of fertility in a country, usually the TFR. From this perspective, childcare provision seems to be positively related to fertility levels, as it allows mothers to participate in the labor market (Esping-Andersen 2000; Ahn and Mira 2002). This assumption was supported empirically in a study on the relationship between structural aspects and macro-level fertility conducted by Castles (2003). Using OECD data, his bivariate analyses showed that childcare provision is positively correlated with period total fertility rates.

Some authors accounted for childcare policies in an indirect way or combined it with other family policy measures. These analyses showed that policies that support working mothers are positively related to national fertility levels. Esping-Andersen (2000: 70) found a positive relationship between service provision and fertility change in a cross-country regression analysis. The sample in his study consisted of 18 states, and the analysis included the country level of youth unemployment as a control variable. The measure of welfare state services was based on the childcare enrollment levels among children under age three and the level of home help coverage. The study by Ferrarini (2006) of 18 OECD countries investigated the effect of policies on fertility levels based on the two policy dimensions suggested by Korpi (2000). Ferrarini found that an index for dual-earner policies (including the childcare enrollment levels of children under age three) positively affected fertility rates. Moreover, he showed that an index accounting for general family policies (e.g., child allowances) had a stimulating effect on country-level fertility. This indicates that family policies improve the situation of families and thus motivate potential parents to have children, independent of the supported family model. In a multivariate study on the national level, Rovny (2011) found that childcare expenditures are positively related to fertility. On average, countries with high spending on childcare facilities have higher fertility levels than countries with lower spending. More generous maternity and parental leave benefits also have been shown to have a positive impact on fertility, which suggests that policies that reduce the conflict between parenthood and employment seem to encourage higher fertility rates. These studies implied a positive relationship between the provision of childcare services (or policy indices including childcare services) and fertility on the country level. However, all of these papers were rather simple in their design, focusing on cross-sectional differences between countries while neglecting the longitudinal perspective. The relationship between public childcare services and fertility were considered on an aggregate level. Moreover, the limited number of control variables in some of the studies ignores possible confounding factors. It is therefore difficult to draw conclusions about the causal relationship between the two macro-level variables.

The importance of analyzing individuals is shown in a multi-level analysis by Billingsley and Ferrarini (2011). They demonstrated that the policy effects were different for men and women, for individuals with different levels of educational attainment, and for individuals with different birth parities. This indicates that the relationship between policy packages and individual-level fertility intentions is complex, and that individual-level variables should be taken into account.

3.1.2   Individual level studies

Micro-level studies on the effects of public childcare provision account for personal characteristics and the economic, demographic, and social situations of each individual. Many of these individual-level studies analyze the transition to a first, second, or third child. While some studies compared the effect of national childcare levels on individuals' childbearing, others focused on childcare provision on smaller geographical areas. On the one hand, sub-national variation makes it possible to analyze childcare effects in a single country. On the other hand, smaller spatial units improve the measurement of the childcare availability for each woman. In many European countries, childcare is available to only a limited number of children (especially for the under-three age group). Care provision is usually not spread homogeneously over a country, but differs considerably by region. Accordingly, the opportunity to combine work and family via childcare services varies across geographical areas.[18] In this setting, researchers also expect to see a positive effect of childcare on fertility behavior. In the following, I compare the results and methodological differences of a number of European studies.[19]

The micro-level studies (see the list in Appendix A) are similar in terms of their analytical approach: based on multi-level settings, they investigated the effect of municipal, regional, or national childcare enrollment rates on individual-level childbearing. While most authors focused on a specific country, a few investigators chose a comparative approach that includes several countries (e.g., Del Boca et al. 2009; Hilgeman and Butts 2009; van Bavel and Rózanska-Putek 2010). The results differed, however, across studies. Some studies found the expected positive relationship between childcare provision and individual

---

18   The reasons for a geographical variation in childcare provision might be manifold. Despite party political differences, it might also depend on the financial situation of municipalities and the actions taken by parents who demand childcare.

19   In the United States, the effects of childcare prices on fertility (Blau and Robins 1989; Mason and Kuhlthau 1992) and on female labor force participation were the main focus of research (Han and Waldfogel 2001; Michalopoulos and Robins 2002). In many European countries, childcare is state-provided or heavily subsidized, and parents' fees account for only a share of the costs. However, for children under age three there are (or were) only a limited number of childcare places available.

childbearing (Del Boca 2002; Rindfuss et al. 2007; Hilgeman and Butts 2009; Rindfuss et al. 2010). The majority of analyses found no significant effects (Klevmarken and Tasiran 1996; Hank 2002; Hank and Kreyenfeld 2003; Andersson et al. 2004; Brodmann et al. 2007; Del Boca et al. 2009; Lappegård 2010). In other studies the childcare effect turned insignificant after a set of control variables were included (Kravdal 1996) or after female employment rates were controlled for (Baizán 2009: for first births). A cross-sectional study by van Bavel and Rózanska-Putek (2010) on the relationship of country-level childcare enrollment rates and individual's childbearing found a positive effect among highly educated women only. In a study on Finland and Norway, childcare even seemed to have a negative – though very small – effect (Ronsen 2004: first and third births in Finland, first births in Norway). It should be noted that the studies reviewed here did not find systematic differences in childcare effects according to birth order.

In addition to looking at the effect of the public provision of childcare on fertility, researchers also investigated the effect of the availability of informal childcare, often provided by grandparents. Potential parents might anticipate that they will have the option to rely on grandparental childcare. This can be seen as substitute for institutional childcare. In fact, it has been shown for a sample of German men and women that the desire to have another child increases with the option of grandparental care if the respondents disapproved of institutional childcare (Ette and Ruckdeschel 2007). In addition, a study on the U.S. showed that working women who could rely on grandparental care had higher intended fertility levels than those who had to use paid care (Lehrer and Kawasaki 1985). Studies on actual fertility found that the potential availability of grandparents is positively related to childbearing. In western Germany, women who live in the same town as their parents have higher first birth risks (Hank and Kreyenfeld 2003). A study on Italy showed that women who have at least one parent who is still alive have higher fertility risks than those whose parents are not alive (Del Boca 2002). Moreover, grandparental childcare support increased the chances of childbearing in the Netherlands (Kaptijn et al. 2010). In a comparative study based on SHARE data, it was shown that fertility risks are reduced for children whose parents already take care of a sibling's young child (Aassve et al. 2012).

The reason for the ambiguous results for the effect of public childcare provision on individual-level childbearing across different studies could be manifold. First, it seems that the causality behind childcare and fertility is complex. On the one hand, families might move to a municipality with sufficient childcare availability when they plan to have a child. Such selective migration might produce an endogeneity bias when estimating the effect of childcare services on fertility (Rindfuss et al. 2007: 357). On the other hand, there might be a situation of reverse causality, as rising fertility might result in an increase in childcare usage. In case of such endogeneity, we would still expect to see a positive correlation between childcare levels and fertility. However, the existing studies do not consistently show this positive relationship.

Second, it has been argued that, in addition to availability, childcare characteristics such as costs, quality, and opening hours might also have an effect on fertility behavior. Such data are often unavailable. A Swedish study analyzing several childcare characteristics did not find significant effects of quality and cost aspects (Andersson et al. 2004).

Third, the different operationalizations of variables in the articles reviewed complicate the comparison of results. Some studies investigated the transition to first births, while others looked at the transition to higher order births. A third group did not distinguish between the different parities. This might account for some different results as it has been suggested that childcare affects births according to the number of children born previously (Kravdal 1996). Regional childcare enrollment was also measured in different ways across studies: a number of authors used the percentage of children enrolled in childcare, while others used categories based on the distribution of enrollment rates. The size of the regional units also varied: some researchers analyzed municipal childcare enrollment, while others considered the province level or even country level enrollment rates. This might be problematic as childcare is often provided with strong regional variation; i.e., the larger the geographical units, the more regional heterogeneity might be unobserved (Baizán 2009). If there was a strong degree of variation within regions, it could be the case that some parents, such as those living in rural areas, did not have the childcare options that were implied by the regional enrollment rates. The assumption of homogenous childcare availability is more likely to be inaccurate in regions with more diverse structural or ideational characteristics (e.g., a rural-urban divide). Another measurement problem is caused by differences in the age groups of the children enrolled: some studies use numbers of children under age three, others concentrate on the age group three to school entry, while still others focus on all children under age six. Very often, these childcare measurement differences are not the product of deliberate consideration, but are rather selected on the basis of the data available (Baizán 2009).

Another explanation for the difficulties involved in determining the effect of childcare on fertility might be the fact that, in most studies, childcare availability is measured by childcare enrollment rates. As this informs us about childcare usage, enrollment is, technically speaking, a measure of demand rather than of availability. Rindfuss et al. (2007: 351) suggested that this should not be a problem in those countries where childcare provision is (or was) limited. Not all of the parents who wish to use childcare were offered services; i.e., only a limited number of children attend childcare. In this setting, enrollment rates are also a measure of supply, as public facilities do not provide enough childcare to meet the demand.

Moreover, as was explained in detail in Chapter 2.3.3, intervening factors – such as policy options that support full-time mothers and attitudes toward childcare ideals – might complicate the detection of childcare effects.

3.2 Empirical evidence: institutional settings and policy uptake

A central argument in this study is that childcare effects on childbearing interact with alternative policy options. The hypothesis was that public care services have a broad effect on childbearing if the overall family policy strategy favors dual-earner families. If, however, governments offer benefits aimed at male breadwinner families in addition to childcare, women who want to care for their children at home might plan to take advantage of these benefits after having a child. One challenge for researchers in this context is to create a situation of detectable variance of policy options and policy coherence. In the following, studies that attempt to assess the differing policy effects are discussed.

Few studies have focused on varying policy effects on fertility in different policy settings. Others have assessed the policy effects in two (or more) countries, and conclude that diverging effects might be related to institutional differences. Accordingly, some studies have indirectly measured the policy effects of incoherent policies on fertility. Hantrais (1994: 158) suggested that the cohesive policies and coherent family policy objectives of the French government have, in conjunction with other factors, led to a high degree of compatibility between work and family in France, which in turn results in high fertility levels. Hoem et al. (2001) compared third-birth patterns in Austria and Sweden. Although for some Austrian policies Sweden was explicitly taken as a role model, fertility remained on a considerably lower level in Austria. Combined with the fact that some traditional Austrian policies were still in place, the authors detected some policy "ambivalence" (ibid.: 260), which might be the reason for the missing convergence of Austrian and Swedish fertility. A study comparing the effects of parental leave policies on fertility in Norway and Sweden (Duvander et al. 2010) found that couples in which the father did not take any parental leave had lower second-birth risks than those in which the father took at least some leave. Effects of parental leave length, by contrast, differed across the two countries. For Sweden, the results showed that second-birth risks increased with the length of the parental leave a father took with his first child. The authors saw this as a positive effect of gender equality on continued childbearing. In Norway, by contrast, the length of the parental leave taken by fathers was found to be negatively associated with lower second-birth risks. The authors speculated that these different policy effects might be related to the childcare allowance available to Norwegian parents who care for their children at home. As the allowance is usually taken by mothers, fathers might be less likely to take parental leave in Norway.

With a focus on childcare usage, some studies identified national differences in policy effects by directly analyzing policy uptake. This means that these authors investigated not at fertility, but the parents' behavior after having a child. Concerning childcare policies, the questions typically posed in these studies are who makes use of childcare and who makes use of other family policies, such as home care allowances. Many authors focused on the determinants of childcare usage in a single national setting (see Becker, 2007 for a review). Only a few country comparisons exist: a study by Mamolo et al. (2011) investigated the effects of socioeconomic characteristics on the likelihood of childcare usage in the UK, France, Italy, and Spain. The study employed individual-level data from the European Union Statistics on Income and Living Conditions (EU-SILC). While mothers' employment status appeared to stimulate childcare use in all of the four countries, the UK was the only country where fathers' income played a role for childcare usage: the higher the income, the more likely is childcare usage. This implies that, in a liberal welfare state, those with higher family earnings can afford to make use of childcare facilities, while those with lower incomes cannot. As the British system relies on the market, childcare usage depends on the parents' ability to afford the costs of private care. In the other countries, this income effect was not detected. One reason for this might be that in France, Italy, and Spain, childcare is subsidized and family income is less relevant for enrollment in childcare services. This indicates that institutional aspects shape child-care usage, as well as the socioeconomic composition of the group of parents who make use of formal childcare.

In addition, van Lancker and Ghysels (2012) found differences in the social structures of the families who benefited from childcare polices in Sweden and Flanders (Belgium). Although both countries reported high coverage rates, childcare policies have different distributional outcomes in the two countries. Childcare use in Sweden was less influenced by families' financial situations, as all of the income groups used the services to a similar extent. In contrast, in Flanders families with lower incomes used childcare services less frequently than those with higher incomes. The main reason for this gap, the authors asserted, was that government subsidies through tax deductions in Flanders support high-income fami-lies to a greater extent than those with lower incomes. In Sweden, lower-income families benefit more from subsidies than higher-income fami-lies, as they pay lower fees. Thus, parents with lower socioeconomic status can also afford childcare services. This indicates how important institutional design is for the redistributive effects of policies.

Beyond childcare, it has been shown that parents with different levels of socioeconomic status respond differently to specific policy measures. On the one hand, welfare state settings influence women's positions within the class hierarchy in a society. For example, the universalistic policies of the Scandinavian welfare states usually reduce inequalities between men and women. This is, for example, evident in the relatively small gender wage gap in Nordic countries (Mandel and Shalev 2009). On the other hand, even within welfare states, there are differences in the opportunity structures for women in different socioeconomic groups. This means that specific policy options might be used by only a sub-population in a society. Studies have shown this to be the case for the home care allowance in different countries. Mothers with lower socioec-onomic status were found to be more likely to make use of the home care allowance than those with higher socioeconomic status (e.g., Morgan and Zippel 2003; Aassve and Lappegård 2009). For fathers' income and uptake of the home care allowance, Aassve and Lappegård (2009) found an inverse u-shaped relationship. This indicates that the family might be less dependent on the mothers' earnings when the father's income is high. For the higher-income group, this flat-rate benefit might matter less for the overall economic situation of the family, and thus has a reduced effect. In Finland, a country where all of the children under school age are entitled to childcare, a study found that women who did not have a job were especially likely to take the home care allowance (Salmi 2006). In Switzerland, the effect of childcare availability on mothers' employment seems to be strongest for highly educated women (Stadelmann-Steffen 2011) implying that policies that encourage women to return to work after childbirth have different effects based on women's educational levels. Model calculations based on the income of hypothetical couples, Tunberger and Sigle-Rushton (2011) showed that the home care allowance in Sweden was most attractive for families where women earn less than men. For these couples, incentives for full-time work were weakest (ibid.: 231).

Most of the studies discussed above did not explicitly focus on the effects of childcare policies on fertility. The results still indicated that some policy settings lead to a selective uptake of childcare services and other family policies, and that the policy effects are selective depending on the socioeconomic status of a family. Thus, when seeking to understand the effects of policies, it is clearly important that we consider the opportunity structures that evolve from family policy packages, rather than assessing each policy detached from its context.

3.3 Empirical evidence: attitudes and fertility behavior

Within the theoretical model I presented in Section 2.3, attitudes are an important element in the decision to have a first child. I argued that the effect of public childcare on fertility might depend on a person's attitudes toward nonfamily childcare. I expect to find that public childcare has less influence on a woman's decision to have a child if she thinks that care of this kind is inappropriate for children. But data on childcare ideals, and thus studies on the effects of such ideals, are usually unavailable.

However, family-related attitudes and their effect on fertility have been extensively investigated in the literature. Although the focus in this study is on attitudes within the Theory of Planned Behavior, I also review studies using related theoretical concepts. In the following, I present empirical evidence on the effects of the values parents attach to children, their preferences concerning family and working life, and on gender roles within the family.

Studies that focus on the "Values of Children" (VOC) approach proposed by Hoffman and Hoffman (1973) assumed that (potential) parents expect differing levels of benefits from having children. Studies have shown that, across countries, a high economic value attached to children was related to high individual fertility risks, while emotional values were related to lower fertility risks (Kagitcibasi and Ataca 2005; Nauck 2007). Although the VOC approach focuses on the positive expectations from having children, scholars have suggested to include also negative expectations when studying childbearing (Liefbroer 2005).

In this context, the use of the TPB framework (cf. Section 2.3) has increasingly been employed (see Philipov et al. 2009 for a review). One study showed that positive attitudes toward having children are related to higher, while negative attitudes are related to lower chances of having positive childbearing intentions (Billari et al. 2009 for Bulgaria). These results were found among both men and women, and for first- and second-birth intentions. Other studies have found these effects for higher-order birth intentions, but not for first birth intentions (Dommermuth et al. 2011 for Norway). Barber (2001) suggested that fertility depends not only on attitudes toward childbearing, but also on attitudes toward alternative behaviors, such as pursuing a career and investing in education. These life goals compete for time and resources. Thus, attaching importance to one of these competing life domains has a diminishing effect on fertility. Studying the U.S., Barber and colleagues (Barber 2001; Barber et al. 2002; Barber and Axinn 2005) found that individual life goals were of varying importance for the fertility behavior in different subgroups of the population. Attitudes toward children and the family were important for predicting first births among married individuals. Among unmarried respondents, by contrast, attitudes toward career and luxury goods had a negative effect on first birth risks, while attitudes toward children did not show an effect. In terms of intentions, Philipov (2009) also found indications for the competing nature of different life domains for young adults. In a study on Bulgarian males and females, the author showed that the intention to study had a negative effect on both the intention to have a first child and the occurrence of a first birth.

Some studies did not directly employ the TPB as theoretical framework, but investigated to what extent expectations of positive and negative consequences affected childbearing. The study by Liefbroer (2005) found higher risks of entry into parenthood among respondents who

expected that having children would have relatively few negative consequences for their careers. Among women, this effect was only shown
after using a model with interaction effects. A study on Swedish young
adults (Bernhardt and Goldscheider 2006) found that respondents who
associated having children with higher costs were less likely to enter
parenthood. For women, it was also shown that those who expected
higher benefits had a higher risk of having a child, while for men this
effect did not reach statistical significance.

A concept that accounts for the reciprocity of childbearing and working life was provided by Catherine Hakim in her "Preference Theory".
Hakim refrained from explicitly defining preferences in her approach, but
only suggested a close relationship to values, personal goals, and socialization (Hakim 2000; Hakim 2002). Others have suggested that preferences "order choices among behavioral options" (Alwin 2005: 115).
Preferences and attitudes are closely related. Attitudes usually focus on a
single behavior, while preferences reflect women's attitudes toward both
career and family organization. Originally, Preference Theory was used to
understand the variation in women's working careers (Hakim 2000).[20]
Later, it was also employed to explain differences in fertility behavior
(Hakim 2003). The theory suggests that women have heterogeneous
preferences concerning the combination of work and family life. Accordingly, Hakim (2003) showed through a descriptive analysis on women in
the UK that those with a preference for a home-oriented lifestyle had
more children than career-oriented women. The average number of children born to women who want to have both a career and a family, so-
called adaptive women, lies in between. This indicates that personal preferences affect childbearing. Other studies have also shown the existence
of heterogeneous patterns of lifestyle preferences and a correlation with
fertility choices in a number of European welfare states (Ruckdeschel
2008; Vitali et al. 2009). Preference Theory has been at the center of
lively discussions in the literature. Some of the critics of this theory have
pointed out the limits women may face when choosing their preferred
lifestyle. They argued that neglecting these constraints understates the
importance of structural and institutional aspects, such as childcare avail-

20 Hakim suggested that her Preference Theory can also be employed to explain
    differences in men's life-style choices (Hakim 2000: 254ff.). However, the life-
    styles of men are more homogenous, and a minority would prefer to exit the la-
    bor market to care for children (ibid.).

ability, job security, and economic necessities (Fagan 2001; Doorewaard et al. 2004; Himmelweit and Sigala 2004; Tomlinson 2006; Kangas and Rostgaard 2007; Gash 2008; Stähli et al. 2009). Moreover, within the framework of Preference Theory, preferences are assumed to be stable over the life course. However, some critics have argued that individuals adapt their attitudes to their experiences and their personal situations (Steiber and Haas 2009).

In addition to explicit attitudes toward childbearing and career goals, more general attitudes may also affect fertility behavior. More traditional individuals, such as those who believe it is important to be married and to have children, seem to enter parenthood earlier than their non-traditional counterparts (Thomson 2002; Moors 2008). In terms of gender-egalitarian attitudes, the effects on fertility seem to be mixed. Egalitarian women seemed to have weaker childbearing intentions than non-egalitarian women (Kaufman 2000 for Americans). In contrast, egalitarian men had stronger intentions than their non-egalitarian counterparts (Puur et al. 2008 for males in eight countries). For Swedish men, the opposite was found to be the case: those with traditional gender attitudes had a higher risk of entering fatherhood than those with egalitarian attitudes (Bernhardt and Goldscheider 2006). Among Swedish women, the degree of traditionalism did not affect childbearing (ibid.).

One issue that seems to be important when considering the effect of attitudes on behavior is that the causal direction is difficult to disentangle (Lesthaeghe and Moors 2002; Surkyn and Lesthaeghe 2004). On the one hand, individuals might select themselves into specific life course trajectories on basis of their values orientation. On the other hand, life course decisions, such as having a child, might affect the opinion of a person. In studying this life course perspective, Lesthaeghe and Moors (2002) have recommended the use of panel data, which allows researchers to take into account the time component between cause and effect. Some of the above-mentioned studies are based on panel data (Barber 2001; Thomson 2002; Liefbroer 2005; Bernhardt and Goldscheider 2006; Moors 2008), while many are based on cross-sectional data.

To summarize, the research findings presented here suggest that attitudes (or similar concepts, such as costs and benefits of children) are related to childbearing intentions and behaviors. If a woman expects that having children will have positive effects on her life, she is more likely to have a child (or to have stronger intentions to have a child). If, however, she expects that having a child will have negative consequences, she will be less likely to have a first birth (or she will have weaker first birth intentions). Women in this latter group might also be more open to being influenced by policies that reduce the expected costs of having children and adapt their childbearing intentions (Philipov et al. 2009). It should be noted that the studies discussed here did not consider attitudes toward the childcare practices that were identified as being relevant in the theoretical considerations above.

4 Fertility development and the institutional context in Sweden and Germany

In the empirical analyses of this study, I build on the institutional differences between Sweden and Germany. These countries have rather different values and different traditions of family policies. Accordingly, childcare availability might affect behaviors in different ways. In Sweden, family policies support mainly dual-earner households. (Western) Germany has long been seen as the prototypical male breadwinner society, but in recent years the German government has added some dual-earner policies to the country's package of family policies. Eastern Germany deviates from this pattern, with its high female labor force participation rates and relatively high levels of availability of childcare for children under age three. Thus, Germany's current mix of family policies is increasingly pluralistic.

In order to provide a broader picture of Sweden and Germany, I will first outline the developments in childbearing patterns in these countries in recent decades (Section 4.1). I will then describe the family policy systems in the two countries. This includes a description of the historical development of childcare policies and female labor force participation over time.

4.1 Fertility development

In the following, I compare the development of the TFR and the cohort fertility rate at age 40 in Sweden and Germany in recent decades. Following this, I provide an overview of the postponement of first births by presenting the change in age-specific fertility rates for first births for different cohorts.

Sweden has a relatively high total fertility rate compared to other European countries. While the EU-27 average had a period TFR of 1.6 in 2010 (Eurostat 2013b), in Sweden, the level was 1.9. A look at the development of the TFR in Sweden over time (see Figure 5) shows a considerable amount of fluctuation ("roller coaster fertility"; Hoem and Hoem 1996).

Figure 5:   Development of the period TFR in Sweden, 1945-2010.

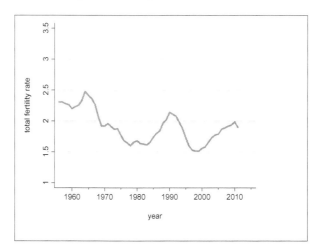

Figure 6:   Development of the period TFR in Germany, 1945-2010.

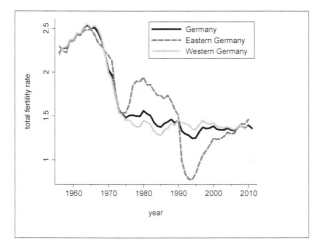

Source (Figures 5 and 6): Human Fertility Database. Retrieved April 7 2013 from www.humanfertility.org.

From 1945, we observe a decline in the TFR, with an increase in the period between 1960 to 1965 followed by a further decrease after 1965. In 1983, the TFR fell to a level of 1.6, but by 1990, the TFR had increased again to a level of 2.1. The decline that followed in the early 1990s was connected to the economic downturn in Sweden during that period (Andersson 2000; Hoem 2000). However, the cohort fertility rate (at age 40) in Sweden had been stable at around two for the last several decades (see Figure 7).

With its history as a divided country between 1945 and 1990, Germany has a special position in Europe. After the Berlin Wall came down, the socialist system in the eastern part of the country was replaced by the economic and political system of West Germany. Over the last 20 years, fertility levels, rates of female labor force participation, and childcare provision have remained different in the two German regions. In both parts of the country, period fertility levels have declined substantially in recent decades (see Figure 6). The TFR developed very similarly between 1956 and 1975 in West and East Germany. From 1976 onward, period fertility was increasing in the East, reaching a TFR of 1.9 in 1982, and then falling thereafter. In West Germany, the TFR stabilized at a low level of around 1.4 starting in the mid-1970s. Fertility in eastern Germany fell sharply immediately after unification in 1990, decreasing to 0.8 in 1992 to 1994. Thereafter it started to increase, reaching a level of 1.46 in 2010. This rate is slightly higher than that of western Germany (1.39).

Figure 8 depicts the development of the completed fertility rates by age 40 in the two countries. In Germany, the cohort total fertility rates by age 40 were declining across the cohorts born between 1940 and 1970 from a mean number of 1.9 to 1.45 children (born to women by age 40). The decline in cohort fertility started earlier in western Germany, with cohort fertility in eastern Germany remaining above 1.7 until 1962.

One dominant factor that shaped the development of fertility in Europe was the postponement of first motherhood (Gustafsson 2001; Sobotka 2004). Women in Sweden have also postponed childbearing to later ages in recent decades. This trend is reflected in the increasing mean age at first birth: whereas in 1970 Swedish women had their first child at a mean age of 24, this value had increased by approximately five years to age 29 in 2010 (Human Fertility Database 2012).

Figure 7: Development of cohort total fertility rates as of age 40 in Sweden. Cohorts born in 1940-1970.

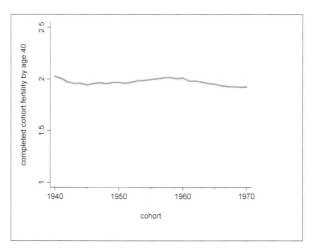

Figure 8: Development of cohort total fertility rates as of age 40 in Germany. Cohorts born in 1940-1970.

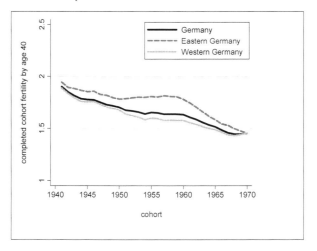

Source (Figures 7 and 8): Human Fertility Database. Retrieved April 7 2013 from www.humanfertility.org.

The postponement trend is also visible in the development of the age-specific fertility rates for first births (Figure 9). Among women born in 1930, the first birth intensities were highest for women at age 24. In contrast, the highest intensities were found at age 29 for birth cohort 1970. The curves reveal that women in Sweden had their first child later, but that the shape of childbearing intensities remained largely the same.

Figure 9:   Age-specific fertility rates; first births in Sweden.

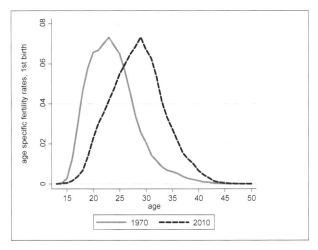

Source: Human Fertility Database. Retrieved April 7 2013 from www.humanfertility.org.

To gain a better understanding of the fertility patterns in eastern and western Germany, it would be interesting to compare the development of age-specific fertility rates for first births. Unfortunately, until recently the necessary data was unavailable for Germany, as vital statistics did not distinguish children by birth order. In order to evaluate the postponement of first births, Table 2 presents the mean age at first birth for selected years, based on different data sources. In 1960 in western Germany, the mean age at first birth was 24.9 years. By 2009, first-time mothers were, on average, more than four years older. While women in eastern Germany also postponed their first births, they were younger than western Germans when they entered motherhood. In 1960, eastern German women were, on average, 22.4 years old when they gave birth for the first time. In 2009, the mean age at first birth was 27.3.

Table 2: Mean age at first birth in Germany. Women ages 15-44. Selected years.

time period	western Germany	eastern Germany
1960	24.9	22.4
1970	23.8	22.1
1980	25.0	21.8
1990	26.0	22.7
1995	26.7	24.9
2001	27.4	26.1
2002	27.6	26.4
2003	27.7	26.6
2004	28.0	26.9
2005	28.1	27.0
2006	28.3	27.1
2007	28.5	27.3
2008	28.7	27.5
2009	29.1	27.2
2010	29.2	27.4

Source: 1960-1995 based on Kreyenfeld (2001: 64), 2001-2008 based on Kreyenfeld et al. (2011a: 214), 2009 and 2010 based on DESTATIS (2012a: 11).

In comparison, the mean age at first birth in Sweden and (West) Germany today is almost identical. However, the differences in childlessness in the two countries are pronounced. In Sweden, childlessness increased slightly for younger cohorts, from 12 percent (cohort born in 1935-39) to 14 percent (cohort born in 1955-59; see Andersson et al. 2009). In Germany, the rates of childlessness are considerably higher. Of the German women born between 1952 and 1961, 19 percent are childless (DESTATIS 2008). Once more, the numbers for eastern and western Germany vary substantially. In eastern Germany, just seven percent of women are childless, compared to 21 percent in western Germany (ibid.). This shows that in western Germany a considerably larger share of women completely forgoes motherhood than in Sweden.

4.2 Family policies in Sweden: dual-earner support

Sweden is often cited as the standard example of a social democratic welfare state (Esping-Andersen 1990). One of the central aims of Swedish family policy is to offer mothers and fathers the opportunity to share responsibilities at work and in the home. As the generous parental leave and childcare policies in Sweden support parents who want to combine family and paid employment, the government's family policy strategy has, in recent decades, favored the dual-earner model (Björnberg 2002; Nyberg 2004).[21]

The Swedish parental leave system offers job protection for 18 months after childbirth. Up to a relatively high ceiling, 80 percent (depending on the employer often 90 percent) of the earnings of parents who were employed before the child was born are replaced. This earnings replacement is granted for 13 months (Ministry of Health and Social Affairs 2007). For a further three months, parents are compensated at a flat rate. In order to promote gender equality, at least 60 days of parental leave are reserved for each parent. Although fathers' use of parental leave has been increasing, in 2010 it still amounted to less than 23 percent of the total parental leave taken by Swedish parents (Duvander and Johansson 2010).

After the leave period, children usually attend public childcare or publicly subsidized daycare.[22] Public care[23] for children below school age (i.e., usually age seven) is organized as a preschool activity for the age group one to five years, and as preschool class for children in the year before they enter school. Today, the municipalities are responsible for providing childcare (Swedish National Agency for Education 2003). Unlike in other

---

21 In addition, there are policies offering financial support for parents, such as a child allowance, a means-tested form of maintenance support, and a housing allowance. In 2008, there were some reforms that included a home care allowance paid to parents who do not use childcare services (Ferrarini and Duvander 2010). Moreover, with the reform a gender equality bonus was introduced, meaning that tax credits were given to parents who shared parental leave equally (Duvander and Johansson 2010).

22 In Sweden, grandparents are involved in childcare to a minor degree (Hank and Buber 2009).

23 Private preschool, which is run by a non-municipal organizer under the supervision of the municipalities, plays a minor role, with a 15.4-percent enrollment of children ages one to five (data provided by SCB).

countries, where the provision is often insufficient, in Sweden the demand for childcare is fully met (European Commission's Expert Group on Gender and Employment Issues 2009). Under the maximum fee rule introduced in 2002, municipalities cannot charge parents more than three percent of gross income for childcare services. The fee decreases with the number of children. Although this rule is voluntary, by 2003 all of the municipalities had adopted this maximum fee system (Skolverket 2007). Childcare quality is usually rated as high in Sweden; child-staff ratio for children age one to five years is 1:5.1 (European Commission's Expert Group on Gender and Employment 2009).

This system of leave and childcare supports sequenced periods of parental care and paid work after a child is born. Less than one percent of children under one year old are in childcare, as virtually all parents take parental leave during this period. Survey data for the years 1991 and 2000 showed that the mean amount of parental leave taken by mothers in Sweden was 15.6 months, although with large variations (Evertsson and Duvander 2011). Children born in 1999 started daycare on average at the age of 1.5 years (Duvander 2006).[24]

The developments in care policies and policy paradigms over time

Starting in the late 1960s, gender equality became a central political issue in Sweden. In order to improve the economic independence of women, a number of policies were introduced. As a means to enable mothers to participate in the labor market, the expansion of childcare availability was largely a feminist issue in Sweden (Naumann 2005). In 1972, an individual taxation system came into force that abolished the joint taxation favoring male breadwinner families (Ahlberg et al. 2008). In the same year, an official report was published that recommended an increase in public childcare provision (Björnberg 2002). Childcare advocates argued that this would both enable women to participate in the labor market, and improve the opportunities of children, as childcare institutions offer a stimulating environment and socialization outside the family (ibid.: 38). Moreover, Sweden was the first country to introduce parental leave in

24 The gap between the parental leave of the mother and the start of childcare might have occurred for different reasons. Most probably, fathers start parental leave after the mother starts working. For an overview of the development of fathers' leave usage over time, see Duvander and Johansson (2010).

1974 (Chronholm 2009: 228). Both parental leave and childcare policies were introduced to support maternal employment and increase women's financial independence. As such, both policies were targeted at promoting gender equality, with a focus on paid work. With the introduction of the "daddy month" in 1995 (which was extended in 2002 to two months) – i.e., parental leave reserved for fathers – gender equality was extended to caregiving (Eydal and Rostgaard 2011).

Childcare policies were also crafted with the goal of improving the prospects of children (Hiilamo and Kangas 2009: 472). This was emphasized by the establishment in 1995 of a legal entitlement to childcare for all children from ages one to 12. From age four to the age of school entry, children are entitled to 525 hours of preschool per year free of charge. Children of unemployed parents (since 2001) or of parents who are on parental leave with a younger child (since 2002) have the right to attend childcare for a minimum of three hours per week (Samuelsson and Sheridan 2004). The goal of equal access weakened the link between childcare and parents' work, as the right to childcare was extended to children whose parents did not participate in the labor market (Pestoff and Strandbrink 2004). Since the 1990s, the Swedish daycare system has undergone considerable changes in terms of organization, fees, curriculum, and access. Today, each municipality is responsible for providing childcare; i.e., a child between the ages of one and 12 will be offered a publicly or privately organized childcare arrangement within three to four months after the family applies (Swedish National Agency for Education 2003). The quality of the childcare facilities is high, and the Swedish system of early childhood services was ranked first among 25 OECD countries (UNICEF 2008). Figure 10 shows considerable increases in enrollment rates in recent decades: in 1975 less than 20 percent of children between the ages of one and school age attended out-of-home care arrangements, while in 2008, the share was 86 percent. For children in the age group one to two, enrollment reached 70 percent; while for those between the ages of three and five, it is 94 percent.

After the national elections in 2006, the center-right government introduced some changes to the family policy system in Sweden. Most prominently, a home care allowance was introduced on July 1, 2008.[25]

---

25 A similar allowance was introduced by the Conservative government in Sweden back in 1994. This policy was abolished in the same year when the Social Democrats won the elections (Nyberg 2010).

Within this scheme, municipalities can pay a specific amount to parents (approx.. 340 euros maximum) who do not use public childcare for children under age three. Such cash-for-care schemes are in practice used mainly by women (Morgan and Zippel 2003), and thus reinforce a gendered division of paid and unpaid labor. As it deviates from the earner-carer model that dominated for decades in Sweden, this reform represents a sharp change in the development of Swedish family policy (Ferrarini and Duvander 2010). Using the rhetoric of "free choice", the conservative government was promoting the home care allowance as an opportunity for women to freely choose whether to return to the labor market or to stay home to care for a child (Nyberg 2010).

Figure 10:   Development of enrollment rates in public (or publicly subsidized) childcare in Sweden 1975-2008.

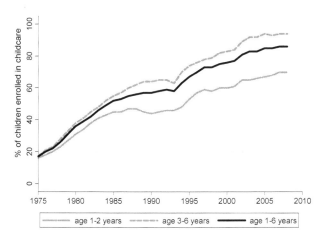

Notes: Numbers in the graph before 1999 refer to the age group 1-6 years, and to the age group 1-5 years from 1999 onward. Source: Swedish National Agency for Education. Author's presentation. Retrieved April 7 2013 from http://www.skolverket.se/sb/d/1664.

By 2011, 37 percent of all municipalities had introduced a home care allowance scheme, and 2.5 percent of parents with one- and two-year-old children were receiving it (Ellingsæter 2012). As the childcare enrollment rates have changed little over the past few years, it appears that the introduction of the home care allowance did not greatly affect parental behavior. In fact, the increasing childcare enrollment rates for children under age three (see Figure 10) indicate a stable acceptance of non-family care for this age group. The majority of Swedish parents use childcare but there are differences in the ages at which children start preschool. It seems that the care ideals among Swedish parents are mainly concerned with the length of the parental leave and the age at which children should start attending formal childcare. An early assessment has shown that, among the few parents who are using the home care allowance in Sweden, immigrants and parents with lower incomes seem to be overrepresented (Nyberg 2010). This is in line with the calculations of Tunberger and Sigle-Rushton (2011), who showed that for mothers with lower earnings, the relative income reduction related to the home care allowance is smaller than for middle- or high-income mothers.

Female labor force participation

The postponement of first births in Sweden is associated with the increasing share of women who attain higher education and who intend to have a professional career (Tesching 2012). Indeed, female labor force participation in Sweden has increased considerably in recent decades (see Figure 11). It should be noted that the female labor force participation rate refers to the share of women in the working-age population (ages 15 to 64) who are available to participate in the labor market; i.e., it includes unemployed women. Another option would have been to use the employment rate, which only refers to women who actually work. This number is, however, sensitive to fluctuations in the unemployment rate. For my argument, it is more interesting to look at how the self-perception of women as workers has changed over time. I therefore focus on the female labor force participation rate, which is independent of the development of unemployment.

Whereas in the period after World War II only 54 percent of Swedish women were available to participate in the labor market, the share increased over time, and reached 82 percent in 1990. It decreased thereafter and was at a level of 77 percent in 2008. Over the time period observed, the labor force participation rate of men was decreasing from 90 percent to 82 percent. This represents a substantial reduction in the employment gap between men and women in Sweden. In 2008, 77 percent of women participated in the labor market, while 70 percent of children between one and two years of age were enrolled in childcare (SCB

2010a). Of the working mothers with one- and two-year-olds, 40 percent were in part-time[26] employment (SCB 2010b).

Figure 11: Development of labor force participation among men and women in Sweden over time. Ages 15-64.

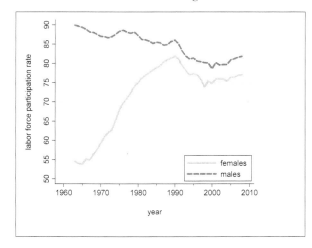

Source: Generations and Gender Programme (2013). Retrieved April 7 2013 from www.ggp-i.org/contextual-database.html.

4.3 Family policies in Germany: departure from male breadwinner support

The German welfare state was classified as conservative (Esping-Andersen 1990). Usually, no distinction is made between western and eastern Germany (Schmitt and Trappe 2010). However, regional differences persist, especially concerning the provision of childcare services since unification in 1990. In western Germany the level of support for male breadwinner families has traditionally been high (Lewis and Ostner 1994). The joint income taxation system provides incentives for married

---

26 Part-time employment in Sweden is defined as less than 35 working hours per week.

women to exit the labor market (Gustafsson and Bruyn-Hundt 1991). In addition, the legal entitlement to kindergarten for each child between the ages of three and six refers to part-time daycare, which is incompatible with the full-time employment of mothers. For children under age three, public childcare options have been very limited (but have increased in recent years). The reduced childcare options can be seen as structural constraints to maternal (full-time) employment (Kreyenfeld and Hank 2000; Klement et al. 2007).

By contrast, in pre-unification East Germany (1945 to 1990), female labor force participation remained at a relatively high level after World War II (Sørensen and Trappe 1995). A number of policies promoted the combining of work and family (Hagemann 2006). The provision of full-time childcare for children under age three was well established (Frerich and Frey 1996). After German unification in 1990, the family policies and labor market regulations changed drastically for eastern Germans, as the family policies of the western part of the country were applied to the new states (*Länder*). Childcare provision decreased in the years after unification, mainly in response to the decline in births and the reduced number of children in care (Sternitzky and Putzing 1996; Hank et al. 2001). Today, enrollment rates in the east are still substantially higher than in the west (DESTATIS 2011a).

At the moment, reforms of the family policy system are underway in Germany, and these changes represent a paradigm shift away from support for male breadwinner families, and toward support for dual-earner families (Henninger et al. 2008). The shift is partly driven by the parental leave reform of 2007, which introduced a leave system similar to that of Sweden (Erler 2009; Ostner 2010). In 2005 and 2008, the German government enacted two laws to increase public childcare provision and subsidized family daycare, especially for children under age three. Since August 2013, childcare access for children between the age of one and the age of school entry should be guaranteed. Before the legal entitlement went into effect, certain groups[27] had had privileged access in regions with a shortage of childcare. Childcare costs are tied to family income and the number of children in the family (Lange 2008). As municipalities are responsible for childcare fees, there is a strong variation in

---

27   According to the law, these privileged groups include children whose well-being is not secured, or whose parents are looking for or are starting a job, or are participating in job-creating measures.

prices. Thus comparison is difficult. Based on a survey in 2005, the average, childcare fee for children under age three was 119€ per month[28] (Lang 2007: 110). Since 2006, two-thirds of childcare fees have been tax deductible, up to a ceiling of 4,000 euros annually (Ehlert 2010). Childcare quality is difficult to assess. The average staff–child ratio for children under age three in 2010 was 1:5.8 in Germany (Autorengruppe Bildungsberichterstattung 2010).

While almost all mothers in Germany use parental leave, uptake among men is modest. Following the parental leave reform, the uptake of leave among fathers has increased considerably. In particular, highly educated men and those with temporary working contracts are now more likely to take leave than in the past (Geisler and Kreyenfeld 2012). Of the men who became fathers in 2010, 25 percent took advantage of parental leave, with a mean leave duration of 2.8 months (DESTATIS 2012b).

In the current transition phase of the German family policy system, women in western Germany will face a period of discontinuity. In regions where the childcare provision for children below age three is not sufficient, mothers often have to remain outside of the labor market after the end of the parental leave period with an earnings replacement of up to 65 percent (after 12 to 14 months). The attachment to the labor force is interrupted, despite the presence of the parental leave system, which should incentivize women to return to work soon after childbirth. Thus, at the moment, family policies in western Germany are difficult to classify, as they do not consistently support either male breadwinner or dual-earner families. The current policy mix in Germany can be classified as pluralistic family support.

The developments in care policies and policy paradigms over time

Over recent years, the political debate on childcare in Germany has focused on children under age three. Before, public interest was focused on children between age three and the age of school entry. This was reflected in the goals set in the reforms of the Child and Youth Welfare Act (*Kinder und Jugendhilfegesetz*). In 1990, the amendment of the act mainly had the objective to make childcare available to a majority of children starting

---

28 It should be noted that in the survey, some parents included costs of meals in the childcare fees (Lang 2007). Thus, average net costs remain unclear.

from age three. Kindergarten was seen as the "first level of the educational system" (Colberg-Schrader 1994). This was implemented through a legal entitlement to childcare for three- to six-year-old children during the 1990s (Rauschenbach 2007). The entitlement referred to part-time kindergarten, and thus did not support mothers in returning to (full-time) work. Thus the law appears to have been promoting children's development rather than women's employment options.

Figure 12:   Provision of public childcare in eastern (1991) and western Germany (1990).

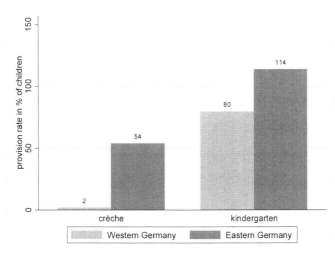

Notes: Provision rates refer to the slots available per 100 children per age group (crèche: children ages 0-2; kindergarten: children ages 3-5). Rates above 100 percent indicate difficulties in assigning kindergarten spots merely to the age group three to school entry. Source: Statistisches Bundesamt 2011a; 2011b.

Figure 12 and Figure 13 display the development of public childcare in eastern and western Germany. It should be noted that a consistent presentation of the yearly level of childcare provision is impossible for Germany, as the definition of the official statistics changed in 2005 (cf. Kolvenbach and Taubmann 2006). The numbers for the years before 2006 (including 1990/1991 depicted in Figure 12) are provision rates; i.e., they refer to the number of slots available to 100 children in the various age groups. In contrast, from 2006 onward, the enrollment rates are reported, i.e., the share of children that actually makes use of childcare services (see Figure 13 for enrollment rates in 2012). These rates differ qualitatively: while provision can be interpreted as supply, enrollment rates reflect demand. Thus, these measures should be compared with caution.

Figure 13:   Enrollment rate in public childcare in eastern and western Germany in 2012.

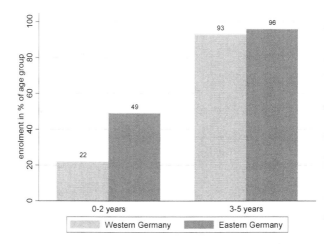

Notes: Enrollment rates refer to the number of children enrolled as a share of all children in this age group. The data refers to March 1, 2012. Source: DESTATIS 2012c.

Children under age three were excluded from the legal entitlement before August 2013. This is visible in the very low provision rate of two percent in western Germany in 1990 (see Figure 12). Children in the age group zero to two were attending crèches, while children in the age group three to five were attending kindergarten. Because of the high level of childcare availability for children under age three during the socialist era, the provision in eastern Germany was, at 54 percent, still high after unification. The provision for children in kindergarten was 80 percent in western and 114 percent in eastern Germany. The provision rates of more than 100 percent are probably not a sign of oversupply; instead, they might indicate problems that occurred when assigning kindergarten slots to children in the age group three to school entry (Kreyenfeld 2004: 10).

The current discussion on childcare focuses mainly on the balance between family and work, which should be improved by sufficient childcare for the under-threes[29] (Leu 2002; Leitner 2010). In addition, the draft legislation for the Act to Support Children Under Three Years in Daycare explicitly mentioned a positive relationship between public childcare provision and the realization of fertility plans (Deutscher Bundestag 2008). Since August 2013, one year old children are legally entitled to childcare services. The expansion of public childcare services and subsidized daycare for children under age three is a reform that enables mothers to delegate childcare to institutions (or family daycare), and is therefore an instrument of de-familialization. Together with the parental leave reform introduced in 2007, the childcare initiative of the German government proposes a policy targeting employed mothers who return to work relatively soon (i.e., after around one year) after giving birth. Interestingly, the introduction of the new parental leave system and the increase in the provision childcare for the under-threes seems to have cross-party political support. Dual-earner policies are associated with social democratic ideas, but they were introduced by a government led by the conservative Christian Democrats (Fleckenstein 2010).[30]

Following several policy initiatives, the availability of childcare for children under age three in western Germany has increased considerably in recent years. This is reflected in the enrollment rate of 22 percent in

29 Moreover, the new law also includes a paragraph focusing on the provision of full-time childcare for children ages three to five tailored to (working) parents' demands.

30 In the coalition agreement it was stipulated that, in addition to the existing reforms of the family policy system, a home care allowance had to be introduced in 2013. This allowance is paid to parents who do not use institutional childcare, but who take a longer break from work in order to care for their children at home. Since August 1, 2013, the amount is paid as lump sum of 100 euros per month. One year later, the benefit will be raised by 50 euros per month (Blum and Erler 2012: 133). It is paid after parental leave benefit until the child's third birthday. The opponents of the allowance expect that particularly low-income mothers and immigrants will take advantage of the benefit, and that existing differences between social groups will thereby be reinforced. To date, no data exist to assess these issues.

western Germany (Figure 13). In eastern Germany, the provision of childcare is more widely spread. A survey on childcare demands among parents in 2011, 49 percent of eastern German respondents wanted to use childcare for their children under age three (BMFSFJ 2012). This matches the share of enrolled children in this age group in 2012, which suggests that the supply meets the demand. In western Germany, 36 percent of parents expressed a desire to use childcare for this age group. By contrast, in 2012 only 22 percent of children were enrolled in care.

Based on the available data, the childcare provision in western Germany for young children still does not meet demand (BMFSFJ 2012). The extent to which municipalities in western Germany have managed to expand their childcare provision to comply with the legal entitlement since August 2013 remains to be seen. Before the policy reform, childcare access for children under age three depended on the family's situation. Preferential access was usually granted to those with special needs, such as working parents (Tietze et al. 1993). The reform abolishes such access criteria and should enable all parents to make use of public childcare.

Overall, even though there has been a marked shift toward the dual-earner family in Germany, male breadwinner policies are still in place. The old approach persists through institutions like the marriage-based joint taxation regime, the pension and health care systems, and the newly introduced home care allowance.

Female labor force participation

In western Germany, female labor force participation has risen substantially (Figure 14 and Figure 15). Between 1959 and 2009, participation levels among western German women increased from 47 percent to 70 percent. In 2008, one-third of German mothers with children under age three were employed (DESTATIS 2010a). However, in 2011 47 percent of women in the age group 25 to 49 years were in part-time employment (see Appendix B).

The share of men in the work force decreased from 91 percent in 1959 to 82 percent in 2009, which might be related to early pension regulations (Manow and Seils 2000). Figure 15 compares the female labor force participation rates in eastern and western Germany since unification. The level of 77 percent among eastern German women in 1991 is considerably higher than among western German women (58 percent).

Figure 14: Development of labor force participation among men and women in western Germany over time. Ages 15-65.

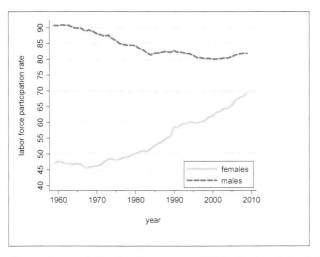

Source: Generations and Gender Programme (2013). Retrieved April 7 2013 from www.ggp-i.org/contextual-database.html.

This indicates that, during the socialist era, women in East Germany were more likely to have been working than women in West Germany (Sorensen and Trappe 1995). Employment among eastern German women decreased in the 1990s, falling to 72 percent in the year 2000. The level then started to increase, reaching 76 percent in 2009. It seems that since unification, the labor force participation rates of women in the two parts of Germany have grown more similar, mainly due to growing female employment in western Germany. This development has been accompanied by a substantial increase of women who work part-time in eastern Germany, which has led to a convergence in the direction of a "male breadwinner/female part-time carer" arrangement (Rosenfeld et al. 2004: 120).

Figure 15:   Development of labor force participation among men and women in western Germany over time. Ages 15-65.

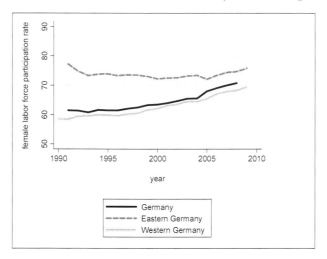

Source: Generations and Gender Programme (2013). Retrieved April 7 2013 from www.ggp-i.org/contextual-database.html.

4.4   Summary: Childcare in Sweden and Germany

In this section, I compared the fertility developments and contextual factors in Sweden, eastern and western Germany. Based on the argument that childcare provision might affect people's behaviors differently in different institutional setting, I provided an overview of the family policy system and the development of public childcare over time. The childcare enrollment rates of one- and two-year-olds over the last 10 years are presented in Figure 16. Moreover, a summary table with all of the discussed features of the childcare and family policy system can be found in Appendix B.

The two countries followed different paths in formulating their general family policy strategies. Sweden offers universal childcare, and the Swedish system of family policies has been regarded as the prototype of the earner-carer model (Ferrarini and Duvander 2010). Western Germany, in contrast, has long been seen as a conservative welfare state with policies supporting single-earner families. Especially in western Germany, childcare for children under age three is not available to all parents who want to use it. However, childcare provision is much higher in eastern Germany. Moreover, in recent years, several reforms introduced policies favoring families in which both parents work; thus (western) German family policies can no longer be classified as supporting the male bread-winner model only. Today, the family policy system is best described as pluralistic.

Figure 16:   Public childcare 2002-2011. Sweden, eastern, and western Germany. Enrollment rates of 1-2 year old children.

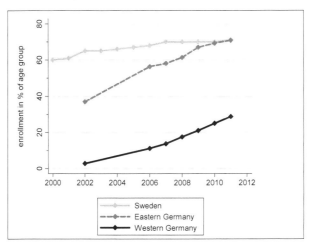

Notes: Author's own calculations. Enrollment rates include public or publicly funded full- and part-time care arrangements in institutions or family day-care. Sources: Sweden: SCB (2010a; 2013). Eastern and western Germany: for 2011: DESTATIS (2012c), for years 2006-2010: (DESTATIS 2011b). For 2002, the number is the provision rate for 0-2-year-old children (DESTATIS, 2004).

Figure 16 shows the development of the official enrollment rates of one- and two-year-old children over time. This age group is of specific interest, as children under age one are usually cared for by the mother. Starting from age one, childcare services become increasingly important in enabling mothers to return to work. Enrollment is lowest in western Germany, where we observe a considerable increase between 2002 and

2010, with enrollment reaching a level of 29 percent in 2011. It is striking that, by 2011, the childcare usage levels for children under age three in eastern Germany were more similar to those in Sweden than to those in western Germany.

Sweden was explicitly cited as a best practice example for the reforms in Germany (Erler 2009; Ostner 2010). The main characteristics of Swedish family policies are the generous parental leave system and universal childcare from ages one to 12. The majority of children (71 percent) in the age group one to two are enrolled in public childcare (SCB 2013). At the same time, Sweden has a relatively high fertility level, with a TFR of 1.9 in 2011 (Eurostat 2013b). Childcare fees in Sweden and Germany are low, i.e., also parents with low income can afford using care services for their children.

5 Excursus: Who uses public childcare? The policy context in Sweden and western Germany

Before exploring the question of how public childcare availability and fertility are related, it is interesting to learn more about who actually makes use of childcare. This provides us with information about the social, economic, and demographic characteristics of the families who make use of childcare services. Moreover, these characteristics are indicative of childcare norms in society. A country comparison offers us the opportunity to identify national differences in the socioeconomic composition of the families who use childcare. This does not allow us to draw conclusions for childbearing, but it might shed some light on the opportunity structures and normative constraints parents with young children face.

This excursus is devoted to the analysis of public childcare usage for two-year-old children in different family policy settings. In this comparison of parental behavior in Sweden and western Germany, the main research questions are: Who uses childcare for very young children? How does the pattern of childcare usage differ for working and non-working mothers? And, finally, are there national differences based on the prevailing family policies of a country?

It has been shown that there are country differences in the socioeconomic composition of the families who make use of childcare services across countries (Mamolo et al. 2011; van Lancker and Ghysels 2012). This might indicate that institutional differences play a role for usage patterns. Similarly, in the following I argue that social differences in childcare use might be associated with the degree to which government policies support parents' (usually mothers') labor force participation. Based on the concept of policy coherence discussed in Section 2.1.3, I expect to find that support for dual-earner families results in virtually universal use of childcare services; i.e., all children have access to childcare, independent of their family backgrounds. In this environment, most parents will participate in the labor market and make use of daycare services, irrespective of their socioeconomic characteristics. In contrast, in countries that offer an incoherent set of family support policies (i.e., both dual-earner and male breadwinner policies), a large share of mothers do not participate in the labor market for a number of years after childbirth.

In this setting, I expect to find that socioeconomic factors affect child-care usage.

Family policies in western Germany and Sweden differ considerably concerning the access to childcare and parental leave policies. However, both countries provide childcare at comparably low prices (less than 10% of average income; see Appendix B). Moreover, as a measure for care quality, the child-staff ratio is 1:5.1 in Swedish pre-schools and 1:5.8 in external care arrangements for children under age three in Germany (cf. Appendix B). Although this data is difficult to compare, it seems that in both Germany and Sweden, childcare quality is on a comparably high level. Differences in childcare usage should thus be affected only to a minor degree by quality and price issues in both countries. In fact, I argue that usage patterns depend on the existence of other family policies.

The empirical analyses are based on data from the European Union Statistics on Income and Living Conditions (EU-SILC) for the years 2005-2008 for two-year-old children. It was impossible to pool the data of the two countries due to confidentiality issues concerning the German dataset, which was analyzed via remote data analyses. Therefore, each country was analyzed separately using logistic regression analyses. As indicated in Section 4.3, childcare usage patterns in eastern Germany differ considerably from those in western Germany. Therefore, the analysis of a third sample would have been ideal. As the sample size for eastern Germany in EU-SILC is too small for meaningful analysis, eastern German respondents were excluded.

In the following, I first present theoretical considerations on the relationship between coherent family policies and the usage of public childcare services. This section also includes the research hypotheses of this study. In Section 5.2, the results of prior research on the determinants of childcare usage are discussed. Section 5.3 is devoted to a description of the methods, data, and variable measurements of my analyses. This is followed by a presentation of the results of the logistic regression models. In Section 5.5, I discuss the findings of the analyses.

5.1 Coherent family policies and public childcare usage

To understand the usage of public childcare for very young children, we must start by considering maternal employment. For working parents, non-family childcare is usually essential.[31] When women with (young) children decide to work, they face competing demands on their time. The availability of non-parental childcare reduces parental care time and offers mothers the opportunity to combine work and family. Female labor force participation depends on socioeconomic status. At the macro level, more women are employed in countries with higher female educational attainment (Jaumotte 2004). Given that working mothers in particular make use of childcare, it is possible that the social composition of childcare users simply reflects the social composition of working mothers. However, public childcare usage might also depend on other family policy instruments. The provision of care is only one family policy instrument, and it may interact with other measures (Lewis 2001; Neyer 2003a; Neyer and Andersson 2008). Policy options that support different family arrangements might affect the decision to work and the decision to use childcare services.

Based on the concept of policy coherence (cf. Section 2.1.3), I expect to find that, in a country with a consistent family policy strategy favoring dual-earner families, childcare usage might be less affected by socioeconomic characteristics, as all mothers are encouraged to work. Given that the services are provided at a low cost, even parents with lower incomes can afford childcare. As neither mothers who stay home nor male breadwinners are supported for a long period, mothers usually return to their jobs after the parental leave period.

According to Korpi's classification (2000), public childcare for children under age three supports dual-earner families, while discouraging the male breadwinner model. In a country that offers both male breadwinner and dual-earner support, socioeconomic characteristics might affect childcare usage. On the one hand, mothers who prefer to participate in the labor market profit from support for dual-earner families. On the other hand, mothers can choose to take advantage of homemaker support, and thus stay out of the labor market. As has been shown, women with lower levels of income and educational attainment are more likely to opt for homemaking in countries offering a cash-for-care program than are those with higher incomes or educational levels (Aassve and Lappegård, 2009; Morgan and Zippel, 2003; Salmi, 2006). This might

31 Other family members, such as grandparents, can also provide daily childcare. However, this is the case only for a limited number of children in Sweden and Germany (Arpino et al. 2010).

be related to the fact that, in a pluralistic setting, maternal employment seems to be strongly related to women's characteristics. For western Germany, for instance, it has been shown that mothers with higher levels of education are more likely to work (Konietzka and Kreyenfeld, 2010). Given that working mothers use childcare more often than non-working mothers, childcare usage might also vary with education. The higher the educational attainment of the mother, the more likely she is to participate in the labor market and to rely on public childcare. Applying these results to childcare usage, I expect to find that, in a country with different family policy options, mothers with high levels of education use childcare more often than those with low levels of education.

In this study, I compare usage patterns in Sweden and Germany. Swedish policies offer strong dual-earner support, including universal childcare for children starting from age one. In contrast, German policies have long favored the male breadwinner family, with relatively little care available for children under age three. However, in recent years, German government enacted a parental leave reform and greatly expanded the provision of public childcare for children under age three. Today, German family policies support both dual-earner and single breadwinner families, creating a situation of ambiguous family support for German parents. This offers us the opportunity to compare a country with coherent dual-earner policies (Sweden) with an increasingly incoherent system (western Germany).

5.2 Prior research on the determinants of childcare usage

Previous research focused mainly on the determinants of childcare usage in a single national setting (see Becker 2007 for a review). The few country comparisons that exist found varying effects of socioeconomic characteristics across different nation-states (Mamolo et al. 2011; van Lancker and Ghysels 2012). The results of these studies imply that institutional aspects might play a role in childcare usage. Research on the determinants of the use of childcare services often focuses on mothers' characteristics. These papers frequently refer to the finding that children benefit from childcare services (see e.g., Biedinger and Becker 2006 for reviews;

Bennett 2008)[32], and point out that children who do not have access to childcare might be disadvantaged and socially excluded.

The decision to use childcare services, especially for young children, is closely related to maternal employment. Studies on childcare hours show that mothers still provide considerably more infant and toddler childcare than fathers (Craig and Mullan 2010; Gauthier and DeGusti 2012). The take-up rates of parental leave also indicate that mothers take the majority of available leave days (De Henau et al. 2007). This is also found to be the case in countries that are usually seen as gender-egalitarian societies, such as Sweden (Duvander et al. 2005). This indicates that it is still mainly mothers who face competing demands of caregiving and paid work. If women want to engage in employment, they usually have to outsource care duties. Accordingly, it has been shown that working mothers are more likely to make use of childcare services than non-working mothers (Huston et al. 2002; Geier and Riedel 2008). Some studies investigated the reverse relationship, and showed that childcare is an important determinant for female labor force participation (Gornick et al. 1998; Kreyenfeld and Hank 2000; van der Lippe and van Dijk 2002; Jaumotte 2004). This indicates that the direction of causality between maternal employment and childcare usage is difficult to disentangle. Do women use childcare because they work, or do they work because they have the option to use childcare services? To overcome this endogeneity problem, some studies model the labor force participation of mothers and childcare use as joint decisions (Andrén 2003; Del Boca et al. 2005; Coneus et al. 2008; van Gameren and Ooms 2009).

Another determinant of childcare usage is the educational attainment of mothers (Kim and Fram 2009; Kreyenfeld and Krapf 2010). Highly educated mothers are more likely to use external care for their children than those with lower levels of education. There are two mechanisms that might be at work in this context. On the one hand, women with higher levels of education are more likely to participate in the labor market (Konietzka and Kreyenfeld 2010). On the other, research has shown

32 Although this finding is widely accepted for children from age three onwards, there are doubts about whether this is also the case for younger children. Evidence on the effects of childcare on the development of very young children is more diverse. Current research results imply that the age at the start of formal childcare for children under age three has neither positive nor negative effects on children's outcomes (Jaffee et al. 2011).

that highly educated women in Germany have more positive attitudes toward non-family childcare and working mothers with young children (Geier and Riedel 2008). This implies that the educational level also influences childcare usage through the acceptance (or non-acceptance) of childcare institutions.

The financial situation of the family is also related to childcare usage. Parents with lower family incomes use external childcare to a lesser extent than those with higher incomes (Durfee and Meyers 2006; Vandenbroeck et al. 2008). One possible reason for this gap is that the cost of childcare services may be less affordable for parents with lower earnings. This argument is especially relevant in market-oriented countries such as the U.S. However, in countries where childcare fees are based on family income, the cost factor is less important. This is the case in, for example, Sweden (van Lancker and Ghysels 2012) and Germany (Kreyenfeld and Hank 2000). Another factor related to childcare usage and income is the prevailing attitude toward non-family childcare for infants and toddlers. A qualitative study on Norway showed that middle-class parents are more likely to use childcare than working-class parents (Stefansen and Farstad 2010). In qualitative interviews, middle-class parents indicated that they appreciate the educational value of childcare services, and reported using institutional care for their children relatively early. In contrast, working-class parents said they prefer to offer their children a safe and calm place to develop, and argued that this environment is best provided within the family (ibid.).

Ethnic background, nationality, and migration background also seem to influence childcare usage. Foreign children in Germany are less likely than German children to be enrolled in childcare (Becker 2007; Böttcher et al. 2010). This relationship seems to have been weakening since the 1980s (Krapf and Kreyenfeld 2011). For the U.S., several studies found that childcare usage varies according to the ethnicity of the mother (Fuller et al. 1996; Hirshberg et al. 2005; Radey and Brewster 2007), with Hispanics being less likely to use formal childcare than whites or African-Americans. A multitude of reasons for these ethnic differences in childcare usage have been discussed in the literature (see Brandon 2004 for a short review). In addition to language problems impeding access, a woman's ethnic background may shape her childcare preferences, as some groups appear to favor maternal childcare. Moreover, ethnicity may be related to other socioeconomic characteristics, such as family income and parents' education. This finding was supported by a study for the U.S., which showed that the effect of the mother's nationality on childcare usage vanished after controlling for education (Kahn and Greenberg 2010).

To summarize, childcare uptake seem to depend to a large extent on a mother's employment, education, income, and migration background. Some economists have argued that the employment and childcare decisions are endogenous, implying that those mothers who work are also those who use childcare for the under-threes. Such an approach does not allow us to take into account the choices of non-working mothers who make use of non-family childcare (Davis and Connelly 2005).

5.3   Method and data

In this study, the comparison of childcare usage patterns in Sweden and western Germany is based on logistic regression models (cf. Hosmer and Lemeshow 2000) run separately for each country. As it focuses on the composition of childcare users and non-users, this approach makes it possible to identify the relevant socioeconomic characteristics related to the use of childcare services in the two family policy settings. In the analyses, I focused on mothers' characteristics. Although male partners participate in the childcare decision-making process (Kim and Fram 2009), I am also interested in single mothers. Thus, I refrained from reducing my sample to mothers who are in a relationship.

As discussed above, maternal labor force participation is closely related to childcare usage for children under age three. Accordingly, some studies model the labor force participation of mothers and childcare use as joint decisions (Andrén 2003; Del Boca et al. 2005; Coneus et al. 2008; van Gameren and Ooms 2009). However, it has been shown that the socioeconomic characteristics that are related to childcare usage differ between working and non-working mothers (Davis and Connelly 2005). In order to identify these differences, I also analyzed separate samples by women's employment status. This results in six models: for both countries, I estimated a full model including all women, and separate analyses for working and non-working mothers.

Data and sample selection

The analyses are based on four cross-sectional survey waves of the European Union Statistics on Income and Living Conditions (EU-SILC), including the years 2005 to 2008. The survey is conducted yearly and has been conducted since 2004 by the national statistical offices of most of the EU-27 countries. The harmonized dataset can be obtained from Eurostat. The general aim of the project is to collect cross-sectional and longitudinal micro-data on the incomes and living conditions of different types of households. Although this is not the focus of the survey, the cross-sectional questionnaire also includes several items concerning the usage of childcare arrangements that allow for country comparisons.

The data for Sweden were provided by Eurostat.[33] For Germany, due to confidentiality issues, not all of the variables were included in this dataset. Therefore, I used the complete German dataset from the German Statistical Office via remote data analyses based on the German EU-SILC data 2005 to 2008. The analyses were conducted by the research data centers of the Federal Statistical Office and the statistical offices of the *Länder*. The drawback of using this procedure was that the creation of a pooled dataset controlling for country effects was not possible. Therefore, I analyzed the two countries in separate samples.

The main parts of the questionnaire were harmonized across countries, but there were several differences, particularly in the sampling design and data collection methods (for details, see Eurostat 2010a, 2010b, 2009a, 2009b, 2008). In Germany, households filled in a postal questionnaire. In Sweden, phone interviews were supplemented by information from administrative registers. Eurostat demands that all countries collect a stratified random sample for EU-SILC. By derogation until EU-SILC 2008 in Germany, the sampling procedure was a combination of quota sampling and random sampling of households based on a sample of respondents generally willing to participate in social surveys identified in the German Microcensus (DESTATIS 2010b). Some scholars have pointed out that in the German sample, problems might arise due to the systematic underrepresentation of migrants, large families, and individu-

---

33 The data are based on the following versions: EUSILC UDB 2005 (version August 2009), 2006 (version 4 of March 2010), 2007 (version 4 of August 2010), and 2008 (version 2 of August 2010) provided by Eurostat. For a discussion of the methodological issues, see Eurostat (2010a; 2010b; 2009a; 2009b; 2008).

als with low levels of education (Hauser 2008; Schneider and Müller 2009). This is of specific concern for the creation of aggregate level indicators that depend on the socioeconomic composition of the sample. This should not be problematic here as in the following analyses I am mainly interested in the individual-level usage of childcare arrangements, and do not focus on aggregate measures.

As was mentioned above, the multivariate analysis focuses on two-year-old children. There are several reasons for taking this approach. First, it seemed inappropriate to analyze all children under age three in a single sample, as I found considerable differences in childcare usage depending on the children's age in both Sweden and western Germany (see Figure 17). Less than two percent of children under age one were found to be in daycare. Only 15 percent of households in western Germany were shown to use childcare for one-year-old children. It is unclear whether parents with a one-year-old child have the same reasons for using childcare as parents with a two-year-old child. Moreover, a pooled sample produces a methodological problem. As the cross-sectional EU-SILC datasets are not linked over years, it is impossible to identify the same child in different survey years. However, uncontrolled nesting of observations might result in biased estimates (Rabe-Hesketh and Skrondal 2008). Analyzing a single age group would prevent the clustering of individuals. Another strategy for accounting for the differences in usage patterns based on children's ages would be the separate analysis of one-year-old children. As separate samples for working and non-working mothers were analyzed, this was not an option. In these sub-samples, the number of children in care was too small for meaningful analysis.

Children who did not live with their mothers were excluded from the samples. The full sample in Sweden includes 697 mothers and the western German sample includes 1,025 mothers.

Dependent variable: childcare usage

In this study, the dependent variable refers to whether a woman reports that she is using some form of public childcare for her two-year-old child. The childcare data in EU-SILC are provided as the number of weekly hours spent in the respective arrangements (Eurostat 2009b). The weekly hours refer to a usual week, and information is given for each child under age 13 currently living in the household. The use of institutional care is reflected in variable RL040: that is, "childcare provided at day care centers, including all kinds of care organized or controlled by a public or private structure". In Sweden and Germany, family daycare is publicly funded or subsidized, and can be considered part of public childcare provision. Family care was measured in variable RL050. In some countries, this variable also includes private childcare arrangements, such as babysitters and au pairs. However, in the questionnaires in Sweden and Germany, it refers to family daycare. Moreover, for the sake of completeness, I additionally considered three German children who were enrolled in preschool (variable RL010).

Figure 17:   Children enrolled in non-family care. Percentages of the respective age groups.

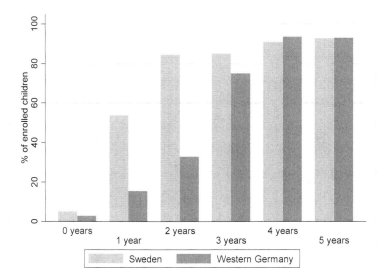

Source: EU-SILC 2005-2008, unweighted data. Author's own calculations.

Focusing on the difficulty of aggregating enrollment rates at the national level, Keck and Saraceno (Saraceno and Keck 2008; 2011) discussed a number of critical issues concerning the childcare items in EU-SILC. For the assessment of national enrollment levels among children under age three, a problem arises due to the possibility that, if a respondent provided information about more than one child, each sibling will contribute as a single observation, which violates the assumption of independent observations. This should not be problematic in this study, as I am not interested in aggregate measures of enrollment but childcare usage for a single child.

The childcare variable in this study is coded "one" if a child was attending childcare for one hour a week or more, and "zero" otherwise. The daily duration of childcare usage would have been an interesting phenomenon to study, as it would show to what extent the provision of childcare services contributes to work-family balance. Unfortunately, there are serious shortcomings in the measurement quality in the German data. As was noted by Keck and Saraceno (2011), the distribution of childcare hours indicates that a considerable number of German respondents reported the number of weekly instead of daily hours. This measurement error makes a comparison of national hourly data difficult. Thus, I relied on the dichotomous variable as the measure for childcare usage.

Figure 17 presents the share of children of different age groups attending some form of publicly funded childcare, based on EU-SILC data. Sweden had higher enrollment rates for children in each age group under age four than western Germany. For the older age groups, the picture was reversed, with western Germany showing slightly higher enrollment rates.

Control variables

The choice of covariates in the analyses was based on the variables identified as important for childcare usage in other studies. The descriptive statistics are shown in Table 3. The first control variable was the number of children under age six living in the household. It is assumed that women with a larger number of children might decide to stay out of the labor market completely, thus reducing the demand for external childcare (Huston et al. 2002; Geier and Riedel 2008). Few children had more than one sibling under age six; thus they were excluded from the analyses. Analyses of the western German sample indicated that having two children was positively related to childcare usage, while having three or more children yielded a negative coefficient (results not shown here). This nonlinear relationship of number of children and childcare usage prevented a grouping of families with two and more children in one category.

Concerning the age of children, studies have shown that children become more likely to attend childcare as they grow older (Huston et al. 2002; Hirshberg et al. 2005). Within the age group of two-year-olds, the models controlled for the child's age in months, based on the assumption that a child who has just turned two years old has a lower probability of being in childcare than a child on the verge of his or her third birthday. While the German dataset provided detailed age data (year and month of birth), they were not included in the harmonized dataset for Sweden. Indeed, other than the year of birth, the only data included in the dataset were the quarter of the year in which the child was born and the quarter of the year in which the respondent was interviewed. On this basis, I randomly assigned one month of the respective quarter to each Swedish child, and created an age variable for the two samples.

Studies have found that mothers with migration backgrounds (Becker 2007; Kahn and Greenberg 2010) or of minority ethnicities (Radey and Brewster 2007; Fram and Kim 2008) use childcare less often than mothers with the prevalent ethnic background of the country where they live. The reasons for this gap might include language problems and different attitudes toward childcare and mothering. To account for this, the citizenship of the mother was controlled for. Unfortunately, the sample sizes were small in the sub-samples of working and non-working mothers. Thus, respondents with foreign citizenship were excluded from the analyses of non-working mothers in Sweden, and in the samples of working mothers in western Germany.

Several studies have shown that mothers' education is positively associated with childcare use (Kim and Fram 2009; Greenberg 2011; Krapf and Kreyenfeld 2011). There are two mechanisms through which education might affect childcare use. (1) The higher the level of education the mother has, the higher her opportunity costs are when she leaves the labor market. Thus, highly educated mothers are more likely to work and to use childcare. (2) Highly educated mothers might also make use of childcare because they appreciate the developmental effects of childcare (Mamolo et al. 2011: 177). In EU-SILC, the International Standard Classification of Education (ISCED-97) is used to measure each respondent's educational attainment. Based on this classification, I created the variables "lower secondary or lower education" (ISCED levels 0, 1, and 2); "upper secondary", including post-secondary non-tertiary education (ISCED levels 3 and 4); and "tertiary education" (ISCED levels 5 and 6).

Table 3:   Childcare usage. Descriptive statistics. All mothers. Column percent.

	Sweden	western Germany
year of survey		
2005	21%	29%
2006	24%	25%
2007	26%	23%
2008	30%	23%
age of child	2.52 years	2.48 years
mean (std. deviation)	(0.30)	(0.29)
number of children in the		
household (under age 6)		
one child	53%	51%
two children	47%	49%
citizenship of mother		
local	95%	95%
foreign	5%	5%
partnership status of mother		
single	2%	7%
married	55%	88%
cohabiting	43%	5%
education of mother		
lower secondary or lower	6%	7%
upper secondary	48%	58%
tertiary	46%	36%
employment status of mother		
full-time	54%	8%
part-time	22%	29%
unemployed	4%	4%
homemaker or other inactive	21%	59%
number of children (total)	697	676
number of children in care	598	220
% of children in care	86%	33%

Source: EU-SILC 2005-2008 data. Unweighted frequencies. Author's own calculations

In the sample of working mothers in western Germany, the number of women with lower secondary (or lower) education was very small. In line with other results for Germany (Konietzka and Kreyenfeld 2010), this indicates that the groups of working and non-working mothers differ systematically in their educational levels. In the German sample of working mothers, the low and the upper-secondary education groups were combined.

The employment status of the mother is also closely related to childcare usage. As mentioned above, other authors have modeled the employment of mothers and childcare usage as joint decisions accounting for the endogenous relationship of the two variables (Andrén 2003; Del Boca et al. 2005; Coneus et al. 2008; van Gameren and Ooms 2009). The study at hand focuses on the composition of the group of childcare users. In order to analyze whether the characteristics of users persist for working and non-working mothers, two separate samples for working and non-working mothers were estimated in addition to the full sample including all mothers for each country. According to several studies, children with mothers in full-time employment use childcare services more frequently than those whose mothers are in part-time employment or are inactive (Huston et al. 2002; Geier and Riedel 2008). In the following analyses, the information on employment status was based on the current employment situation, as defined by the respondent. Four categories were distinguished: full-time employed, part-time employed, unemployed, and homemaking mothers, with the latter group including others who were inactive, such as retired or disabled respondents. As there are differences in the national definitions of full- and part-time jobs, I used the information on respondents' working hours. Mothers who reported working less than 30 hours per week on average were classified as part-time employed, while those who said they worked 30 or more hours per week were coded as full-time employed. Because in the western German sample the number of students with a two-year-old child was too small for meaningful analysis, respondents who were enrolled in education were excluded.

Concerning maternity leave, employed mothers on leave were usually classified as working in the EU-SILC dataset. In the context of my study, however, women on leave with a younger child did not face competing time demands at work, and might have been taking care of older children as well. Thus, the categorization of women on leave as working might be misleading. To address this problem, I re-classified women on parental leave by taking into consideration the age of the youngest child living in the household. All of the mothers with very young children were categorized as homemakers.

Table 4:   Childcare usage. Descriptive statistics Separate samples for working and non-working mothers. Column percent.

	Sweden		western Germany	
	working	non-working	working	non-working
year of survey				
2005	19%	27%	24%	33%
2006	23%	25%	32%	21%
2007	26%	24%	24%	22%
2008	32%	24%	21%	24%
age of child	2.52 yrs	2.52 yrs	2.51 yrs	2.46 yrs
mean (std. deviation)	(0.30)	(0.29)	(0.30)	(0.29)
number of children in the				
household (under age 6)				
one child	64%	16%	62%	45%
two children	36%	84%	38%	55%
citizenship of mother				
local	97%	-	-	93%
foreign	3%	-	-	7%
partnership status				
single	-	4%	7%	7%
married	56%	55%	87%	89%
cohabiting	44%	41%	6%	4%
education of mother				
lower secondary or lower	4%	11%	-	9%
upper secondary	49%	44%	55%[b]	61%
tertiary	47%	45%	45%	31%
employment status				
full-time	72%	-	23%	-
part-time	28%	-	77%	-
unemployed	-	15%	-	7%
homemaker or other inactive	-	85%	-	93%
number of children (total)[a]	522	155	238	426
number of children in care	478	105	125	88
% of children in care	92%	68%	53%	21%

Notes: [a] The numbers of children in the single samples do not sum up to the total number as those with foreign citizenship were excluded from some sub-samples. [b] Includes lower secondary education. Source: EU-SILC 2005-2008 data. Unweighted frequencies. Author's own calculations.

Accounting for differences in minimum legal entitlements for maternal or parental leave, the classification is based on different ages of the youngest child (Sweden: youngest child under 11 months old; Germany: youngest child under three months old). The procedure differs across the two countries.

In Sweden, the period mentioned refers to the parental leave period, as the question on employment status refers to previous December. In this study, I am interested in the employment status at the time of the interview. As virtually all mothers in the EU take the full maternity and parental leave period (Moss 2010), the age of the youngest child indicates whether women are on leave. In Germany, respondents are asked about their employment at the time of the interview. For the years 2005 and 2006, women on maternity leave were coded as working in EU-SILC. For this period, I used the shorter maternity leave period to identify women who were staying at home with their infants. In 2007, a new parental leave law was introduced in Germany and from that year onwards, women on maternity and parental leave were coded as working. Thus, for younger siblings born in 2007 and 2008, women are considered as being on leave for the first year after childbirth.

In a second step, based on the information on employment, the samples of working and non-working women were separated. These sub-samples differed considerably in size and composition over the two countries (see Table 4).

Taking into consideration the partnership status of the mothers, I distinguished between single, married, and cohabiting mothers. Research has shown that in the U.S. unmarried mothers are more likely to use childcare than married mothers (Hirshberg et al. 2005). Partnership status is of specific interest for Germany because, in the period before August 2013, which is analyzed here, single parents who work have priority access when childcare services are limited (Heimer et al. 2009). I expect to find that German single mothers were more likely to have been using childcare than mothers with a partner. In the Swedish sub-sample of working mothers, all of the respondents were in a partnership; i.e., the category of single mothers was empty.

5.4   Regression results

The results of the basic logistic regression models on childcare usage in Sweden and western Germany for two-year-old children are shown in Table 5, and the separate analyses for working and non-working mothers are displayed in Table 6.

Table 5:   Logistic regression results for childcare usage. Two-year-old children. Odds ratios. All mothers.

	Sweden Model 1	western Germany Model 2
year of survey	1.25**	1.19**
age of child	1.61	3.10***
number of children		
one child	1	1
two children	0.69	0.94
citizenship of mother		
local	1	1
foreign	0.82	0.75
partnership status of mother		
single	1	1
married	1.37	0.65
cohabiting	1.32	0.62
education of mother		
lower secondary or lower	0.97	0.75
upper secondary	1	1
tertiary	0.86	1.51**
employment status of mother		
full-time	1	1
part-time	0.64	0.42**
unemployed	0.30**	0.68
homemaker or other inactive	0.19***	0.11***
number of children in the sample	697	676
likelihood-ratio-χ^2	64.33***	123.42***
McFadden's Pseudo R^2	0.11	0.14

Notes: *p = 0.10; **p = 0.05; ***p = 0.01. Source: EU-SILC 2005-2008 data. Author's own calculations.

113

The effects are displayed as odds ratios.[34] Table 5 shows that, in Sweden and western Germany, the year of the interview had a positive effect on childcare use, which implies that childcare usage among two-year-old children has increased over time.

The exact age of the child was important only in western Germany. There, the odds ratio of 3.10 indicates, as expected, that older children were more likely to be in childcare than younger children. The analyses do not show a significant effect for the number of children living in the household in the two countries. The coefficients of citizenship and partnership status of the mother were also shown to be insignificant.

In Sweden, education was not shown to significantly influence childcare usage. In contrast, in western Germany children whose mother had tertiary education had higher odds of being in childcare than children whose mother had secondary education (western Germany: odds ratio=1.51). The findings further indicated that childcare usage did not differ significantly for mothers with lower secondary education.

Concerning employment status, the results showed that, with a significant odds ratio of 0.42, children in western Germany with part-time employed mothers had lower odds of being in childcare than those with full-time employed mothers. The difference was insignificant in Sweden. Children of both unemployed and homemaker mothers were found to be less likely to be in childcare than full-time employed mothers in both countries. One exception was unemployed women in western Germany, who did not significantly differ from full-time working mothers.

The results for the separate samples of working and non-working mothers are displayed in Table 6. For Sweden, the results for the sub-samples generally confirmed the findings for the full sample. In the Swedish sample of working mothers (Model 3), none of the household characteristics had a significant impact.

Moreover, the likelihood ratio test was insignificant, which indicates that considering the variables in the model did not improve the model fit compared to a model without control variables. In other words, Swedish children with working mothers were in childcare irrespective of their mother's education and their family situation.

---

34 It has been discussed in the literature that the interpretation of odds ratios might be problematic because of unobserved heterogeneity (Mood 2010). For the analyses here, calculating average marginal effects as alternative measure (results not shown) did not yield substantially different results.

Table 6: Logistic regression results for childcare usage. Two-year-old children. Odds ratios. Samples separated into working and non-working mothers.

	Sweden		western Germany	
	working	non-working	working	non-working
	Model 3	Model 4	Model 5	Model 6
year of survey	1.10	1.43**	1.25*	1.12
age of child	0.94	3.15*	1.86	5.08***
number of children				
one child	1	1	1	1
two children	0.60	0.76	0.66	1.31
citizenship of mother				
local	1	-	-	1
foreign	1.54	-	-	0.75
partnership status of mother				
single	-	1	1	1
married	1	2.16	0.35*	0.86
cohabiting	1.04	1.50	0.40	0.62
education of mother				
lower secondary	1.03	0.78	-	0.44
upper secondary	1	1	1ᵃ	1
tertiary	1.31	0.57	1.58*	1.34
employment status of mother				
full-time	1	-	1	-
part-time	0.72	-	0.51**	-
unemployed	-	1	-	1
homemaker or other inactive	-	0.60	-	0.11***
number of children	522	155	238	426
likelihood-ratio-χ^2	4.68	12.77	19.94***	38.71***
McFadden's Pseudo R^2	0.02	0.07	0.06	0.09

Notes: *p = 0.10; **p = 0.05; ***p = 0.01. ᵃ Includes lower secondary education. Source: EU-SILC 2005-2008 data. Author's own calculations.

Among non-workers (Model 4), both the year of the survey and the age of the child had a significant effect on childcare. For all other characteristics, the odds ratios and the likelihood ratio test remained insignificant. However, it is important to note that this sub-sample was rather small, as relatively few of the Swedish mothers with two-year-old children did not work.

In western Germany, among working mothers, the coefficients for the child's age and the number of children were found to be insignificant (see Model 5). The significant odds ratio of 0.35 indicated that married mothers were less likely to use childcare than single mothers. This might reflect the fact that, by law, single working mothers have priority access to childcare. This effect is not significant for cohabiting mothers.

Concerning education among working mothers, women with tertiary education had a significantly higher chance of using childcare (odds ratio=1.58) than the combined group of those with lower- and upper-secondary education. In other words, the likelihood that a working mother would use childcare services was positively related to the mother's education. Children whose mothers were employed part-time had lower odds of childcare usage than those with mothers who worked full-time (odds ratio=0.51).

In the sample of non-working mothers (Model 6), the odds ratio of 5.08 indicates a strong effect of children's age on childcare usage. None of the other demographic characteristics showed significant effects in the sample of non-working German mothers. The children of homemaker mothers, with an odds ratio of 0.11, had significantly lower chances of being in childcare than children with unemployed mothers. Among German employed mothers, having tertiary education had a positive effect on childcare usage. This is in line with Geier and Riedel (2008), who also found a positive correlation between educational attainment and childcare use. According to these authors, highly educated mothers use childcare more often because they have positive attitudes regarding the effects of childcare on children's development. Among non-working mothers in Germany, unemployed mothers were found to be more likely to use childcare than homemaker mothers. This might be related to the fact that unemployed mothers might need some time to search for a new job, and may thus use childcare to reduce the amount of time they spend on childcare duties (cf. Vikman 2010). Moreover, unemployed mothers expect to start working in the near future, and they might therefore see childcare usage during unemployment as preparation for the time when they have a job (ibid.). In contrast, homemaker mothers do not plan to (re-)enter the labor market. They might have a preference for caring for their very young children at home, and are thus intentionally not using childcare.

In Sweden, working mothers and childcare usage for very young children are widespread; thus, there was no significant education effect among Swedish mothers. This finding contradicts the results of other studies that have found that childcare usage in Sweden is affected by socioeconomic characteristics (e.g., Östberg 2000). Such effects may have diminished over time, in part because several policies were introduced in the early 2000s that enhanced childcare access (for a summary of these reforms, see Skolverket 2007).

Some of the findings were unexpected. For example, according to the analyses, the citizenship of mothers was not significantly related to childcare usage in either Sweden or western Germany. Other studies have shown that children of mothers, who are not citizens of the country where they reside, use childcare less frequently than children of citizens. A recent U.S. study found that the immigrant effect vanishes when controlling for other socioeconomic characteristics of the mother (Kahn and Greenberg 2010). This could also be the case in the EU-SILC samples under study. Another reason for this finding could be that the sample sizes were simply too small to identify robustly the effect of citizenship.

5.5   Discussion

The aim of this study was to compare the socioeconomic composition of childcare users in different family policy settings. The analyses were based on childcare usage among two-year-old children in Sweden and western Germany. These countries are similar in childcare prices and quality, but vary in terms of childcare access and other family policy measures.

The results of the logistic regression models on basis of EU-SILC data for 2005-2008 generally show that the relationship between family factors and childcare usage differ across the two countries. For the Swedish sample, the only important factor affecting childcare usage was whether the mother worked. However, the group of non-working mothers was small, making up only about one-quarter of the sample. Within this group, children with homemaker mothers were found to be less likely to attend childcare than children whose mothers were unemployed. Other family characteristics, such as the child's age and the mother's partnership status or education, did not significantly affect childcare usage.

In western Germany, by contrast, the analyses revealed an effect for maternal education. Children whose mothers were highly educated had a greater chance of being in non-family childcare than children of mothers with lower levels of education. This was found among working mothers in western Germany. The coefficient for tertiary education remained insignificant in the sample of non-working German mothers. A look at the composition concerning mother's education indicates that highly educated women are more likely to be working mothers.

Overall, the education effect implies that children had access to or were excluded from public childcare based on their mothers' education levels. Other factors of social structure, such as citizenship and the number of children under age six in the household, did not yield significant results in the countries analyzed here. As this might be related to the small sample sizes, it is difficult to draw final conclusions on the effect of these variables on childcare usage based on EU-SILC. Moreover, other factors might affect childcare choices; with larger sample sizes, information on the women's partners and the income situation of the family would be interesting to analyze.

Although the analyses did not explicitly account for the effects of the institutional peculiarities in the countries, I suggest that the observed differences in childcare usage patterns are related to family policies. In Sweden, dual-earner support is very pronounced, and there are virtually no incentives for maternal homemaking. Thus, mothers' employment is widespread even when children are very young, which results in childcare usage independent of mothers' educational attainment. German policies, in contrast, support not only male breadwinner families, but also, increasingly, dual-earner families. In the analysis presented here, I found that mothers with low levels of education had low levels of employment, and that working mothers with tertiary education were more likely to use childcare than those with lower levels of education. These findings are in line with those of studies in other countries, where it has been shown that less educated parents are more likely to make use of the home care allowance, while highly educated parents tend to use non-family childcare (e.g., Morgan and Zippel 2003), which results in a selective use of day care. These results might be relevant for the design of family policies in a country. If parents do not make use of childcare services, the policy might fail to attain its goal. Public childcare is a relevant social policy as it is seen as investment in children's human capital reducing social inequalities in early life and as a means to increase maternal employment rates (Esping-Andersen 2002).

In both Germany and Sweden, it will be interesting to observe the effects of a cash-for-childcare program for children under age three. In Germany, since August 2013, the government has introduced a home care allowance for parents who stay home to take care of their children. This policy reform supports the male breadwinner model, and might counteract the reforms introduced since the mid-2000s that provided additional support for dual-earner families. Meanwhile, in Sweden, cash-for-care has been introduced by a considerable number of municipalities since 2008. In the political rhetoric, it is expected that, in the long run, this policy will provide "free choice" to parents (Eydal and Rostgaard 2011). However, a look at Finland that also offers both universal childcare and home care allowance, indicates that mother's choice is related to her socio-economic status. Finnish mothers with lower levels of education are less likely to use childcare services than others (Krapf forthcoming). This is worrying, as children from disadvantaged backgrounds have been found to benefit the most from childcare services (Barnett 2011). In Sweden, the stable childcare enrollment rates indicate that, since its introduction, only a minority of Swedish parents have been making use of the allowance. But initial observations show a higher uptake of the home care allowance among immigrant parents (Ellingsæter 2012). In Germany in 2013, a lively debate about the usefulness of a home care allowance continues. When considering the issue, policy makers should keep in mind that parents' freedom to choose might result in a polarization of employment and segregated childcare usage.

The approach followed in this study does not completely rule out other factors that might be of importance for the national differences in childcare usage. In Finland, for instance, while free choice is promoted, the limited availability of part-time work leaves women with only two options: either work full-time or stay home full-time (Repo 2003). Mothers who would prefer to work part-time might decide to stay out of the labor market, resulting in a smaller share of children in childcare. Another factor influencing the acceptance of childcare policies is the prevailing idea of appropriate childcare in a country (Duncan et al. 2004; Kremer 2007; Saraceno 2011). It is important that non-family childcare (for young children) is positively evaluated. Parents who believe that a child in public care suffers (or that others think so) are less likely to make use of it. If, conversely, childcare is perceived as positive for children's development, a majority of children will participate. So far, it seems to be difficult to test such normative effects across countries; in the EU-SILC data, for example, there are no normative questions included. However, as research has shown, family policies are often in line with attitudes toward the family held by the population (Sjöberg 2004; Ferrarini 2006), and may thus reflect normative differences across countries.

6 How do attitudes and childcare availability affect fertility in Germany and Sweden?

The main research question of this thesis looks at the effect of childcare availability and attitudes on fertility. Based on the theoretical discussion in Section 2, the opportunity to use childcare services should reduce the conflict between career and family, and thus encourage childbearing. I further hypothesize that this expected positive effect depends on whether a woman has positive attitudes toward non-family childcare and working mothers (cf. Section 2.3.4). Among women with more traditional family values, the availability of childcare services should not stimulate fertility. Another interaction is expected between childcare availability and education: childcare is particularly attractive for the highly educated. This education effect is especially clear in countries with policy alternatives that support full-time mothers.

In the following chapter, I investigate whether women who live in a region with high childcare availability are more likely to enter parenthood than women who live in regions with lower childcare availability. Employing discrete-time hazard models, the age of the mother at first birth or pregnancy is central. The event of interest is the occurrence of a first birth or pregnancy among female respondents before the next survey interview. The data is arranged as person-years (see Singer and Willett 1993) for up to three survey waves.

The analyses in this section are based on two separate datasets for Germany and Sweden. The German Family Panel *pairfam* (including the eastern German supplement DemoDiff) and the Swedish Young Adult Panel Study (YAPS) offer new opportunities to investigate first births. In many surveys, the values and preferences of respondents are measured at the same time as their fertility . However, while it is clear that a woman's attitudes affect the probability that she will have a child, it also seems plausible that the occurrence of a birth may change her attitudes (cf. Lesthaeghe 2002). Based on cross-sectional data it is difficult to disentangle mutual relationships which might cause inaccurate estimators due to endogeneity bias. In order to minimize such reverse causality issues, I take advantage of the panel structure of the data and investigate the effect of a woman's opinions and attitudes at one point in time on her childbearing thereafter.

As was noted in Chapter 3.1, it is unclear to what extent childcare provision is related to childbearing. Prior research on Sweden

(Andersson et al. 2004) and also studies on public childcare and fertility in western Germany (Hank 2002; Hank and Kreyenfeld 2003) did not find the theoretically expected effect. Investigating these countries might show whether childcare availability has a different influence on childbearing in the two different settings. Moreover, based on the traditional contrasts between Germany and Sweden, a comparison might shed light on the similarities and differences in attitudinal effects.

In the following, I first discuss the discrete-time hazard models which I use in the analysis of both datasets. For the German dataset, I also account for the multi-level structure of the data. This turned out to be unnecessary for Sweden, where the consideration of the regions did not significantly help to explain the variance in first births. Section 6.2 is devoted to the analysis of the German dataset, while Section 6.3 presents the Swedish case. The last Section summarizes results on both countries.

6.1   Method: multilevel discrete-time hazard model

In order to identify the effects of childcare services and attitudes on first birth behavior, I used a discrete-time hazard model for the transition to first motherhood and first pregnancy. The process time was the age of the respondent at the time of the interview. The information on the timing of first births was based on the self-report of the age in years at the time of interview; i.e., the time scale is discrete. Assuming that the underlying latent time variable was continuous, I specified the hazard rate as complementary log-log (cloglog) regression (cf. Allison 1982: 74f.). Moreover, the data were interval-censored, and cloglog models allow me to account for this (Rabe-Hesketh and Skrondal 2008: 356).

The data were organized in person-year format, with each person potentially contributing one entry per year. The information retrieved from the earlier wave was used to investigate childbearing in the next wave. Whether a woman gave birth between the two waves was reported in the next interview. That means that the variables measured in one wave were used to predict childbearing reported in the next wave.

The data were analyzed using multilevel methods. First, the research question analyzed in this chapter focuses on the effect of regional-level childcare availability on individual-level childbearing. Accordingly, in the analyses I investigated the effects on both the lower- (individual) and the higher-level units (regions). In order to accurately estimate the effects of the regional-level variables on individual-level first birth occurrences, it is necessary to account for this hierarchical structure of the data (Raudenbusch and Bryk 2002). Second, a basic assumption of regression analyses is that observations are independent of each other. If observations are clustered, the independence assumption is violated and the estimation of effect sizes might be inefficient (Diez-Roux 2002). Based on the assumption that individuals living within a region behave more similarly than individuals living in different regions, I used a multilevel specification for the regression analyses. A random-effects model accounts for the clustering of individuals in regions. In this model, it was assumed that, in addition to a fixed-error term for all units, there was a group-specific error term for each regional unit (Barber et al. 2000). Multilevel analyses estimate the effects on the individual level and on the regional level.

In order to investigate whether childcare affects childbearing differently for specific groups in the population, I also ran models that accounted for possible interaction effects. Of primary interest were women with specific attitudes, which I modeled as multiplicative interaction effects in the regression analyses. Moreover, according to our theoretical considerations, it might be expected that childcare effects would be shown to vary across educational groups. I therefore also ran models that controlled for an interaction between childcare and the educational attainment of respondents.

6.2   Case study: Germany

Germany is an interesting case for studying childcare effects. For many years, Germany was the prototype of a conservative country that supported male breadwinner families. Since the 1970s, fertility rates in western Germany (and, later, also in eastern Germany) have been very low (TFR below 1.5)[35], and childlessness has been relatively high (Konietzka and Kreyenfeld 2007; Dorbritz 2008). The incompatibility between work and family has often been cited as the reason for this low level of fertility.

---

35   Note that the TFR is sensitive to postponement of births. Accounting for this, a tempo adjustment results in higher period fertility levels (Goldstein and Kreyenfeld 2011).

However, Germany is increasingly transitioning to dual-earner policies (cf. Section 4.3). In the 2000s, childcare for children under age three appeared on the political agenda. Care services for this age group have grown rapidly; albeit at different speed in different regions of the country. At the same time, it is generally expected that the traditionally conservative values of German society will persist, at least in part. If there is indeed a "cultural lag" between the implementation of political institutions and values, this should be mirrored in enduring traditional attitudes among respondents. The historical differences between eastern and western Germany also increase the variance in both the childcare data and in the attitudes questions asked in the *pairfam* dataset. This might give us some insights into the relationship between childcare, attitudes, and fertility decisions.

6.2.1 Data and sample selection

The analyses were based on the first three waves of the survey "Panel of Intimate Relationships and Family Dynamics" (*pairfam*), release 3.0 (Nauck et al. 2012)[36]. Moreover, I used an additional oversample of eastern German respondents, called "Demographic Differences in Life-Course Dynamics in eastern and western Germany" (DemoDiff), relase 2.0. The questionnaire used in DemoDiff is almost identical to the *pairfam* survey. A detailed description of the *pairfam* study can be found in Huinink et al. (2011) and more details on DemoDiff have been provided by Kreyenfeld and colleagues (2012a; 2012b). The panel is conducted annually among randomly selected men and women in three age groups. In the first wave in 2008/2009, 12,402 respondents (so-called anchors) participated in *pairfam*. The first wave of DemoDiff was conducted with a one-year delay, and had an initial sample size of 1,489. The interviewed cohorts were born in 1991-1993, 1981-1983, or 1971-1973. Researchers asked the anchors for permission to also interview the anchor's partner.[37]

---

36 This study is based on data of *pairfam*, which is coordinated by Josef Brüderl, Johannes Huinink, Bernhard Nauck, and Sabine Walper. The study is a long-term project funded by the German Research Foundation (Deutsche Forschungsgemeinschaft – DFG).

37 In the second and subsequent waves of the panel survey, parents and children were also interviewed (Huinink et al. 2011).

Both data projects, *pairfam* and DemoDiff, were initiated to improve the data available for family research in Germany.

In the present study, I used the first three waves (2008/09, 2009/10, and 2010/11) of *pairfam* and the first two waves (2009/10 and 2010/11) of DemoDiff in a pooled dataset.[38] For the purposes of this study, I considered only female respondents. In addition to using information on the female anchors, I also considered female partners of male anchors. My research design included the retrospective information taken from the later wave about whether a first birth had occurred since the last interview. Women who participated only in the first wave but not in one of the later waves were excluded. The analysis was restricted to respondents older than 20 and younger than 40 years of age. As first births can be experienced only once, women who already had children or who were pregnant at first interview were excluded; i.e., they were left-truncated (Rabe-Hesketh and Skrondal 2008). In the analyses, I consider 1,738 person-years.

The measure of childcare used in this study was based on the official statistics on regional childcare enrollment rates (district level). These data were provided by the German Federal Statistical Office (DESTATIS 2009a). I combined the individual data of *pairfam* and DemoDiff with the enrollment rate on the district level.

6.2.2 Dependent variable and data structure

The dependent variable in the analyses would ideally be "proceptive behavior". As was explained in Section 2.3.1, the actual behavior of interest was "stopping contraception" or "having sexual intercourse" rather than the birth itself. However, such proceptive behaviors are difficult to measure. In demographic research, births are seen as outcomes or consequences of behaviors that lead to conception (Ajzen 2011), and thus can be used as a proxy for behavior (Dommermuth et al. 2011).

In the analyses on Germany, I focus on the conception of a first child since the last interview. The *pairfam* and DemoDiff questionnaires include an item on whether the female respondent (or the partner of a male respondent) is pregnant. As pregnancy is the direct consequence of suc-

---

38 Note that the first wave of DemoDiff was conducted with a one-year delay relative to *pairfam* (Kreyenfeld et al. 2011b).

cessful conception, I considered it, in addition to childbirth, as a proxy for fertility behavior. Women who were pregnant in the first wave were excluded from the analyses. A conception since the last interview was indicated in one of two ways. A person reported either that (a) she had given birth to her first child since the last interview, or (b) that she was pregnant at the time of the current interview. As no information about the date of conception was provided, the data were interval-censored. For births, I also did not consider the exact age of the mother at the time of birth, but rather treated the observation as interval-censored, with a conception occurring between interview t and t+1.

In addition, women who participated in waves one and two but not in wave three entered the risk set as a censored observation. *pairfam* has a non-monotonous design; i.e., respondents who participated in wave 1 but skipped the survey in wave 2 could re-enter the sample in wave 3. Taking advantage of this design, I also considered women who did not participate in wave two but who participated in wave three. For the DemoDiff supplement, only two waves were available.

6.2.3 Childcare availability

One key variable in this analysis was childcare availability. The research question referred to a woman's beliefs about childcare availability for her (unborn) child. However, *pairfam* and DemoDiff did not include information on respondents' perceptions of the childcare situation in their environment. Instead, I used childcare statistics that provided information on the actual childcare provision in a region. As I was especially interested in the effect of childcare for young children, I used the district-level[39] enrollment rates of children under age three. Enrollment rates refer to the percentage of children using public childcare among all children in a specific age group. These numbers include full- and part-time care arrangements. Moreover, in addition to institutional care (*Kindertages-stätten*), family daycare (often provided by the so-called *Tagesmutter*) is subsidized in Germany. In order to capture the overall supply of publicly supported childcare, I considered the enrollment rates of children under age three in both publicly funded institutions and subsidized daycare.

---

39   The districts refer to German *Kreise*. After the reform came into effect on August 1, 2008, there were 413 districts.

This means that the enrollment rates provided information on both publicly provided and publicly funded care arrangements.

Figure 18: Enrollment rates of children aged 0-2 years. German districts 2008.

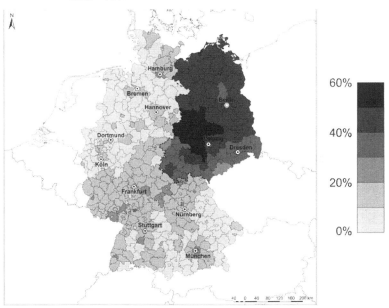

Source: DESTATIS 2009a. Illustration: Sebastian Klüsener.

In this analysis, I used enrollment rates as measure of childcare availability. This is debatable as it can be argued that enrollment tells us about
usage rather than about availability. In the case of (western) Germany,
the supply of childcare for children under age three still does not meet
the demand. In this situation, enrollment rates can serve as proxy for
provision (Rindfuss et al. 2007: 351). In collecting data for *pairfam* and
DemoDiff, the research institute in charge (TNS infratest) combined the
individual-level data with the Community Identification Number
(Brüderl et al. 2012: 38).

While the information in *pairfam* and DemoDiff on respondents' place of residence refers to the municipality[40], the childcare enrollment rates are available on the district level. From the community-id, I generated the district-id, merging the individual data with the official statistics. I considered childcare data for the year 2008 for *pairfam* and for the year 2009 for Demo-Diff. This means that, in both cases, the level of childcare refers to the year at or before the interview.

The childcare enrollment rate of children under age three varies considerably over German regions, as can be seen in Figure 18. With an average enrollment rate of 46 percent in eastern Germany and 15 percent in western Germany in 2008, the difference between these two parts of the country is still pronounced (DESTATIS 2009a; see Section 4.3 for more information on the development of childcare services in East and West Germany).

For the multivariate analyses, the enrollment rates were categorized into three groups. Regions with enrollment rates below 10 percent were classified as "low", those with rates between 10 and under 20 percent as "medium". Regions with enrollment levels above 20 percent were categorized as "high". In the sample under study, one third of respondents live in a region with low, 39 percent in a region with medium and 28 percent in a region with high childcare enrollment (see Table 11).

6.2.4 Attitudes toward children and family life

The second key variable in this analysis was attitudes toward family arrangements. Theoretically, I argued that the effects of childcare policies on fertility depend on attitudes toward non-family childcare. Unfortunately, the *pairfam* and DemoDiff questionnaires do not contain an explicit question on the respondent's views on childcare arrangements.

The data did, however, contain responses to a number of questions concerning (1) attitudes regarding family values, (2) the expected positive and negative aspects of having children, and (3) the importance attached to different life domains. I assumed that these values were related to attitudes toward children. Research has, for example, shown that more

40   This information on the municipality in which a respondent lives is excluded from the scientific use-file of the data due to confidentiality issues. Therefore, this part of the data analysis was done with the help of the *pairfam* data service team, who conducted the analyses via remote execution.

traditional values are associated with a preference for maternal care (Mason and Kuhlthau 1989). Attitudes toward the family and children are multidimensional and overlapping. In order to identify the items in the questionnaire that are related to the underlying constructs, I conducted a factor analysis (see Kim and Mueller 1978a; 1978b). For the current study, I aimed to create indices based on a number of variables that, conceptually, measure similar things. Based on the whole sample of anchors (including male and female respondents participating in wave 1 in *pairfam* and in DemoDiff; n=13,891), this procedure resulted in two indices: "traditional family values" and "expected cost of having children". According to the factor analysis, the scale "expected benefits of having children", which theoretically refers to the positive aspects of having children within the VOC approach, was not valid. For the sake of completeness, I present below the summary statistics of the items related to the positive aspects of having children. Appendix C contains a more detailed description of the factor analysis and its results, including Cronbach's alpha as measure of scale reliability (Streiner 2003).

There are several reasons to prefer an index to single items. First, theoretical constructs in the social sciences are often multi-dimensional. Indices capture a number of facets that are part of the latent phenomenon. Second, the measurement of single attitude items in a questionnaire is prone to measurement error (Bertrand and Mullainathan 2001). A combination of variables might reduce such errors.

Attitudes toward family life

In Table 7, the summary statistics for the single items of the traditional family index are presented.[41] These descriptions refer to the response patterns in wave one. The sample consisted of female respondents also considered in the multivariate analyses; i.e., only childless women between ages 20 and 39 were considered. Because of missing values on single items, the number of observations differed slightly.

---

41 The *pairfam* and DemoDiff questionnaire do not include a large number of questions on a person's values. Only one item refers to gender role ideology, which was excluded after the factor analysis.

Table 7:   Summary statistics for the survey items related to traditional family values. Female respondents. First wave. Germany.

Traditional family values – *To what extent do you agree with the following statements?*

Item	number of observations	mean (std. deviation)	min	max
You should get married if you permanently live with your partner.	1791	2.98 (1.38)	1	5
Women should be more concerned about their family than about their career.	1793	2.46 (1.13)	1	5
A child under age 6 will suffer from having a working mother.	1772	2.48 (1.24)	1	5
Marriage is a lifelong union that should not be broken.	1784	3.12 (1.46)	1	5
Couples should marry at the latest after a child is born.	1787	2.19 (1.39)	1	5

Notes: The descriptive statistics refer to only those women who are considered in the multivariate analyses and only to the first panel wave. The degree of agreement to the statements ranges from "1-Disagree completely" to "5-Agree completely". Source: *pairfam* wave 1, DemoDiff wave 1. Varying numbers of observations might occur due to different numbers of missing values. Unweighted data. Author's own calculations.

The answers to the five items varied from one to five. The mean value of the answers ranged between 2.19 and 3.12, which indicates that, on average, the respondents did not have extreme attitudes regarding family.

In creating the index, I built the mean of the answers to the respective question. As the variables under investigation all had the same magnitude ranging from one to five, I constructed indices by building the average score on the referring items. If there were missing values on one of the items, I used the information of the remaining items. The value on the index for each individual was based on a minimum of two of the identified items. In order to further compress the index, they were reduced to three categories. Those respondents who had a value between one and 2.49 on the index "traditional family values" were re-categorized as one ("non-traditional"). Those with a value of between 2.5 and 3.49 were assigned to the second category ("neither traditional nor non-traditional"), and those with a level of between 3.5 to five were classified as three ("traditional"). The questions that constitute the "traditional family values"-index were asked only in wave one. In the regression models, the answers were also used to analyze whether a first birth (or pregnancy) occurred after wave two.

The value of children: cost and rewards of having children

Another group of items were based on Hoffman and Hoffman's "Value of Children" (VOC) approach (Hoffman and Hoffman 1973. Cf. Section 2.3.1). The VOC looks at the perceived positive aspects of childbearing.

Table 8:   Summary statistics for the survey items related to the benefits of having children. Female respondents. First wave. Germany.

Benefits of having children - *How strongly do you expect....*

item	number of observations	mean (std. deviation)	min	max
... that with children you will stay young longer?	1729	3.18 (1.26)	1	5
... to have an especially close emotional relationship with your children?	1760	4.58 (0.71)	1	5
... that your standing in your social network will increase because of your children?	1753	2.07 (1.09)	1	5
... that your adult children will be there for you when you are in need?	1758	3.82 (1.08)	1	5
... that you will get new ideas from your adult children?	1739	3.76 (1.00)	1	5

Notes: The descriptive statistics refer to only those women who are considered in the multivariate analyses and only to the first panel wave. The measure ranges from "1-Not at all" to "5-Very strongly". Varying numbers of observations might occur due to different numbers of missing values. Source: *pairfam* wave 1, DemoDiff wave 1. Unweighted data. Author's own calculations.

In Table 8, the summary statistics for the response patterns to the referring items are presented. The minimum and maximum values for the "benefits" items were one and five, respectively. On average, the respondents strongly indicated that they expect to have an emotionally close relationship with their children (mean=4.58). In contrast, the women in the sample did not think that having children would improve their standing in their social network (mean=2.07).

The responses to the other items had a mean value of between 3.18 and 3.82, indicating that, on average, the attitudes regarding the benefits of children were rather neutral. It should be noted that the factor analysis showed a moderate relationship between the items related to the benefits of having children (see Appendix C). However, the factor loadings were under the threshold of 0.5 that is used here as a benchmark indicating a considerable association between a number of variables. This result showed that the single items did not strongly load on the same factor; i.e., that from a statistical point of view, an indexation was unjustified. While this finding was in line with the VOC's recognition of different aspects of the value of children, such as affect and comfort (Nauck 2001), it also indicated that the single dimensions were not strongly correlated. I therefore refrained from creating an index based on these items.

In addition to measuring these positive aspects, the VOC approach also considers the perceived disadvantages of childbearing. Based on the factor analysis, five items were loading on the respective factor. These were subsumed in the index "cost of having children". The summary statistics of the single items are shown in Table 9. Again, the values ranged from one to five. The mean scores of around two or three indicated that, on average, the respondents did not have strong attitudes regarding the negative effects of having children. One exception was the response pattern to the item: "How strongly do you worry that with children you will stand out in a negative way in public?" The mean value of 1.62 and the standard deviation of 0.88 indicated that, on average, the respondents did not think that having children would negatively affect their standing in public. For the index "cost of having children", category 1 included the respondents who expected that having children would be associated with a "low cost" (values between one to 2.49). Category 2 was made up of the respondents who expected "neither a high nor a low cost" (values ranging from 2.3 to 3.49), while category 3 consisted of the respondents who anticipated a "high cost" (values 3.5 to 5.0).

Table 9:   Summary statistics for the survey items related to cost of having children. Female respondents. First wave. Germany.

Cost of having children - *How strongly do you worry...*

item	number of observations	mean (std. deviation)	min	max
... that you will be able to afford less with children?	1782	3.15 (1.18)	1	5
... that children will put you under nervous strain?	1789	2.74 (1.16)	1	5
... that with children you will not accomplish your professional goals?	1782	2.55 (1.26)	1	5
... that with children you will stand out in a negative way in public?	1788	1.62 (0.88)	1	5
... that children will limit your personal freedom?	1792	2.69 (1.19)	1	5

Notes and source: see Table 8.

Importance of different life domains

Another attitude dimension that might be of interest in studying the effect of childcare on fertility is the importance a person attached to different life domains at the time of the interview. The respective question in the *pairfam* (and DemoDiff) survey asks the respondent to assign a total of 15 "importance points" to five life domains. This means that the five response options could sum up to no more than 15. Those participants whose responses did not meet this requirement were set to missing. Table 10 reports the descriptive statistics of the respective items. The item responses to the life domains "education and career", "hobbies", and "partnership" ranged from zero to 15, indicating that some interviewees assigned none or all of their importance points to these domains. The relevance attached to "friends" and "having a child" had a maximum value of 10, which shows that, in the sample at hand, these domains never received the total number of available points. The mean values ranged from 1.75 to 3.81. These rather low values are related to the fact that the 15 relevance points could be allocated to five categories. Interestingly, in the sample under study, the lowest mean importance was assigned to

133

having children, while the highest average importance was assigned to living in a partnership.

Table 10: Summary statistics for the survey items related to the importance attached to different life domains. Female respondents. First wave. Germany.

Importance of different life domains - Please look at these five life goals and life domains. How important are these to you personally at the moment?

item	number of observations	mean (std. deviation)	min	max
Pursuing my education or career interests.	1790	3.64 (1.77)	0	15
Pursuing my hobbies and personal interests.	1790	2.62 (1.23)	0	15
Keeping in touch with friends.	1790	3.17 (1.17)	0	10
Living in a partnership.	1790	3.81 (1.08)	1	15
Having a(nother) child.	1790	1.75 (1.72)	0	10

Notes: The descriptive statistics refer to only those women who are considered in the multivariate analyses. The question was asked only in the first panel wave. Respondents were asked to assign a total of 15 importance points to the five life domains. Responses that sum up to more than 15 points seem to indicate a measurement error and the observations were excluded. Source: *pairfam* wave 1, DemoDiff wave 1. Unweighted data. Author's own calculations.

For the analyses of the relationship between childcare and fertility, the importance attached to (a) education and career and (b) to having a child appeared to be of particular interest. Both education and work and caring for children were assumed to be time-consuming and to compete for a woman's time. In order to distinguish between women who attach high, middle, or low importance to each domain, I grouped the two items into three categories based on the terciles among childless women between ages 20 and 39. The descriptive statistics (Table 11) for the variable "importance of career/education" showed that it was impossible to split the sample into three equal groups. For more than half of the respondents, job- and education-related goals were of low importance (i.e., three or less importance points), while 40 percent assigned medium relevance to career goals (four to five points), and only 10 percent indicated that career was very important (more than five points).

It should be noted that the response patterns reported here referred to those respondents who were considered in the multivariate analyses below. The attitudes questions were asked at the time of the first or second interview, while the birth information was used from the interview thereafter. This means that for those who had a child or were pregnant, the attitudes were observed before conception.

6.2.5 Control variables

In the discrete-time hazard models, I controlled for the confounding effects of a number of demographic and socioeconomic variables. The descriptive statistics are presented in Table 11 and refer to person-years. The share of missing values on each variable was less than one percent; observations with missings on one of the relevant variables were excluded from the sample.

A standard variable included in the discrete-time hazard model was the age of the women. I considered respondents aged 20 to 39 and placed them into four groups: 20 to 24, 25 to 29, 30 to 34, and 35 to 39. The age variable was based on the self-reported age of respondents when asked at the time of the interview. The number of women fluctuated considerably over age groups, which is related to the fact that the anchors were selected on the basis of their birth cohort and not randomly over age. Moreover, the group of childless women in the higher age groups was naturally smaller than among younger women.

Another control variable was woman's educational attainment. Women with higher levels of education might be less likely to enter motherhood because they stay in the education system longer, and because it takes them more time to get established in the labor market for highly educated women (Liefbroer and Corijn 1999). In *pairfam*, the respective variable has five categories and is created on the basis of the International Standard Classification of Education (ISCED-97) and its adaptation to the German educational system (Brüderl et al. 2012: 31). The category "in education" included all respondents who reported being currently enrolled.

Table 11: Descriptive statistics. Column percent of person-years. Germany.

age group	
20-24 years	6%
25-29 years	70%
30-34 years	2%
35-39 years	22%
educational attainment	
low	40%
medium	17%
high	35%
in education	9%
nationality	
German	95%
foreign	5%
region	
western Germany	77%
eastern Germany	23%
availability of parents	
grandparents available	77%
grandparents unavailable	23%
partnership status	
living apart together	24%
cohabiting	47%
married	28%
family attitudes	
non-traditional	46%
neither traditional nor non-traditional	37%
traditional	17%
perceived cost of children (VOC)	
low	48%
medium	40%
high	12%
importance of children	
low	36%
medium	49%
high	15%
importance of career/education	
low	51%
medium	21%
high	28%

Table 11:   Continued: Descriptive statistics. Column percent of person-years. Germany.

childcare level (1- and 2-year-olds)	
low level (<10% enrolled)	33%
medium level (10 to <20% enrolled)	39%
high level (20% or more enrolled)	28%
number of individuals	1,041
number of observations (person years)	1,738
number of events	226
number of districts	240

Notes: Female anchors and female partners in a partnership. Frequencies refer
to the number of observations considered in the analysis. Source: *pairfam*
(2008/09, 2009/10 and 2010/11) and DemoDiff (2009/10 and 2010/11) data.
Unweighted data. Author's own calculations.

The category "low education" included all respondents without a school
diploma, those with a school diploma but without a vocational diploma,
and those with a vocational diploma and lower schooling. (ISCED levels
1 to 5). The women classified as having "medium education" had a vocational diploma and higher schooling; i.e., they first qualified for university
and then did an apprenticeship (ISCED level 6). Those with "high education" had a university or college degree or had earned a doctorate
(ISCED level 7). The descriptive statistics showed that 40 percent of the
women in the sample belonged to the low education group, and 17 percent had medium education, or post-secondary and vocational education.
One-third had tertiary education (35 percent) and nine percent of the
women in the sample were in education at the time of interview (cf. Table 11).

A variable concerning the nationality of the respondent was also included. It has been shown that women with a migration background
have higher first birth risks than Germans (Milewski 2007). According to
the socialization hypothesis, this is usually attributable to the more traditional family values in the country of origin. In the sample analyzed here,
the vast majority of respondents were German (95 percent), while five
percent had foreign citizenship.

The variable accounting for living in eastern or western Germany was created on the basis of the place of residence at the time of the interview[42]. This information is important, as western Germans still have more traditional attitudes toward women's roles and working mothers than eastern Germans (Bauernschuster and Rainer 2012). These differences are generally attributed to the persisting influence of the different political systems of the FRG and the GDR. In the sample at hand, about one-quarter (24 percent) of the respondents lived in eastern Germany.

Another variable that might affect first birth or pregnancy is the availability of grandparents to help care for the child. As I mentioned above, potential parents might anticipate that they will have the option of relying on grandparental childcare. This can be seen as substitute for institutional childcare. In fact, it has been shown for a sample of German men and women that the desire to have another child increases if there is an option of arranging informal care in the event that the respondent disapproved institutional childcare (Ette and Ruckdeschel 2007). Moreover, studies have shown that the availability of grandparents might be positively related to fertility (Del Boca 2002; Hank and Kreyenfeld 2003). The *pairfam* questionnaire does not include a direct question on grandparental availability. As a proxy, I used travel time to the parents of the respondent, as it is difficult for the grandparents to help with childcare on a regular basis if they live far away. In *pairfam* and DemoDiff, the respondents and their partners were asked how long it takes them to travel to see their parents. I distinguished between respondents who needed less than 30 minutes ("grandparents available"; category 1) to travel to one of their parents from those who needed 30 minutes or more ("grandparents unavailable"; category 2). The first category also included those who were living in the same house with at least one of their parents. Those whose parents had died before the time of the interview were assigned to category two. Moreover, I took into consideration the respondent's level of attachment to her parents. If the interviewees indicat-

---

42   Between 1990 and 2006, 2.8 million people migrated from the East to the West; Vatterrott (2011: 11). Eastern Germans migrated to the western part of the country after German unification. It is unclear whether these migrants are more similar to non-mobile eastern Germans, or whether they adapted their attitudes and behaviors to those of their western German non-mobile compatriots. Concerning female fertility, the first and second birth risks of East-to-West migrants lie between those of the non-mobile eastern and western populations (ibid.).

ed that they were in contact with their parents less than monthly, I assumed that the parents would not be available for grandparental caregiving. Respondents who felt "not at all" close to their parents were assigned to category 2. If the partner was interviewed in *pairfam* wave 2, I also used the information about travel distance to the partner's parents; i.e., if at least one of the four potential grandparents were living within a distance of less than half an hour, the respondent was assigned to category 1.[43] A look at the frequencies reported in Table 11 shows that the vast majority of grandparents (77 percent) were theoretically available to care for their grandchildren, while 23 percent of grandparents were unavailable.

Another variable of interest is the partnership status of respondents. In the sample under study, 24 percent of respondents were living apart together with their partner. The largest share of respondents (47 percent) was cohabiting while 28 percent reported to be married.

6.2.6 How important is public childcare in the decision to have a child?

The second wave of the *pairfam* anchor questionnaire included a question on the willingness to have an additional child if specific policy measures were enacted. The list of items included the option of guaranteed full-time daycare for children under age three. The question was asked only at the second wave and only to the anchor person in *pairfam* (not in Demo-Diff); the number of childless women was too small for an analysis of first birth risks in wave three. However, describing the response patterns might provide some insights into how important childcare might be for individuals' childbearing decisions. Therefore, in the following, the response patterns were described.

I distinguished between male and female answers, and also between childless respondents and parents. From the 9,069 anchor persons in the second wave, 37 percent were not asked the question about a possible influence of family policies. The ones who were filtered – i.e., the group of participants who were not asked this question – were underage, ho-

---

43 Note that the distance to partners' parents was available only for *pairfam* wave 2. In DemoDiff, partners were not asked about the travel distance to their parents. If no partner information was available, I relied on the anchor's travel distance only.

mosexual, or either infertile or with an infertile partner. In the following, this group was not included; i.e., the proportions referred only to the respondents who were asked the question.

Table 12:   Family policy options that might support childbearing. Response patterns in percent. Weighted data. Germany.

Please tell me which of the following family policies would be most likely to positively influence your decision to have a(nother) child. Please indicate a maximum of two policies.

		total	women	men
(1)	Guaranteed all-day daycare for children under 3 years old.	29%	31%	27%
(2)	Universal availability of all-day schools.	12%	10%	13%
(3)	An increase of the child allowance from 170 euros currently to 300 euros per child.	22%	21%	23%
(4)	An increase of the parental leave benefit "Elterngeld" from 67 to 80 percent of net income.	11%	12%	11%
(5)	Making childrearing years count more toward one's pension.	8%	8%	8%
(6)	More flexible working hours for working parents with small children.	32%	35%	28%
(7)	More opportunities for part-time work for mothers and fathers.	17%	18%	15%
(8)	More tax reductions for parents.	18%	12%	23%
	None of the mentioned policies would have an influence.	11%	10%	12%
	I do not want a(nother) child under any circumstances.	10%	13%	8%
	missing	2%	2%	2%
	n (unweighted)	5,852	3,089	2,763

Notes: Weighted data (combined weight based on *dxpsweight* and the longitudinal weight *lweight*). Percentages refer to only respondents who are age 18 or older, heterosexual, fertile, and with a fertile partner. Source: *pairfam* wave 2, only anchor persons. Author's own calculations.

As the analyses remain purely descriptive, I used the post-stratification weight (in combination with the cohort weight, *dxpsweight*) and the longitudinal weight for non-response in the second survey wave (*lweight*) by multiplying the weights (for more details about the weighting procedure, see Brüderl et al. 2012: 45ff.). In the interview, the respondents were asked to answer the following question: "Please tell me which of the following family policies would be most likely to positively influence your decision to have a(nother) child. Please indicate a maximum of two policies". There were eight policies from which respondents could choose a maximum of two. In Table 12, the shares of respondents who opted for each policy are presented. The largest proportion of parents chose "more flexible working hours for working parents with small children" as the policy that would most incentivize them to have children (32 percent of respondents). Childcare provision for the under-threes was ranked second (29 percent). This indicates that parents would value policies that make it easier to balance working and having children. The third-most popular policy was an increase in child allowances (22 percent), while the fourth-most popular was more tax deductions (18 percent). These two policies are designed to reduce the financial costs of having children. The least-popular measure concerning childbearing was a policy that would count childrearing years more heavily toward the parent's pension (eight percent). A share of 11 percent said that none of the presented policy options would change their childbearing plans, and 10 percent stated that they did not want (more) children, irrespective of family policies. The response patterns among male and female respondents were similar. The biggest difference was found for tax reductions for parents: 23 percent of men opted for this policy option, while only 12 percent of women did so.

In order to determine whether childcare policies were perceived and valued differently by respondents according to their number of children, I compared the response patterns among the childless, parents with one child, parents with two children, and parents with three or more children (see Table 13).

It might be argued that childless individuals do not take into consideration the childcare situation when they think about having children as they are inexperienced in everyday live with children. In contrast to this hypothesis, childless respondents were the most likely to indicate that childcare provision would have a positive effect on their decision to have a child (33 percent). More than half (51 percent) of respondents in this group did not opt for childcare policies but for other policy measures. These shares were slightly reduced among respondents with one child.

Table 13: Influence of guaranteed daycare for children under age three on individuals' childbearing decisions. Response patterns in percent. Weighted data. Germany.

Please tell me which of the following [eight] family policies would be most likely to positively influence your decision to have a(nother) child. Please indicate a maximum of two policies.

Guaranteed all-day daycare for children under 3 years old.

	total	women	men
childless respondents			
selected "childcare policy"	33%	37%	30%
did not select "childcare policy"	51%	48%	53%
none of the policy options	11%	9%	12%
I do not want to have (more) children	3%	4%	2%
missing	3%	2%	3%
n (unweighted)	3,340	1,696	1,844
parents with one child			
selected "childcare policy"	31%	34%	27%
did not select "childcare policy"	48%	44%	54%
none of the policy options	10%	9%	11%
I do not want to have (more) children	10%	12%	8%
missing	0.4%	1%	0%
n (unweighted)	1,080	681	399
parents with two children			
selected "childcare policy"	16%	16%	16%
did not select "childcare policy"	39%	38%	42%
none of the policy options	14%	13%	15%
I do not want to have (more) children	30%	33%	27%
missing	1%	1%	0.5%
n (unweighted)	1,059	671	388
parents with three or more children			
selected "childcare policy"	9%		
did not select "childcare policy"	36%		
none of the policy options	13%		
I do not want to have (more) children	41%		
missing	0.5%		
n (unweighted)	369		

Notes and source: see Table 12

The share of parents who said they did not want to have more children, irrespective of family policies, increased with the number of children (two children: 30 percent; three or more children: 41 percent), while the expected positive effects of childcare provision decreased (two children: 16 percent; three or more children: nine percent). The response patterns varied slightly by sex. More women than men selected childcare policies. For childless respondents and parents with one child, the response patterns of men and women were significantly different. For parents with two children, the difference diminished, and was not statistically significant.

Table 14: Importance of daycare and educational attainment. Response patterns in percent. Weighted data. Germany.

Please tell me which of the following [eight] family policies would be most likely to positively influence your decision to have a(nother) child. Please indicate a maximum of two policies.

Guaranteed all-day daycare for children under 3 years old.

	total	women	men
low education (n= 2,541)	25%	25%	25%
medium education (n= 579)	32%	33%	32%
high education (n= 1,421)	31%	34%	28%
enrolled in education (n= 1,311)	31%	36%	27%
all respondents (n= 5,852)	29%	31%	27%

Notes and source: see Table 12.

As a next step, I investigated whether the response patterns concerning childcare policies differed according to a respondent's educational attainment (see Table 14). Based on the theoretical considerations above, it might be expected highly educated women in particular would have a preference to return to work soon after childbirth, and would thus value childcare provision for the under-threes. As was discussed in more detail in Section 6.2.5, I distinguished between four categories: those with a low level of education, those with a medium level of education, those with a high level of education, and those currently enrolled.

A comparison of these four groups showed that respondents with a level of low education were the least likely to indicate that a policy guaranteeing public childcare would positively affect their decision to have a

143

child (25 percent). Among the respondents with medium education, 32 percent said they see childcare policies as supportive of childbearing; while among highly educated respondents and students, this share was 31 percent. Interestingly, male and female response patterns were slightly different. The share of women who said they view childcare policies as supportive of childbearing increased with higher levels of education, and was highest among students (36 percent). More men with medium education (32 percent) said they see childcare policies as supportive, while the shares were lower among highly educated men (28 percent) and male students (27 percent).

Another interesting question is whether respondents living in eastern and western Germany agreed on the importance of childcare policies. It might be expected that childcare is more widely accepted in the eastern part of the country, and that the perceived importance of childcare would therefore be higher. Table 15 presents the shares of respondents who said policies guaranteeing access to childcare would positively influence their decision to have a child. In eastern Germany, 35 percent of respondents said they see childcare policies as supportive of childbearing; while in western Germany, the share was 27 percent. In eastern Germany, 36 percent of women and one-third of men said childcare policies would encourage them to have a child. Among western Germans, these shares were smaller.

Table 15:   Importance of daycare in eastern and western Germany. Response patterns in percent. Weighted data.

Please tell me which of the following [eight] family policies would be most likely to positively influence your decision to have a(nother) child. Please indicate a maximum of two policies.

Guaranteed all-day daycare for children under 3 years old.

	total	women	men
living in eastern Germany (n= 1,303)	35%	36%	33%
living in western Germany (n= 4,549)	27%	29%	25%
all respondents (n= 5,852)	29%	31%	27%

Notes and source: see Table 12.

To summarize, approximately 30 percent of the young adults surveyed in Germany indicated that a policy guaranteeing childcare for children under age three would encourage them to have children. In a ranking of family policies that respondents perceived as supportive of their decision to have a(nother) child, childcare policies placed second. (A policy that offers more flexible working hours for parents received the highest share of votes.) Childcare policies were slightly more popular among childless respondents than among parents. This indicates that individuals do anticipate the future care arrangements in the family before having children. Moreover, slightly more women than men selected childcare policies. A positive relationship of education was found only among female respondents: more women with higher education (and female students) said they see childcare policies as supportive of childbearing than women with lower levels of education. Eastern Germans were more likely than western Germans to indicate that guaranteed childcare would encourage them to have a child. It would be interesting to investigate the extent to which family policy preferences are related to actual childbearing. The item was included only in the second survey wave of *pairfam*, which leads to sample size problems for the analyses of order-specific transitions to birth in the third wave. As soon as there are more waves available, such analyses will be possible.

6.2.7 Regression results

This section presents the results of the discrete-time hazard models on the transition to a first conception in Germany. Models that included only individual-level variables were calculated based on simple cloglog models. For specifications that also consider regional childcare levels, I estimated random-effects models accounting for the multilevel structure of the data. Model 1 included all of the individual-level covariates without attitudes and childcare. Model 2 presented the multilevel model controlling only for age and childcare effects on the district level. In Model 3, all of the individual-level control variables were added to the multilevel model. The effects of the four different attitudes variables were presented in eight separate models (Models 4 to 11). Although both the risk of first birth and first pregnancy were considered in these regressions, for convenience I refer only to first births.

In Model 1 (Table 16), concerning age, the respondents aged 25 to 29 were the reference category. Compared to this group, those aged 35 to 39 had a significantly lower first birth risk (RR=0.37). Members of both age group 20 to 24 and age group 30 to 34 also had negative risks; however, these were statistically insignificant.

Table 16: Discrete-time hazard models. Transition to first birth. Relative risks. Basic model. Germany.

	Model 1	Model 2	Model 3
age group			
20-24 years	0.91	0.78	0.87
25-29 years	1	1	1
30-34 years	0.79	1.09	0.68
35-39 years	0.37***	0.58***	0.32***
educational attainment			
low	0.84		0.84
medium	1		1
high	0.67**		0.68*
currently enrolled	0.15***		0.14***
nationality			
German	1		1
foreign	1.39		1.55
region			
western Germany	1		1
eastern Germany	1.54**		1.68
availability of grandparents			
parents are available	1		1
parents are unavailable	1.17		1.24
partnership status			
living apart together	0.54**		0.55**
cohabiting	1		1
married	2.71***		3.18***
childcare level (1- and 2-year-olds)			
low level (<10% enrolled)		1.37	1.32
medium level (10 to <20% enrolled)		1	1
high level (20% or more enrolled)		1.55**	1.19
number of observations (1st level)	1,738	1,738	1,738
sigma_u (std. deviation random effect)		0.81	0.74
rho (residual intra class correlation)		0.28	0.25
χ^2 of likelihood-ratio test		0.00	0.00

Notes: Female respondents in a partnership. Model 1: discrete-time hazard regression using a complementary log-log (cloglog) model. Models 2 and 3: discrete-time hazard regression using a multi-level cloglog model with random effects. *p = 0.10; **p = 0.05; ***p = 0.01. Source: *pairfam* waves 1, 2, and 3; DemoDiff waves 1 and 2/3. Regional childcare data provided by the German Federal Statistical Office (DESTATIS). Author's own calculations.

For educational attainment, a lower risk of having a child was found among the highly educated than among those with a medium level education. Those who were currently enrolled in education also had lower first birth risks (RR=0.15), a result which is in line with findings in other studies (Blossfeld and Huinink 1991; Kreyenfeld and Konietzka 2008). Women in the low education group had no significantly differing risks. Having a non-German nationality had a positive but insignificant effect on the transition to a first birth. This might be related to the fact that the share of migrants in the sample under study was small (cf. Table 11).

For region, Model 1 found a 54 percent higher risk of first births among women living in eastern Germany than among women in western Germany. This finding is consistent with the results of Goldstein and Kreyenfeld (2011), who found higher age-specific birth rates for first births in eastern than in western Germany.

Concerning the influence of the availability of grandparents, the analysis indicated that there was a negative, though insignificant effect. This contradicts the findings of studies that have shown a significant (and positive) relationship between grandparents who can potentially help with childcare and entry into motherhood (Del Boca 2002; Hank and Kreyenfeld 2003). The category "grandparents are unavailable" was very heterogeneous, as it included women whose parents and whose partner's parents lived farther away than 30 minutes' travel time, those whose parents were not alive, and those who did not have close contact to their parents. These subgroups were too small for separate analyses.

The last variable under consideration in Model 1 was partnership status. As expected, women who did not live with their partner had a lower first birth risk than cohabiting women. Married respondents were most likely to enter motherhood (RR=2.71).

Model 2 referred to a random-effects model and included the district-level childcare variable. The results for the individual control variable age were largely the same as those described for Model 1. Concerning the childcare effect, the analysis revealed a u-shaped relationship. However, only the positive effect of high compared to a medium childcare availability (RR=1.55) was significant. This means that women living in a region with high levels of care provision had a higher first birth risk. For the low level, the counter intuitively positive effect remained insignificant. The fact that the model did not prove an effect for the low childcare category might indicate that potential mothers perceived services as unavailable when childcare levels were very low. Accordingly, Hank and Kreyenfeld (2003) argued that childcare might have an effect on childbearing only when the supply is large enough that parents can realistically expect to get a place for their child. Based on the analysis here, this threshold might be reached at a childcare level of more than 20 percent.

When all of the individual-level control variables in Model 3 were added together, the childcare effect was reduced to a relative risk of 1.19 and turned insignificant. All of the other variables had a similar effect on conception risks as in Model 2 with one exception: the effect of living in eastern Germany was not significant in this specification. The regional variables were closely related; in fact, almost all of the districts in eastern Germany fell into the high childcare category.

The goodness of fit measures (see Rabe-Hesketh and Skrondal 2008) given in the last rows of the regression tables implies that the multilevel approach used in Models 2 and 3 was appropriate. The standard deviation of the random effect was 0.81 (0.74, respectively), and indicated that the districts varied considerably from the mean effect. The *rho* was a measure of intra-class correlation, which measures to what extent women living within the same district were similar in terms of their transition to the first births. In Models 1 to 3, the null hypothesis that rho=0 was not accepted (see χ^2-test statistic of the likelihood-ratio test given in Table 16). This supported the choice of a multilevel model.

Effects of attitudes

In order to account for the effects of the different measures of attitudes toward the family, children, and career, I estimated six different models presented in the following tables. Models 4 and 5 included the level of traditional family attitudes. In Models 6 and 7, I considered the effects of the perceived costs of children. The last two models (Models 8 and 9) accounted for the importance a woman attaches both to having children, and to having an education and a career. The first model in each table referred to the simple model, while the second accounted for the multilevel structure of the data. The control variables had largely the same effects as in the models described before across all of the models. The finding that eastern Germans had a significantly higher risk of experiencing a first birth was also robust in the simple cloglog models, but it turned insignificant in the multilevel analyses. In the following, I focus on the description of the attitudinal and the childcare effects.

Table 17 presents the analyses that investigate the effect of traditional family attitudes on first births. Concerning the effect of family attitudes, the results imply that women with non-traditional opinions had a lower risk of having a first child than the reference group (neither traditional nor non-traditional).

Table 17: Discrete-time hazard models. Transition to first birth. Relative risks. Traditional family attitudes. Germany.

	Model 4	Model 5
family attitudes		
non-traditional	0.54**	0.62**
neither traditional nor non-traditional	1	1
traditional	2.47***	1.59***
childcare level (1- and 2-year-olds)		
low level (<10% enrolled)		1.33
medium level (10 to <20% enrolled)		1
high level (20% or more enrolled)		1.12

Notes: Female respondents in a partnership. Model 4: discrete-time hazard regression using a complementary log-log (cloglog) model. Model 5: discrete-time hazard regression using a multi-level cloglog model with random effects. *p = 0.10; **p = 0.05; ***p = 0.01. Source: *pairfam* waves 1, 2, and 3; DemoDiff waves 1 and 2/3. Regional childcare data provided by the German Federal Statistical Office (DESTATIS). Author's own calculations.

Those who had traditional attitudes, in contrast, had a higher risk of entering motherhood. This effect was less pronounced in the multilevel model, where the relative risks were smaller than in the simple model. This positive effect of traditionalism on the first birth is in accordance with the results of Moors (2008) and Thomson (2002). For childcare, the effect was again u-shaped but insignificant.

In Models 6 and 7 (see Table 18), I investigated the effect of a woman's perception that having children would have negative consequences for her life. Again, the coefficients of the control variables were very similar to those in the first models. In line with the theoretical argument, potential mothers who associated low costs with having children had a higher first birth risk than those who expected medium costs. Those who said they believe that having children has many negative consequences had lower first birth risks, but this effect was insignificant.

Table 18:   Discrete-time hazard models. Transition to first birth. Relative risks. Negative VOC. Germany.

	Model 6	Model 7
perceived cost of children (VOC)		
low	1.61***	1.63**
medium	1	1
high	0.88	0.86
childcare level (1- and 2-year-olds)		
low level (<10% enrolled)		1.34
medium level (10 to <20% enrolled)		1
high level (20% or more enrolled)		1.22

Notes and source: see Table 17. Model 6: discrete-time hazard regression using a complementary log-log (cloglog) model. Model 7: discrete-time hazard regression using a multi-level cloglog model with random effects.

This might be related to the fact that only 12 percent of the respondents in the sample had negative views on having children. Other authors have also found that perceived high costs negatively affects entry into motherhood (Liefbroer 2005; Bernhardt and Goldscheider 2006). The childcare effect remained insignificant.

Table 19:   Discrete-time hazard models. Transition to first birth. Relative risks. Importance of children. Germany.

	Model 8	Model 9
importance of children		
low	0.43***	0.40***
medium	1	1
high	2.46***	2.55***
childcare level (1- and 2-year-olds)		
low level (<10% enrolled)		1.25
medium level (10 to <20% enrolled)		1
high level (20% or more enrolled)		0.92

Notes and source: see Table 17. Model 8: discrete-time hazard regression using a complementary log-log (cloglog) model. Model 9: discrete-time hazard regression using a multi-level cloglog model with random effects.

The effects of the relevance women attached to having children are presented in Table 19. Women who said they see children as rather unimportant for their life at the moment had less than half the risk of having a first child relative to those who attached medium importance to starting a family. The women who rated having children as very important had more than double the childbearing risks of women who rated the importance as medium. These results were found in both the simple and the multilevel analyses. In Model 9, childcare was negatively related to childbearing risks; however, this effect was statistically insignificant.

While it seems rather unsurprising that the importance attached to children affects childbearing, the results for the value of education and career are less intuitive. As Table 20 reveals, the expected negative effect of the career/education variable on first births was found only for the group that attached relatively low importance to career (RR= 2.66; reference group: medium level of importance attached to career). For women who were strongly career-oriented, the unexpectedly positive relative risks were insignificant. The childcare variable did not yield significant results.

Table 20: Discrete-time hazard models. Transition to first birth. Relative risks. Importance of education and career. Germany.

	Model 10	Model 11
importance of career/education		
low	2.66***	2.65***
medium	1	1
high	1.52	1.51
childcare level (1- and 2-year-olds)		
low level (<10% enrolled)		1.28
medium level (10 to <20% enrolled)		1
high level (20% or more enrolled)		1.23

Notes and source: see Table 17. Model 10: discrete-time hazard regression using a complementary log-log (cloglog) model. Model 11: discrete-time hazard regression using a multi-level cloglog model with random effects.

For all of the multilevel models, the measures for the model fit were similar to those in Model 3 (not shown here). It appears that the district-level variation contributes to explain the variances in childbearing behaviors. Thus, the decision to employ multilevel models seems to have been appropriate.

Interaction effects

In order to investigate whether childcare effects vary for women with specific attitudes and educational levels, I specified interaction effects. Based on the theoretical considerations discussed in Chapter 2, I expected that women who believe that family is very important might react to childcare policies to a lesser extent than women who want to pursue their careers. In addition to the direct attitude questions, a woman's education might also reveal her interest in job-related goals. I further assumed that having a higher level of education indicates that a woman attaches greater importance to her career. Moreover, the development of childcare provision and the persisting deviation in eastern and western Germany might indicate that the availability of care services affects childbearing in the two regions in different ways. However, the sample sizes were too small to allow me to run models with an interaction effect between childcare and region.

Table 21 presents the interaction effects of the different dimensions of family-related attitudes and childcare provision. All of the models are random-effects specifications, and the individual-level variables discussed above were controlled for. The reference categories differed over the models, and were based on the respective hypotheses on the expected relationship.

In the model that accounted for women's traditionalism (Model 12), the reference category chosen consisted of those women who had non-traditional attitudes about family and who lived in an area where childcare provision was high. For this group, according to the theoretical expectations formulated above, childcare should have had the strongest effect on childbearing. The first birth risks for women in this category were found to be lower than among non-traditional women living in regions with lower levels of childcare provision. But these effects were statistically insignificant. All of the other categories had higher childbearing risks than the reference group; many of the effects were also insignificant.

The highest relative risk was found among those women who were traditional and lived in a region with low levels of childcare provision (RR=3.06). This effect was significant, and implies that women with more traditional family attitudes had a considerably higher risk of transitioning to first birth than those who are non-traditional. It appears that, as traditional women believe that a mother should stay home and care for her family rather than pursue her own career, childbearing is high even in a situation in which the availability of childcare is very low.

Table 21: Discrete-time hazard models. Transition to first birth. Relative risks. Interaction models (woman's attitudes and regional childcare provision). Germany.

| | childcare level (1- and 2-year-olds) | | |
	low level (<10% enrolled)	medium level (10 to <20% enrolled)	high level (20% or more enrolled)
Model 12:			
family attitudes			
non-traditional	0.91	0.88	1
neither traditional nor non-traditional	1.81	1.17	1.58*
traditional	3.06**	2.15	1.83
Model 13:			
perceived cost of children (VOC)			
low	1.87	1.18	1.50
medium	0.98	0.84	0.93
high	0.48	0.82	1
Model 14:			
importance of children			
low	0.53	0.65	1
medium	2.18	1.70	1.46
high	5.24**	3.83**	3.60***
Model 15:			
importance of career			
low	1.59	1.25	1.58
medium	0.54	0.81	0.34**
high	1.05	0.52	1

Notes and source: see Table 17. All models discrete-time hazard regression using a multi-level cloglog model with random effects.

The second interaction model in Table 21 considered the combined effect of the perceived costs associated with children and childcare (Model 13). The reference category in this analysis consisted of those respondents who said they believe they would incur high personal costs by having children, and who lived in a region with a high level of childcare availability. I assumed that parents may perceive children as costly if they need to provide childcare privately, and that public childcare provision might change this negative attitude. For this group I expected to find that childcare had a positive effect on childbearing. Indeed, the lower the availability of childcare, the lower the first birth risks were for this group. But none of the effects was significant. Women who associated having children with low costs had a higher risk of entering motherhood, which would indicate that, for these women, childcare was less relevant. Again, the effects were insignificant, and I could not draw any definite conclusions from these findings.

When interacting the importance of children and childcare availability (Model 14), I chose as a reference group those respondents who did not attach great importance to having children, and who lived in an area with a high level of childcare provision. In the low importance group, childcare had a positive but insignificant effect. Those who attached medium and great importance had higher first birth risks, with significant and very pronounced differences for the latter group. Interestingly, among those who said they see having children as very important, their first birth risk decreased with higher childcare availability.

Model 15 referred to the combined effect of the importance a woman attached to education and career on the one hand, and childcare on the other. The reference category consisted of those to whom career was very important and who lived in a region with a high level of childcare availability. Women who attached low importance to career-related goals had higher first birth risks than the reference group; however, this effect was insignificant for all three childcare levels. The other groups also did not differ significantly from the reference group. One exception were women who rated having a career as being of medium importance and who lived in a region with high levels of childcare. This group had a significantly lower first birth risk than the reference (RR=0.34). This finding was difficult to interpret in light of my theoretical expectations.

The last model showed the interaction effect between childcare availability and the educational attainment of women (Model 16). Figure 19 displays this interaction effect, with women who were living in a region with a low level of childcare provision and who had low educational attainment serving as the reference group. Interestingly, the graph reveals that, for women in both the low and the medium education groups, the first birth risks declined with increasing childcare availability. It has to be noted that almost all of these effects were not significantly different from the reference group. In contrast, for highly educated women living in a region with low childcare provision had a significantly lower risk of having a first birth than women in the reference category (RR=0.44). This negative effect was reduced among highly educated women who live in a medium level childcare region (RR=0.57). The effect in high childcare regions remained insignificant.

Figure 19:   Model 16. Interaction effect of childcare level and education. Transition to first births. Multilevel cloglog model. Relative risks. Germany.

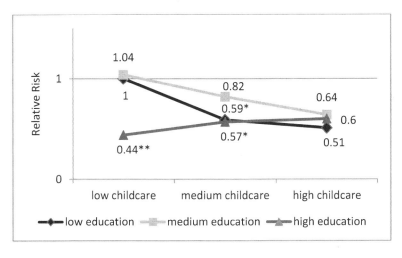

Notes: *p = 0.10; **p = 0.05; ***p = 0.01

To summarize, the findings of the models accounting for interaction effects were mixed. Many of the effects shown here were statistically insignificant, which might be related to the small number of observations in some of the categories under study. We found a pattern in which those who were "family-oriented" (i.e., those with traditional family attitudes) (Model 12), those who perceived the costs of having children as being low (Model 13), and those who attached great importance to the family (Model 14) and low importance to education and career (Model 15) had higher childbearing risks than those who were less family-oriented. This seems to have been the case regardless of the level of childcare provision. In contrast, those who were the least family-prone were also the group who had elevated first birth rates in regions with higher childcare availa-

155

bility (Models 13 and 14). This trend was also visible in the model with education: among highly educated women, the availability of public childcare had a positive effect. Another interesting finding was that, for family-oriented respondents, the childcare effect was actually negative (Models 12, 14, and 16). The group of women who were categorized in the intermediate attitudes groups sometimes had the same childcare effects as the family-oriented group (Models 12 and 14). In contrast, in Model 13, the effects in the intermediate group were more similar to those of the less family-oriented group. Concerning the interaction with education, first birth risks of those with medium levels and those with low levels did not differ significantly. However, the negative effect of high education seemed to be slightly decreasing for women living in regions with medium levels of childcare compared to those living in low childcare regions (Figure 19). Again, these effects should be interpreted with caution because the majority of coefficients were insignificant in the models.

6.3   Case study: Sweden

Sweden is an interesting country for comparison. Swedish family policy was used as a blueprint for the parental leave reform introduced in 2007 in Germany (Erler 2009). The legal entitlement to childcare from age one in Germany, which has become effective in August 2013, also resembles the Swedish childcare policy. Family policies in the Nordic countries were not designed to influence fertility behavior, but rather to promote gender equality (Naumann 2005). In spite of this, there is substantial evidence that the policy arrangements in Sweden and other Scandinavian societies reduce the incompatibilities of work and family, and are thus positively related to fertility (Hoem 2005; Andersson 2008; Ellingsæter 2009; Rønsen and Skrede 2010). At the same time, Sweden is known as a country with relatively egalitarian gender role attitudes (Dorius and Alwin 2010; Pampel 2011).

It should be noted that the analyses based on Sweden differ from the German case study. First, the Swedish dataset is considerably smaller than the German data and no partners were interviewed. Second, the panel survey was conducted not yearly but after four years. Thus, I considered also respondents who were single at time of first interview. Third, the Swedish questionnaire differs from the German one, e.g. the Swedish data do not include a question on expected positive effects of single policies, for instance. Fourth, the childcare data refers to provinces. As these are much larger regions than German districts, I refrain from an extensive discussion of interaction effects between childcare and attitudes or education in the Swedish case study.

6.3.1 Data and sample selection

In the empirical analysis on Sweden, I use the individual-level dataset "Young Adult Panel Survey" (YAPS).[44] This survey consists of a two-wave panel study collected in 1999 and 2003.[45] The dataset has a focus on the family and working lives of young men and women, and includes a large set of questions on attitudes. In the first wave, 2,283 young adults who were born in Sweden and whose parents were also born in Sweden participated in the survey. Moreover, 537 Swedish-born respondents with at least one parent born either in Turkey or Poland were also surveyed. Like in *pairfam*, three birth cohorts were included in YAPS: namely, those born in the years 1968, 1972, and 1976. The data were collected via paper and web questionnaires. Moreover, some information, such as information on the income of the respondents, was added from official register data merged to individuals' survey responses. Due to panel attrition, the number of respondents in the second wave was smaller than in the first wave, leaving 2,089 individuals for analysis in panel format. The response rate for the overall sample in 1999 was 65 percent, while in 2003 it reached 70 percent (see Goldscheider and Bernhardt 2011; Wanders 2012).

As I mentioned in the context of the German case study, I would have been interested in learning how each woman evaluates the availability of public childcare in her environment. Such information was not included in the YAPS questionnaire but there is a variable on the region (*län*) where a person lives. I therefore make use of regional-level childcare enrollment rates. These data were provided by Statistics Sweden.

44 The survey was designed by Eva Bernhardt at Stockholm University with Statistics Sweden in charge of the field work. Data are provided by the Swedish Social Science Data Service (SSD) and are available at http://www.ssd.gu.se/.
45 In the second wave, a fourth cohort born in 1980 was interviewed (number of observations: 1,194). A third wave was collected in the year 2009 but was not yet available for public use by March 2013.

In principle, the data set-up would have allowed me to conduct an analysis of fertility behavior for the period from 1999 to 2003. However for the years 1999 and 2000, information on regional childcare is unavailable. Such data are available only from 2001 onwards. Therefore, births occurring in the years 1999 and 2000 were omitted from the analysis. Instead, I predicted women's rate of entry into first births for the period 2001 to 2003, excluding all women who had a child before the year 2001. The data were organized in a person-year format, with each woman contributing one entry per year. If the woman had a child she dropped out of the sample. Respondents who had children prior to 2001 were left-truncated; i.e., they never entered the risk set.

As the dependent variable refers to women's first childbearing, the male respondents and women who already had children before 2001 were excluded from the analyses. I thus considered 665 individuals in the analyses.

6.3.2   Dependent variable and data structure

For the current analysis, I used individual data from the first survey wave (1999) to predict childbearing behavior reported in the second wave (2003). As I discussed above (Section 2.3.1), I would actually be interested in investigating proceptive behavior; i.e., behavior that may lead to contraception. But since this behavior is not covered in the questionnaire of YAPS, I considered all births[46] that occur in the years 2001, 2002, and 2003. Within the data, I found 133 entries into motherhood occurring during the period of observation. Arranging the data in a person-year format resulted in the data structure presented in Table 22. A woman dropped out of the analysis after she had experienced a birth. If this did not happen in the year 2001, the woman contributed another observation in the year 2002. If the woman did not give birth in 2002, she entered the data one more time for the year 2003. If she did not have a child over the entire observation period, her record was censored in 2003.

It should be noted that (in contrast to the German dataset) YAPS was not conducted yearly, but only in 1999 and 2003. Information on chang-

---

46   In contrast to the German case study, I refrained from considering pregnancies at the time of the second interview. In the Swedish dataset, I analyzed births in each year under consideration (2001, 2002, and 2003). Unfortunately, I do not have information about pregnancies during the single years.

es in individual-level characteristics is therefore unavailable, and these characteristics are thus time-invariant (denoted as z in Table 22). The data on childcare enrollment rates are, however, available on a yearly basis, and vary over time.

Table 22: Exemplary data structure analyzed in the discrete-time model. YAPS data.

id	cohort	year	childcare	z	first_child	...
1	1972	2001	71.0	3	1	...
2	1968	2001	69.3	4	0	...
2	1968	2002	72.1	4	1	...
3	1976	2001	59.7	2	0	...
3	1976	2002	60.4	2	0	...
3	1976	2003	60.3	2	0	...
...	...	...	...	...	...	...

Source: own illustration.

6.3.3 Childcare enrollment

A key variable in this study is an individual's perception of the public childcare situation in her environment. Such data are not collected in the YAPS dataset. To measure childcare, I used regional childcare enrollment rates provided by Statistics Sweden. These numbers refer to both child-care services (*förskola*) directly provided by the municipalities, as well as arrangements that are overseen by the municipalities, but organized by a private provider. Moreover, family daycare (*familjedaghem*) is included.

The regional level refers to the so-called *län*. Sweden is divided into 21 such provinces. The childcare data refer to children between one and two years of age who are enrolled in childcare as a percentage of all children in that age group. Less than one percent of parents with children under one year old make use of childcare, which indicates that Swedish parents care for their infants at home. This might be related to the generous parental leave system in Sweden. I therefore excluded the childcare enrollment of children under one year old.

Figure 20:   Enrollment rates of children aged 1-2 years. Swedish provinces 2002.

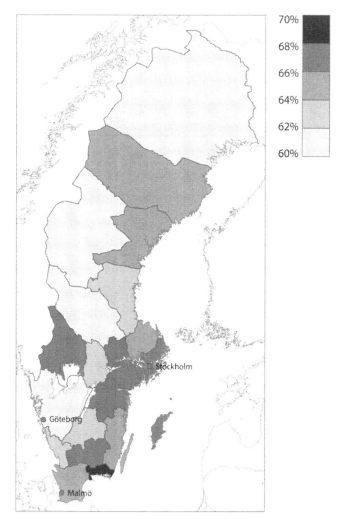

Source: Data provided by Statistics Sweden (SCB). Illustration: Ruben Apitz.

The rates for the 21 regions in the years from 2001 to 2003 varied between 56.8 percent and 70.4 percent, with a mean of 64 percent. In Figure 20, the regional variation is illustrated for the year 2002. The exact enrollment rates in each province over the three years under study are provided in Appendix D. Based on the enrollment rates, I created three provision levels along the terciles in the sample, including all regions in the three years under study. In the first tercile, there are all regions with an enrollment rate under 63 percent (low childcare level), the second tercile ranges from 63 to 65.7 percent (medium childcare level) and regions with rates above 65.7 percent are classified as high childcare level. As I mentioned above, the data are available only from 2001 onwards.

The measurement of childcare usage is problematic, as the regions are not homogeneous entities. The average percentage of children enrolled in a province might be inadequate to give exact information on childcare enrollment in the precise area where a respondent lived. As some of the provinces cover a rather large area, they might include some rural areas with low childcare enrollment rates and urban areas with high childcare enrollment rates.[47] Using municipality-level enrollment rates would help to reduce this lack of precision. Unfortunately, in the YAPS data, there is no detailed information on each woman's municipality. Other studies also used enrollment rates to investigate the effect of childcare availability on childbirth (see e.g., Del Boca 2002; Hank and Kreyenfeld 2003; Andersson et al. 2004; Rindfuss et al. 2007). The argument is that childcare provision does not meet parents' demand in many countries; i.e., that not all children can access childcare because demand exceeds supply.

In Sweden, childcare provision now is universal; i.e., all children between the ages of one and 12 can attend childcare if the parents apply. Thus, it is often assumed that childcare provision does not vary across Sweden. However, in the time period under study (2001-2003) the principle of universalism had just been introduced. Before this time, mothers who were unemployed or who stayed at home with a newborn were excluded from public childcare usage (see Section 4.2).

---

47 The differences between rural and urban areas in their childcare provision are shrinking. In 2005, the enrollment rates of children between ages one and five in rural municipalities and big cities differed by nine percent (Neumann 2009).

6.3.4 Attitudes toward family and career

The second central aspect of interest for this study is the attitude toward public childcare. Such information was unavailable in the YAPS dataset. However, a large set of questions about related attitudes concerning family and working life were posed in the survey. Again, I created two indices on the basis of a factor analysis: importance of family, and importance of work. Moreover, I consider gender role attitudes.

Importance of having a family

Nine attitudes items were identified to load on a factor I call "importance of having a family". Like in the *pairfam* dataset, the variables ranged between one and five.

Table 23: Descriptive statistics for the items related to the importance of having a family. Female respondents in Sweden.

People have different opinions about what is important in life. Can you tell us how important it is to you to achieve the following? Answers range from 1 for "unimportant" to 5 for "very important".				
	number of observations	mean (std. deviation)	min	max
To have children.	655	3.83 (1.17)	1	5
To live in a good cohabiting or married relationship.	658	4.48 (0.89)	1	5
Here are some statements about children and family. What do you think? Answers range from 1 for "don't agree at all" to 5 for "agree completely".				
I enjoy children.	655	4.12 (1.06)	1	5
I think I can be satisfied with my life if I am a good parent.	592	3.75 (1.11)	1	5
Spending time with the family is more rewarding than work.	573	4.10 (0.89)	1	5
Children need siblings.	644	3.58 (1.27)	1	5

Table 23: Continued. Descriptive statistics for the items related to the importance of having a family. Female respondents in Sweden.

Having children is a confirmation of a good partner relationship.	640	1.81 (1.19)	1	5
What is your view of the following statements? Answers range from 1 for "don't agree at all" to 5 for "agree completely".				
Having children is part of what gives life meaning.	640	3.77 (1.23)	1	5
Something is missing if a couple never has children.	640	2.14 (1.33)	1	5

Notes: Women who are considered in the multivariate analyses. Varying numbers of observations might occur due to different numbers of missing values. Source: YAPS wave 1 (1999). Unweighted data. Author's own calculations.

Most of the items had a mean value score above three, which indicates that many of the respondents agreed with the respective statement (see Table 23). The highest mean value of 4.48 shows that, for the majority of young Swedes in the sample, having a good relationship with a live-in partner was very important. In contrast, the level of agreement with the statement "to have children is a confirmation of a good partner relationship" was low (mean= 1.81). The average values of these items were used to create an additive index, which varied between 1.3 and 5, with a mean value of 3.4. Based on the terciles, I subdivided the family index into three categories (low, medium, high). These categories were used as covariates in the multivariate analyses.

Attitudes toward having a career

Another set of items that might be related to attitudes toward public childcare concerns the relevance a woman attaches to having an occupational career. Women who want to pursue a career might be more interested in public childcare provision, as I assume that having access to childcare enables them to combine work and raising children.

Based on the factor analysis, I identified the six items presented in Table 24. The response patterns for these items revealed that the mean value of five items was higher than four. This indicates that, for a majority of young Swedish women, it was important to be successful at work.

163

The lowest mean score among the items (3.94) was found for the item referring to the relevance attached to a high salary.

Table 24:   Descriptive statistics for the survey items related to the importance of being successful at work. Female respondents in Sweden. First wave (1999).

People have different opinions about what is important in life. Can you tell us how important it is to you to achieve the following? Answers range from 1 for "unimportant" to 5 for "very important".

item	number of observa-tions	mean (std. devia-tion)	min	max
To do well economically.	659	4.53 (0.67)	2	5
To be successful in my work.	657	4.07 (0.84)	1	5

What does a good job mean to you? Answers range from 1 for "unimportant" to 5 for "very important".

That I can think and act independently.	664	4.55 (0.64)	2	5
That it offers good opportunities to advance.	657	4.01 (0.94)	1	5
That I can be proud of my work.	658	4.57 (0.72)	1	5
That I get a high salary and/or other benefits.	658	3.94 (0.84)	1	5

Notes and source: see Table 23.

Homogeneous response patterns to single items were also reflected in low levels of variance in the additive index. In order to still find a meaningful grading in the index, I distinguished between those who scored four or higher (categorized as "high level of importance attached to job") and those who scored under four ("lower level of importance attached to job"). The first category comprises 76 percent of respondents in the sample, while 24 percent belong to the second category.

Gender role ideology

The third attitudinal variable that might be related to childcare ideals and to childbearing is gender role ideology. According to the literature, egalitarian women might be less likely to have a child than traditional women (Mills et al. 2008). Accounting for individuals' attitudes toward gender equality, I did a factor analysis which revealed four items that were loading on the same factor. Table 25 shows that the variation in the variables is very low. All four of the items show a mean value of above 4.5. This indicates that the majority of young women in Sweden have strongly egalitarian views, which is in line with the literature (Oláh and Bernhardt 2008).

Table 25: Descriptive statistics for the survey items related to gender equality. Female respondents in Sweden. First wave (1999).

What is your view of the following statements? Answers range from 1 for "don't agree at all" to 5 for "agree completely".				
item	number of observations	mean (std. deviation)	min	max
It is as important for a woman as it is for a man to support herself/himself.	663	4.92 (0.40)	1	5
A society in which men and women are equal is a good society.	659	4.71 (0.60)	1	5
Men can perform as well as women in caring jobs.	663	4.87 (0.43)	1	5
Women can perform as well as men in technical jobs.	661	4.83 (0.51)	1	5

Notes and source: see Table 23.

Due to the negligible variation in this variable, I did not consider it in the following hazard models. In order to take into account the degree of gender egalitarianism when considering families with children, I created a second measure of gender equality based on the question: "What do you think would be the best arrangement for a family with preschool children?" The dichotomous variable "both carers" reflects whether a respondent opted for the answer: "Both parents work roughly the same hours and share the responsibility for home and children equally". On this variable as well, a vast majority (86 percent; see Table 26) answered in an egalitarian way. In order to investigate whether the few respondents who did not agree with the equal family arrangement differ in their fertility behavior, I included this variable in the analyses below.

6.3.5 Control variables

In order to account for the effects of other individual characteristics on having children, a number of covariates based on the response patterns in the first wave were included in the discrete-time hazard model. Because the individual-level information was reported at one point in time only (1999), these covariates were time-constant. The frequencies of these variables are shown in Table 26.

To control for a woman's age, I included her birth cohort in the analyses. As only three of the cohorts included in YAPS were considered in the years 2001 to 2003, each cohort can be seen as a single age group. As is apparent in Table 26, more than half of the respondents belonged to the youngest cohort (1976), one-third were born in 1972, and 12 percent were born in 1968. Many of the respondents in the older cohorts had already had children before 2001. As we considered only first births, many of the women in the older cohorts were not considered here.

Education influences childbearing behavior through a number of channels (Lappegård and Ronsen 2005). Research has shown that having a high level of education is related to a postponement of having a first child (Tesching 2012). Among the mechanisms behind this delay might be the relatively long amount of time it takes for these women to complete their education and to become established in the labor market (Liefbroer and Corijn 1999). Moreover, having a higher level of education might be correlated with attitudes toward work and family that center on career-related goals (Blossfeld and Huinink 1991; Kravdal and Rindfuss 2008). The information on respondents' educational attainment was coded into three categories. Women in the "low" education category include those with lower-secondary or lower levels of education (17 percent). Women with upper secondary education were assigned to the "medium" group (47 percent of the respondents), while women with tertiary education were placed in the "high" category (36 percent of the respondents).

Table 26:   Descriptive statistics. Column percent of person-years.

birth cohort	
1976	55%
1972	33%
1968	12%
educational attainment (in 1999)	
low	14%
medium	26%
high	17%
in education	42%
migration background	
Swedish	77%
foreign (Turkish or Polish)	23%
metropolitan area (in 1999)	
lives in non-metropolitan area	52%
lives in metropolitan area	48%
partnership status (in 1999)	
single	58%
in relationship	42%
importance of children (in 1999)	
low	33%
medium	38%
high	29%
importance of career goals (in 1999)	
low	33%
medium	35%
high	32%
gender role ideology (in 1999)	
non-egalitarian	15%
egalitarian	85%
childcare level (in 2001, 2002 and 2003)	
low level (<63% enrolled)	34%
medium level (63 to <65.7% enrolled)	38%
high level (67.7% or more enrolled)	28%
number of individuals	665
number of observations (person-years)	1,827
number of events	131
number of regions	21

Notes: Frequencies refer to the number of observations considered in the analysis. Female respondents. Source: YAPS data. Unweighted frequencies. Author's own calculations.

Additionally, women who reported that their main activity is being a student were assigned to a category labeled "in education". This is based on the assumption that young adults generally wait to start a family until they have finished their education, usually for economic reasons (Thalberg 2009). Another reason why being a student could lead to a postponement of entry into motherhood is the design of parental leave in Sweden. Benefits are paid on the basis of the individual's income in the calendar year before childbirth; i.e., the higher the income in the year before birth, the higher the parental leave benefit. A woman who did not work for a minimum of 240 days before the leave receives a basic payment. Students often receive this minimum payment. In order to receive a parental leave benefit the minimum, a woman might choose to have a child when she is earning a reasonable amount of money; i.e., after she has finished her education.

Studies have shown that many immigrant groups in Sweden have higher first birth propensities than Swedish-born women (Andersson and Scott 2005). Although all of the respondents in the YAPS data were born in Sweden, 22 percent had at least one parent who was born in either Poland or Turkey. As migrant parents might transfer the culture and values of their country of origin to their children, the second generation of immigrants might have accelerated childbearing. I therefore controlled for migrant status in the discrete-time hazard models.

As there might be differences in childbearing behavior between women who live in urban and in rural areas, I included a variable on the type of area of residence. Studies have shown that, although the difference is diminishing over time, fertility decreases as the settlement size increases (Kulu et al. 2007). Moreover, it can be assumed that childcare provision is better in cities than in rural areas. I therefore included a variable for "living in a metropolitan area;" i.e., living in Stockholm/Södertälje, Malmö, Lund, Trelleborg, or Gothenburg.

The relevance of marital status for first births seems to be shrinking in Sweden, which is visible in the high levels of non-marital childbearing (nearly 60 percent; see Oláh and Bernhardt 2008: 1114). As being in a relationship is a prerequisite for having children, I controlled for having a partner (including living apart together, cohabiting, and married partnerships). In the sample under study, 58 percent of women were in a relationship in 1999, while 42 percent were single.

6.3.6 Regression results

In the following section, the results of the discrete-time hazard models for Sweden are presented. Again, the presented coefficients are relative risks (RR). The data were analyzed on the basis of cloglog models. Moreover, I also used a random effects model to analyze the influence of the province level. Using such models allowed me to take into consideration the multilevel structure of the data as individuals are clustered within regions. However, in contrast to the German models discussed in Section 6.2.7, the random-effects design did not lead to an improvement of the model fit when considering provinces as a second level. This means that women in the same region were not more similar concerning their childbearing behavior than women across regions (Rabe-Hesketh and Skrondal 2008). Therefore, in the six models presented here, I did not apply random-effect models to the Swedish dataset. First, I show three models without the attitude indices. In Models 4 to 6, I included the three attitudes dimensions discussed above. For each attitude a separate model was estimated.

In Table 27, the results of the basic models are displayed. First, I ran a model with only individual-level covariates (Model 1). The results for birth cohorts show that women born in 1976 did not differ significantly in their first birth risks from those born in 1972 (reference group) while the cohort born in 1968 had significantly lower rates of entry into motherhood.

The results for educational attainment show that Swedish women in the low education category had significantly lower first birth risks (RR=0.47) than those in the medium category. Highly educated women also had lower childbearing risks but the effect remains insignificant. Respondents who were in school had lower first birth risks (RR=0.39) than those with a medium level of education. In line with Andersson (2000: 304), who observed that young adults in Sweden are expected to "establish themselves properly in society" before planning a family, students in the YAPS sample had a low probability of entering parenthood.

Respondents with a migration background – i.e., those with at least one parent born in Turkey or Poland – did not significantly differ in their first birth risks. This might indicate that second-generation women are well integrated into Swedish society, and that their family behavior is similar to that of Swedes.

The results on the place of residence indicate that respondents living in a metropolitan area had lower first birth risks (RR=0.71) than those

169

who lived outside the big cities. This fits with similar results showing that women in rural areas have higher fertility risks than women in urban areas (Kulu et al. 2007). Moreover, as expected, the relationship status of a woman also had an influence on her childbearing. The results show that women who had a partner in 1999 were three times more likely to enter motherhood than those who reported being single.

Table 27:   Discrete-time hazard models. Transition to first birth. Relative risks. Basic models. Sweden.

	Model 1	Model 2	Model 3
birth cohort			
1976	1.27	1.55*	1.27
1972	1	1	1
1968	0.55***	0.51***	0.56***
educational attainment (in 1999)			
low	0.47***		0.47***
medium	1		1
high	0.78		0.79
in education	0.39***		0.39***
migration background			
Swedish	1		1
foreign (Turkish or Polish)	0.63		0.62
metropolitan area (in 1999)			
lives in non-metropolitan area	1		1
lives in metropolitan area	0.71*		0.72*
partnership status (in 1999)			
single	1		1
in relationship	3.42***		3.43***
childcare level (in 2001, 2002, 2003)			
low level (<63%)		1.38	1.21
medium level (63 to <65.7%)		1	1
high level (65.7% or more)		0.81	1.14
number of observations	1,827	1,827	1,827
number of occurrences	131	131	131

Notes: *p = 0.10; **p = 0.05; ***p = 0.01. Source: YAPS data. Female respondents. Author's own calculations.

In Model 2, the effect of childcare enrollment rates on first birth-risks is evaluated. Controlling for birth cohort revealed that those born in 1968 had significantly lower birth risks, and those born in 1976 had significant-

170

ly higher first birth risks than the reference group (birth cohort 1972). Contrary to the theoretical expectation, the analysis shows that women living in a region with a low level of childcare enrollment had higher first birth risks than those living in a region with a medium level of childcare enrollment. In regions with high childcare enrollment, the fertility risks were lower than in the medium category.

However, both effects are statistically insignificant. The picture remains similar when controlling for the individual-level covariates discussed before. The relative risks displayed in Model 3 differ only marginally from the results in Models 1 and 2. In this model specification women in the high childcare category have higher birth risks, but again, the effect of the childcare variable is insignificant.

Table 28 presents the results of the cloglog models, including the attitude variables and childcare. For each attitudes dimension a separate analysis is conducted. Starting with the index on the relevance attached to children, Model 4 shows a positive effect on the transition to first birth. The more important children were to a woman, the higher her birth risk. This effect is significant for both higher and lower levels of importance attached to children (reference group: medium importance). Interestingly, in this model, the negative effect of having a high level of education also turns significant. All of the other control variables vary only slightly compared to Model 3. Again, the childcare effect remains insignificant.

In Model 5, the effect of the importance a woman attaches to job-related goals is assessed. First birth risks did not differ significantly for women who indicated that having a career was less important to them. This might reflect the fact that for the Swedish women in the YAPS-data, the majority attaches a high level of importance to their occupational success (see Section 6.3.4).

The last attitudes variable that we considered concerned the question of whether a woman agreed with the statement that the dual-earner/dual-carer family is the best arrangement for a family with preschool children. Model 6 shows that the women who agreed ("egalitarian") had lower first birth risks, but this effect is insignificant. This finding is in line with the results of Bernhard and Goldscheider (2006: 33), who also analyzed the YAPS data. The effect of childcare on the transition to first birth was also insignificant in Model 6. All of the other variables had effects similar to those of the models presented above.

Table 28: Discrete-time hazard models. Transition to first birth. Relative risks. Models including different attitudes indices and childcare. Sweden.

	Model 4	Model 5	Model 6
birth cohort			
1976	1.58*	1.28	1.29
1972	1	1	1
1968	0.46***	0.56***	0.56***
educational attainment (in 1999)			
low	0.43***	0.47**	0.46***
medium	1	1	1
high	0.73*	0.79	0.80
in education	0.40***	0.39***	0.39***
migration background			
Swedish	1	1	1
foreign (Turkish or Polish)	0.58*	0.62	0.62
metropolitan area (in 1999)			
lives in non-metropolitan area	1	1	1
lives in metropolitan area	0.73*	0.72*	0.72*
partnership status (in 1999)			
single	1	1	1
in relationship	2.94***	3.44***	3.45***
importance of children (in 1999)			
low	0.50**		
medium	1		
high	1.59**		
importance of career goals (in 1999)			
lower		0.96	
high		1	
gender role ideology (in 1999)			
non-egalitarian			1
egalitarian			0.84
childcare level (in 2001, 2002, 2003)			
low level (<63%)	1.15	1.21	1.20
medium level (63 to <65.7%)	1	1	1
high level (65.7% or more)	1.14	1.14	1.14
number of observations	1,827	1,827	1,827
number of occurrences	131	131	131

Notes: *p = 0.10; **p = 0.05; ***p = 0.01. Source: YAPS data. Female respondents. Author's own calculations.

In the German case study, after the attitudes analyses, I investigated whether childcare effects vary across different groups of women by analyzing interaction effects. In the Swedish case, childcare measurement is not very precise as it refers to large regions, and the analyses of conditional effects appear less promising. Therefore, I do not discuss the results of the interaction analyses at length but present them in Appendix E. The models included the interaction effects between different attitude variables and childcare enrollment rates and those between education and childcare. Each model was run separately and included the set of control variables also used in the models in Section 6.3.6. However, most of the interactions remained statistically insignificant.

6.4 Summary of findings

This chapter was devoted to three analytical goals. First, I analyzed whether women living in regions with high levels of childcare provision were more likely to have a first birth than women living in regions with lower childcare availability. Second, I was interested in investigating to what extent the effect between childcare and fertility was mediated by individuals' attitudes and education. Third, I compared two countries in order to identify national differences in childcare effects on fertility. To investigate women's transition to a first birth, I conducted discrete-time hazard models, partly using multilevel techniques, on a German and a Swedish panel dataset. The panel structure of the data allowed me to analyze the relationship between a woman's attitudes at one point in time and her fertility behavior thereafter.

A descriptive analysis revealed that about 30 percent of the respondents in the German dataset opted for childcare policies when asked which policy they would find supportive for having a(nother) child. A simple multivariate analysis confirmed this result: women living in regions with high enrollment rates had higher first birth risks than women in regions with medium enrollment rates. This effect turned insignificant after I controlled for individual-level variables. The interaction effects between education and childcare enrollment rates were found to be partly insignificant, but a slightly positive effect of childcare was shown among highly educated women. These findings are in line with the expectation that women who pursue a career – i.e., women with higher educational attainment – are likely to have an interest in the level of childcare provision, and to have a first birth in response to childcare availability. van Bavel and Rózanska-Putek (2010) also found this education effect on first births in their analysis of national childcare levels. The results on attitudes showed that having traditional family views had a strong, positive effect on the likelihood of having a first birth. The importance a woman attached to having children was also shown to be positively related to childbearing risks. This finding was robust also after I controlled for childcare provision. Obviously, among German women, having traditional family values was a relevant factor for the transition to motherhood, regardless of the level of childcare availability. Although German policies currently target working mothers, there may still be a non-negligible group of women who have more traditional values concerning the family, and who might not respond to childcare policies.

For Sweden, on the basis of the YAPS data and the childcare provision at the province level, I concluded that childcare had no effect on first birth timing. According to my theoretical expectations, a woman's attitudes toward children and career could interact with childcare availability. But because of the coarse measurement of childcare services on the province level, results on interaction effects are difficult to interpret. Although these results did not meet my theoretical expectations, it is in line with Andersson et al. (2004), who found no childcare effects on the transition to a second birth in Sweden. Studies for other countries have also found insignificant effects of childcare enrollment rates on fertility behavior (Klevmarken and Tasiran 1996; Hank and Kreyenfeld 2003; Brodmann et al. 2007; Del Boca et al. 2009; Lappegård 2010). One possible reason why my analyses did not yield significant results for Sweden is that the legal entitlement to childcare was extended in Sweden during the period under study.[48] Today, childcare provision is universal, which means that all families can use childcare services if they wish to do so. Thus, childcare *provision* is invariant (because all families have access to it), while *usage* varies. In this context, the level of demand might provide some insights into the different opinions about the best age for children to start childcare. Although Swedish society is supportive of the dual-earner family and the level of acceptance of childcare in the country is generally high, less than 50 percent of parents made use of formal child-

---

48 Since 2001, universal childcare has also been provided to children whose parents are unemployed; and since 2002, children whose parents have taken parental leave for a sibling are also entitled to care (Skolverket 2007).

care for one-year-old children in 2003. This implies that a considerable share of parents prefer to take parental leave and care for their young children at home, while others prefer to make use of formal childcare arrangements. A lower regional enrollment rate might indicate that more mothers in that region attach importance to the family, as they stay on parental leave longer. By contrast, a higher regional enrollment rate might suggest that more mothers in that region want to return to work soon after childbirth. However, even when we consider childcare enrollment as measure of the level of acceptance of childcare for very young children, there is a second problem concerning the province level. Although Swedish provinces vary in size, they are large, which can conceal the actual heterogeneity of the population they cover. Therefore, the enrollment rate in a province might be an insufficiently precise measure to use in assessing a woman's perceptions of the childcare situation in her area.

Analyzing Germany and Sweden shows how difficult it is to compare individual behavior across countries. As was shown in Sections 4.2 and 4.3, the share of women participating in the labor market has increased considerably in both countries, and reached a level of almost 70 percent in Germany and 77 percent in Sweden in 2008. As the analyses in this chapter indicated, the attitudes toward family in the two countries are still quite different. In Germany, the share of young adults who reported that education and career were very important to them was rather small. In Sweden, virtually all respondents in the sample under study assigned high values to the items related to the importance of career success. In the German sample, by contrast, 17 percent of women reported having rather traditional family values. The results did not show that childcare had a significant effect in Sweden. Among young Swedes, career aspirations and having a family were not seen as competing life domains, but rather as complementary phenomena. With their focus on gender equality and work-family balance, Swedish family policies seemed to create a climate of family friendliness that did not discourage women from pursuing a professional career. According to my results, the fact that childcare was used to varying degrees in different regions was not connected to having children. In (western) Germany, where childcare provision still does not meet the demand, highly educated women seemed to slightly shorten the length of time they postponed their first birth if childcare availability was medium compared to those living in a region with low childcare availability.

7 Conclusions

The aim of this study was to analyze the effect of public childcare availability on entry into motherhood in Germany and Sweden. Care services for children under age three are on the political agenda of many European countries and the European Union. The main reasons for the expansion of services are to encourage maternal labor force participation and to improve the education of children. While it is seldom mentioned as a policy goal[49], providing access to childcare is also expected to have positive effects on fertility behavior. However, prior research on the relationship between childcare and fertility produced ambiguous results.

My main argument was that intervening factors might be relevant for understanding the effect of public childcare on individuals' childbearing behavior. On the one hand, the institutional setting in a country is important. While childcare provision for the children under age three supports dual-earner families, it is only one element in a system of family policies. Other policies might support male breadwinner families. In a country with a pluralistic approach to family support, some women who are thinking about starting a family might consider using public childcare, while for others it might be more attractive to be a full-time mother. Childcare availability does not affect childbearing behavior in this latter group. On the other hand, attitudes toward appropriate childcare are important. Potential parents who believe that only mothers can provide appropriate care to children in the early years of life will not consider using formal childcare services. For them, the availability of care services is less relevant when deciding whether to have a child.

This final chapter presents the research contribution and the empirical results of this study. I then suggest some implications of my findings for theory and policy makers. Finally, I discuss the limitations of my research strategy and suggest potential topics for future research.

---

49 In the Nordic countries the provision of childcare was seen mainly as a means of promoting gender equality (Leira 2002; Naumann 2005, Ellingsæter and Leira 2006; Rauhala 2009). In Germany, in contrast, the positive relationship between childcare provision for the under-threes and childbearing decisions was explicitly mentioned in the draft legislation for the *Act to Support Children Under Three Years in Daycare* (Deutscher Bundestag 2008).

7.1 Research contribution and key findings

Previous studies mainly focused on the direct effects of childcare availability on fertility behavior. In this study, I developed a more comprehensive approach. First, I integrated sociological and economic arguments in the framework of the Theory of Planned Behavior. My theoretical model included attitudes and pluralistic policy options to better understand the effect of public childcare on entry into motherhood. This allowed me to also take into consideration education-specific effects of childcare. Second, the fertility analyses for Germany and Sweden were based on panel datasets. Prior studies that analyzed the relationship of attitudes and fertility often had to rely on cross-sectional data, ignoring the possibility that individuals might adapt their attitudes to their experiences. Such reverse causality might lead to biased effect estimation (Lesthaeghe 2002). In this study, I analyzed panel data, which allowed me to test women's attitudes at time t, and their fertility behavior thereafter. Third, a country comparison of Germany and Sweden offers the opportunity to identify childcare effects in different institutional settings. German family policies have traditionally favored the male breadwinner model, although several dual-earner policies have been introduced in recent years (Ostner 2010). In contrast, Sweden is generally seen as the prototypical dual-earner society, with a long tradition of childcare services for children under age three (Ferrarini and Duvander 2010). These settings offer different opportunity structures to (potential) parents in the two countries. A comparison of Germany and Sweden is therefore well-suited for studying country differences in childcare effects.

Who makes use of public childcare?

In order to improve information on the group of parents that makes use of public childcare I first compared usage patterns in Sweden and western Germany. This investigation used EU-SILC data for 2005 to 2008 focusing on mothers with two year old children. Based on my analyses, I found that working women in both countries were more likely to use childcare than homemakers. In the Swedish sample, the group of employed mothers was considerably larger than in the western German sample (Sweden: 75 percent, western Germany: 37 percent). In western Germany, the educational level of mothers was relevant for childcare usage. Working mothers with high levels of educational attainment were more likely to use childcare than those with medium levels of education. In contrast, both working and non-working mothers in Sweden used public childcare independent of their educational attainment.

How does childcare availability affect entry into motherhood?

The central part of the empirical analyses of this study was dedicated to the question whether women living in a region with high public childcare provision have a higher risk to experience the transition to a first child than women living in a region with lower childcare provision. I analyzed the two countries separately based on country specific survey studies (Germany: *pairfam*; Sweden YAPS). In the German case study, childcare provision had a weak but positive effect only among highly educated women. For those with medium or lower levels of education, no effect was found. This indicates that German women reacted differently to childcare services according to their socioeconomic status. The analysis of the Swedish dataset did not show an effect of regional childcare provision on the transition to first births. This is in line with the findings of Andersson et al. (2004), who also found no effect of childcare availability on fertility behavior in Sweden. One reason for this finding might be that public childcare availability and childcare acceptance were high in all regions. This does not necessarily mean that childbearing was in fact unrelated to childcare provision. The resulting low degree of regional variance might be insufficient to statistically detect an effect of childcare on first births.

What role do attitudes toward the family play?

The results for both Germany and Sweden showed that women with traditional family attitudes were more likely to enter parenthood than those with non-traditional attitudes. In addition, I expected that women with less family-oriented attitudes are especially likely to respond to childcare provision. My analyses on Germany refuted this hypothesis: the effect of childcare provision did not vary according to individuals' attitudes. It seems that positive attitudes toward the family are a relevant factor to understanding fertility, irrespective of the availability of public childcare services.

Theoretical implications

The empirical results have some theoretical implications for the hypothe-
sized effects of policies on fertility behavior in advanced societies. Within
the framework of the TPB, family policies were expected to affect
childbearing directly by reducing external constraints. My analyses for
both Sweden and Germany did not show this direct effect. However, I
found a weak but positive impact of childcare on the entry into
parenthood among highly educated women in Germany. Having a high
level of education means that the opportunity costs of childbearing are
high. For this group, childcare availability might reduce perceived obstacles to childbearing, because their childbearing plans are closely related to
their anticipated ability to return to work soon after childbirth.

A woman's educational attainment seemed to be relevant for both
childcare effects on fertility and childcare usage in Germany, but not in
Sweden. This difference might be related to the levels of support each
country offers for various family policy models. In a setting with coherent family policies that favor dual-earner families (Sweden), the majority
of mothers make use of public childcare. By contrast, in a setting with
pluralistic policies that support both male breadwinner and dual-earner
families (Germany), individuals make use of a range of options according
to their life course situations. As an indicator of the importance a woman
places on her career and of her potential opportunity costs, a woman's
education tends to determine whether she plans to make use of childcare
services (high education), or whether she prefers to take advantage of
other policies, such as joint taxation and the home care allowance (lower
education). For the purposes of policy evaluation, this indicates that it is
necessary to analyze how the opportunity structures, and thus the effects
on behavior, vary for different population groups.

Another implication arising from my findings concerns attitudes. The
influence of positive family attitudes on a woman's first birth decision,
which is central in the TPB, was shown in the analyses of both Sweden
and Germany. In addition, I expected to find that attitudes regarding the
family would interact with public childcare provision. In the empirical
analyses, I did not find this mediating effect. My results indicate that the
direct effect of attitudes towards having children on first birth risks was
more important than the interaction effect between attitudes and childcare. However, the sample size in each cell of the interaction term was
limited and the effect should be re-analyzed with a larger dataset.

Policy implications

Many European countries and the European Union have put the expansion of public childcare for children under age three on their political agendas. Disregarding the explicit aims of policies, several authors have pointed out that the effects of a specific program might depend on intervening factors, which makes it difficult to anticipate policy effects (McDonald 2002; Neyer 2003a; Neyer and Andersson 2008).

In line with this assumption, the empirical findings of the current study imply that the effects of public childcare services are not homogeneous across countries or socioeconomic groups. It seems that in Germany, childcare affects fertility behavior among highly educated women, but not among those with lower levels of education. This has two important implications. First, by offering highly educated women the opportunity to combine family and work, childcare policies might encourage them to start a family. Given that this group of women have the highest share of childlessness in western Germany (DESTATIS 2009b), facilitating their entry into motherhood might help to reduce permanent childlessness. Second, the education-specific effect of public childcare implies that in Germany, there are subgroups of women who do not seem to respond to the availability of childcare. For them, taking care of their children might be an alternative to pursuing a professional career. Their motivation might be diverse, such as little interest in a career or joy of rearing children. Accordingly, they may prefer family policies that support homemaking mothers, giving them the opportunity to leave the labor market.

In this context, policy makers should be aware of the goal of each family policy instrument. Do they want to encourage mothers to participate in the labor market, or do they want to offer parents the opportunity to choose whether they want to care for their children at home? A new childcare initiative in Germany offers all children above the age of one a legal entitlement to childcare services since August 2013. According to the political rhetoric, the goal of this policy is to reduce the conflicts between work and family for women and enable women to have the number of children they want. At the same time, alternative policy options create incentives for some groups of women to remain full-time mothers. These policies discourage maternal employment, and may counteract the positive effect of childcare on fertility. One example is the home care allowance, which is paid at a flat rate following the parental leave benefit period until the child is three years old if parents do not use childcare. An allowance of this type was introduced by the Swedish government in 2008 and a similar policy went into effect in Germany in late summer 2013.[50] Although the amount of the benefit is low[51] and it does not replace former wages, it is a contribution to the household income that acknowledges the social value of childrearing. A number of studies have shown that a home care allowance might lead to a change in opportunity structures, encouraging women with lower socioeconomic status to drop out of the labor market (Morgan and Zippel 2003; Leitner 2005; Salmi 2006; Ellingsæter 2012). The political motivation for offering cash-for-care programs may be to enable parents to choose from a number of family arrangements. The selective use of such a program could mean that children from lower socioeconomic backgrounds are excluded from early education opportunities, however. This should concern policy makers, as children from disadvantaged backgrounds have been found to benefit the most from childcare services (Barnett 2011).

Moreover, my analyses for both Germany and Sweden indicated how important attitudes toward children and the family are when it comes to the decision to have a first child. Yet it remains unclear in how far attitudes can be influenced by social policies. It would be interesting to investigate whether it is possible to enhance the value of children and the family on a societal level without reinforcing conservative patterns of a gendered division of labor. Unfortunately, such questions were beyond the scope of this study.

7.2 Critical reflections and research perspectives

My empirical analyses were subject to a number of limitations which need to be addressed. A first shortcoming is related to the complexity of the proposed micro-theoretical model. Sample size limitations and the

---

50 Such a long parental leave with a flat-rate payment had existed in Germany before. With the parental leave reform of 2007, the long leave was abolished in the majority of *Länder*. The re-introduction of a payment of a federal home care allowance was part of the coalition agreement in 2011 (Blum and Erler 2012).

51 The home care allowance in Sweden is a voluntary payment that amounts to a maximum of approximately 340 euros per month (Ellingsæter 2012). In Germany, the amount will be 100 euros per month (which is set to be raised to 150 euros in 2014; see Blum and Erler 2012).

principal of parsimony inhibited a comprehensive investigation of each theoretically relevant element. With a focus on attitudes and policies supporting (or constraining) women's childbearing, some aspects to which the TPB attaches great importance had to be neglected. In the fertility analyses, I did not consider the explicit effect of subjective norms, although it seems that partners' attitudes toward having a child are likely to be relevant in any attempt to understand childbearing decisions (Thomson 1997; Thomson and Hoem 1998; Jansen and Liefbroer 2006; Rosina and Testa 2009). The opinions and expectations of others, such as parents and friends, were also excluded. Moreover, I did not explicitly consider in my analyses the elements "perceived behavioral control" and "childbearing intentions".

A second limitation of this study is related to variable measurement. The ideal information on childcare would have been a woman's perception of how easy (or difficult) it is to find a spot in public childcare in her area. Unfortunately, this information was unavailable. In order to measure childcare availability, I used district(*Kreis*)-level enrollment rates as a proxy in the German dataset. This is an imprecise measure, as there might be strong variations of enrollment in a district. This aspect is even more critical for Sweden, where the regional measure refers to even larger areas (so-called *länen*). Another variable that was measured in an imprecise way was "attitude toward childcare". Based on my assumption that some women might consider institutional childcare inappropriate, a direct measure on the acceptance level of each form of childcare (e.g., full-time maternal care, parental sharing, grandparental care, professional care, and surrogate mothers[52]; see Kremer 2007) would have been ideal. The attitudes toward institutional childcare might have varied according to children's ages; i.e., the question on acceptance of various childcare forms should be asked for different age groups (e.g., for those under one year old, those between one and two years old, etc.). Such items were not included in the surveys used in my analyses. Instead, I had to rely on attitudes toward the family, costs of children, and the importance assigned to children and career-related goals, assuming that these indices were related to attitudes toward public childcare. The index on "traditional family values" in the German *pairfam* dataset did include the level of agreement with the statement: "a child under age six will suffer from

---

52 The term "surrogate mother" refers to a female carer who has her own children (Kremer 2007: 74f.), such as a mother providing family daycare.

having a working mother". Such items did not allow me to distinguish between attitudes toward working mothers and attitudes toward public childcare.

A third problem is related to the country differences observed between Germany and Sweden. In my theoretical considerations, I argued that mainly institutional variations are responsible for such differences. Although it was suggested in the literature that policies and cultural developments are closely related (Strohmeier 2002; Ellingsæter and Gulbrandsen 2007), I could not determine to what extent confounding factors, such as cultural and normative constraints, explained country differences in either childcare usage or fertility behavior. Overall, in order to improve comparability of the results in Sweden and Germany, it would have been preferable to analyze harmonized data that included identical measures of both childcare availability and attitudes.

Moreover, the sample size of the German case study was small when it came to the estimation of interaction effects. This was reflected in the partly insignificant results especially for the interaction between education and childcare.

Suggestions for future research

The results presented in this study indicated that the availability of public childcare has education-specific effects in Germany. More empirical research is necessary to explore whether this effect can be confirmed in a larger sample, i.e. each category in the interaction specification would include a larger number of observations. It would be also interesting to test the robustness of the results across countries. As a first step, it would be interesting to investigate eastern Germany in more detail. In the current study it was impossible to analyze the new Länder separately due to the small sample size. With 49 percent of eastern German children in the age group zero to three enrolled in public childcare (DESTATIS 2012c), the demand for childcare in this age group is largely met (BMFSFJ 2012: 95). In combination with the long tradition of public childcare during the socialist era (Frerich and Frey 1996), the relationship between childcare and fertility behavior in eastern Germany might be more similar to that of Sweden than to that of western Germany.

Moreover, future studies on childcare effects should focus on societies in which work-family conflicts are perceived to be strong, but in which public childcare provision is not universal. Interesting cases would be countries with a large degree of variation in childcare availability across regions (such as in Italy) or over time (such as in Great Britain). Further country comparisons might add to our understanding of childcare mechanisms in different family policy settings. Ideally, such analyses would be based on longitudinal and harmonized datasets, such as EU-SILC, but with some extensions of the question catalogue concerning childcare availability and attitudes. Such data would allow us to study childcare effects in different institutional settings, to identify education-specific effects, and to better understand the role of attitudes in this relationship.

Childcare policies are gaining relevance in many European countries. Public childcare services enable women to return to work soon after childbirth, thus helping to avoid long career breaks. This preserves mothers' employability and promotion prospects. Moreover, childcare is seen as an investment in the human capital of children (Esping-Andersen 2002). Finally, as was argued in this study, childcare might also positively affect childbearing. This manifold linkages and implications underpin the importance to extend our knowledge about effects and underlying mechanisms of childcare policies.

8 Appendix

appendices	content	page
Appendix A: Studies on the effect of public childcare on individual level fertility; refers to **Chapter 3**	- Overview of studies on the effect of public childcare provision on individual level fertility.	188
Appendix B: Institutional comparison of Sweden and Germany; refers to **Chapter 4**	- Overview table with information on family policies in Sweden, eastern and western Germany.	191
Appendix C: Factor analyses; refers to **Chapter 6**	- Description of the factor analysis. - Tables with items and Cronbach's Alpha for the German and Swedish indices.	193
Appendix D: Regional enrollment rates in Sweden; refers to **Chapter 6**	- Regional enrollment rates in Sweden in 2001, 2002 and 2003.	197
Appendix E: Discrete.time hazard models; refers to **Chapter 6**	- Discrete-time hazard models of transition to first birth; interaction effects in Sweden.	198

Appendix A: Studies on the effect of public childcare on individual level fertility

Table A1: List of studies.

Study	Country	Setting	Dep. variable	Childcare variable	Results
Klevmarken and Tasiran (1996)	Sweden	Multilevel analyses with instruments, Data: 1984-1988 HUS-panel.	Transition to 1st, 2nd and 3rd births.	- Public provision rate in municipality - continuous variable - age group and year unclear	All coefficients negative but insignificant.
Kravdal (1996)	Norway	Norwegian Family and Occupation Survey of 1988 was linked with individual register-based migration histories and time-series data on day-care coverage. Observation period: 1974-1987.	Transition to 1st, 2nd and 3rd births.	- Public and private) yearly provision rate by municipality - 1-3 year olds - both continuous and 5-level categorical variable	Mixed results: Negative effect for continuous childcare variable without controls. Turns insignificant after including controls.
Del Boca (2002)	Italy	Bank of Italy's Survey of Households' Income and Wealth (1991-1995) combined with regional data on childcare provision in 16 Italian regions. Simultaneous equation for conditional likelihood of maternal employment and birth.	Births occurring in the observation period (regardless of parity).	- Public childcare provision rates in 16 Italian regions - under 3 year olds - 1991, 1993, and 1995 - continuous variable	Positive effect of childcare on fertility.
Hank (2002)	West Germany	Multilevel perspective; western Germany. Individual-level data from the SOEP (the German Socio-Economic Panel) are linked with regional indicators provided by the	Transition to 1st and 2nd births.	- Childcare provision rates on the level of combined districts (Raumordnungsregionen) - 3 to 6 year olds - 1986 and 1994 - continuous variable	No effect of public childcare.

		Federal Office for Building and Regional Planning (BBR).			
Hank and Kreyenfeld (2003)	West Germany	SOEP 1984-1999, combined with regional official statistics. Multi-level analysis.	Transition to 1st and 2nd births.	- Childcare provision rates on district level - 3 to 6 year olds - 1986 and 1994 - continuous variable (categorical variable in appendix) - grandparental child-care (do parents live in same town?)	No statistically significant effect of public child-care on first and second births; positive effect of grandparental availability on first birth risks.
Andersson et al. (2004)	Sweden	Register data, years 1997+98, consider availability, quality and costs of childcare for children 1-12.	Transition to 2nd and 3rd births.	- (Public) yearly child-care provision rate by municipality - children at ages 1-12 years in full-time child care - 1996 and 1997 - 3-level categorical variable along the quintiles	No effect of childcare on 2nd and 3rd births.
Rønsen (2004)	Norway + Finland	Data: 1988 Norwe-gian Family and Occupation Survey and the 1989 Finnish Population Survey; retrospec-tive for the late 1980s and early 1990s.	Transition to 1st, 2nd and 3rd births.	Norway: - childcare provision rate by municipality - children aged 0-3 - time-series (?) - continuous variable Finland: - national childcare provision rate - children aged 0-6 - period unclear - continuous variable	Mixed results: Negative and significant for first births, no significant effects for 2nd births and negative effect on 3rd births in Finland but no significant effect in Norway.
Aaberge et al. (2005)	Den-mark, Nether-lands, France, Italy, Spain	ECHP, married or cohabiting women, 21-45 years, 1994-1999.	Births occurring in the last two years (regard-less of parity).	- Public childcare provision rates in re-gions - continuous variable	Mixed results: positive effect in the fixed effects model, insignifi-cant when considering countries and time in a random effects model.
Rindfuss et al. (2007)	Norway	Register + census data 1973-1998. Fixed effects model for municipalities.	Transition to 1st births.	- Childcare enrollment rates for 435 municipalities - 0-6 year old children - 4 categories along the quartiles	Positive in the fixed effects model for first births (negative in the naïve model).
Brodmann et al. (2007)	Spain + Denmark	ECHP 1994-2001, couple data.	Transition to 2nd births.	Childcare variable on basis of the survey: time varying dummy varia-ble measuring whether	No effect (negative but insignificant in Denmark,

189

					someone outside the household looks after the first child on a paid basis.	positive but insignificant in Spain).
Del Boca et al. (2009)	Denmark France, Belgium, Netherlands, Italy, Spain, UK	ECHP, Single year: 1999, pooled cross-section, country dummies, only women. Probit analysis.	Births occurring during the year of interview (regardless of parity).	- Childcare enrollment rates for regions - children aged 0-2 - continuous variable	No significant effect of child-care availability for 0-2 year olds on fertility (but on mothers' employment).
Baizán (2009)	Spain	ECHP data for Spain. 1994-2001. Event history models with regional fixed effects.	Transition to 1st births and higher order births occurring in 1993-2000 (backdated by 9 months).	- Childcare enrollment rates for regions (NUTS 1) - children aged 0-2 - both as continuous and categorical variable (4 levels) - 1993-2000	Mixed effects. Positive effect turned insignificant after controlling for female labor force participation for first births. Positive effect increased for second and higher order births.
Hilgeman and Butts (2009)	20 countries	EVS and WVS data. Cross-sectional analysis. Hierarchical Bayesian model. Women ages 18-45.	Total number of children.	- Childcare enrollment on the national level - 0-2 year old children - continuous variable	Positive relationship between childcare enrollment and fertility.
Lappegård (2010)	Norway	Register data between 1995-2002 combined with regional childcare data. Naïve model and fixed effects.	Transition to 2nd and 3rd births.	- Childcare enrollment rates in the municipality where a couple lived when the previous child was born - 1-2 year old children - 1995-2002 - 4 categories along the quartiles	Mixed results according to the model: slightly negative effect for the naïve model, slightly positive but insignificant in the fixed effects model. This pattern is visible for both transitions.
van Bavel and Rózanska-Putek (2010)	23 countries	ESS3 data 2006/2007. Discrete-time hazard analyses of having a second child. Time since birth of the first child. Country random effects.	Transition to 2nd birth.	- National enrollment rates - 0-2 year old children - mainly 2004	Positive effect for highly educated women.

Source: own illustration.

190

Appendix B: Institutional comparison of Sweden and Germany

Table A2: The family policy system in Sweden, western and eastern Germany.

	Sweden	West Germany	East Germany
Total female labor force participation rate 2009 (age 15 to 64 years)	76%[a]	70%[b]	76%[b]
Female labor force participation rate 2009 (age 25 to 49 years)[a]	87%	Germany: 81%	
Female part-time employment rate (<35 hours/week) 2009 (age group 25-49)[c]	37%	Germany: 47%	
Income taxation[d]	Individual	Joint	
Childcare quality: average staff–child ratio	Pre-school: 1:5.1[e]	0-2-year-olds: 1:5.8[f]	
Childcare fees	Since 2003: not more than 3% of family net income due to maximum fee regulation.[g]	Varies across communities. In 2005, the average, childcare fee for children under age 3 was 119€ per month.[h]	
Childcare access	Universal for 1- to 12-year-old children.	Ages 3 to school entry: universal; under age 3: in W. Germany supply does not meet demand. In E. Germany supply largely meets demand.[i]	
Enrollment rate 1 and 2-year-olds (2011)	70%[j]	29%[k]	71%[k]
Job protection after birth	18 months	3 years	
Duration and level of earnings substitution	13 months (80%-90% earnings substitution	14 months (first 14 weeks: maternity	

	up to a ceiling).	leave, 100% earnings substitution; afterwards: 65%–67% earnings substitution up to a ceiling). Introduced in 2007.
After parental leave with wage substitution: cash-for-care	Flat-rate benefit until the child is 18 months old. Since July 2008, some municipalities offer cash for care after parental leave for children between 1 and 3 years old. €320/month max.	Since August 1, 2013: lump sum of 100 euros per month. In 2014, the benefit will be raised by 50 euros per month (Blum and Erler 2012: 133). The care allowance is paid until the child's third birthday.
Reserved for one parent	2 months	2 months

Source:

a   Generations and Gender Programme (2012). Retrieved April 7 2013 from www.ggp-i.org/contextual-database.html.

b   Eurostat 2013a: Labor force participation rates for a given sex and age group (%), variable fsa_argaed.

c   Eurostat 2013c: Part-time employment as a percentage of the total employment for a given sex and age group (%), variable lfsa_eppga.

d   For information on taxation systems, see Daly (2000), Dingeldey (2001) and Immervoll et al. (2009).

e   Information taken from European Commission's Expert Group on Gender and Employment (2009).

f   Autorengruppe Bildungsberichterstattung (2010).

g   Skolverket (2007).

h   Lang (2007: 110). Note that sometimes fees include meals, sometimes not. Thus comparison is difficult.

i   BMFSFJ (2012: 95ff.).

j   SCB (2013).

k   DESTATIS (2012d).

Appendix C: Factor analyses

Factor analyses are used in order to identify variables that are closely related. In the case of my analyses in this dissertation, I was interested in attitudes toward institutional childcare. However, neither *pairfam*/Demo-Diff nor the YAPS survey included such items. Therefore, I included several indices in the multivariate analyses that are assumed to be related to attitudes toward institutional childcare. In order to select items that are relevant for the underlying constructs I decided to follow an empirical strategy. Based on confirmatory factor analysis, I identified the statistical dependencies between variables. Based on the items included in the questionnaires, I identified three theoretical constructs in each country ("traditional family values", "benefits of having children", and "cost of having children" for Germany; "importance of the family", "being successful at work", and "gender equity" for Sweden). In both datasets, I included all respondents participating in the first wave in the factor analyses. That means that these analyses also included men, parents, and respondents born in the youngest cohort. I used a principal component analysis with orthogonal varimax rotation (Kim and Mueller 1978a).

Factors in a factor analysis are unobserved (or latent) variables. The model estimated in a factor analysis refers to the expected values of a number of observed variables as a linear function of the unobserved factors. Factor loadings vary between +1 and -1 and are a measure of how closely an item is related to the underlying construct. Factor loadings of +/- 0.5[1] and higher were regarded as indicator of close relationship and were used to identify relevant items for each index. Items that did not prove relevance for a given factor (i.e., factor loadings under the threshold of +/- 0.5) were excluded from the referring index. A second measure for the degree of interrelatedness of the items is Cronbach's Alpha. A value of alpha=0.6 or higher indicates that each item can be seen as a measure of the same construct. The higher the number of items, the higher alpha, thus the higher the reliability. The questions included in the factor analyses are presented in the following tables. Also the values of Cronbach's Alpha is presented for each scale.

---

1   The critical value of 0.5 as "acceptable factor loading" is debatable (Ford et al. 1986). Some authors define 0.3 as the critical value (de Vaus 2002: 191), while others recommend accepting factor loadings higher than 0.8 (Schnell et al. 1999: 154).

Table A3:   Items identified in the factor analysis and Cronbach's Alpha of the respective scales. *pairfam* and DemoDiff. Germany.

Scale	Items	Cron-bach's Alpha
traditional family values	*To what extent do you personally agree with the following statements (1 Disagree completely .... 5 Agree completely)* • You should get married if you permanently live with your partner. • Women should be more concerned about their family than about their career. • A child under age 6 will suffer from having a working mother. • Marriage is a lifelong union that should not be broken. • Couples should marry at the latest after a child is born.	α=0.73
benefits of having children	*Please indicate how strongly you expect or worry the following things will occur as a result of having children. How strongly do you expect... (1 not at all...5 very strongly)* ... that with children you will stay young longer? (bce2i1) ... to have an especially close emotional relationship with your children? ... that your standing in your social network will increase because of your children? ... that your adult children will be there for you when you are in need? ... that you will get new ideas from your adult children?	α=0.61
cost of having children	*Let's now talk about the unpleasant aspects. How strongly do you worry... (1 not at all...5 very strongly)* ... that you will be able to afford less with children? ... that children will put you under nervous strain? ... that with children you will not accomplish your professional goals? ... that with children you will stand out in a negative way in public? ... that children will limit your personal freedom?	α=0.68

Source: wave 1, *pairfam* and DemoDiff. Author's own calculations.

Table A4:   Items identified in the factor analysis and Cronbach's Alpha
             of the respective scales. YAPS data. Sweden.

Scale	Items	Cron-bach's Alpha
importance of family	*People have different opinions about what is important in life. Can you tell us how important it is to you to achieve the following? Answers range from 1 'unimportant' to 5 'very important'.* • To have children • To live in a good cohabiting or married relationship	α=0.80
	Here are some statements about children and family. What do you think? Answers range from 1 'don't agree at all' to 5 'agree completely'. • I enjoy children. • I think I can be satisfied with my life if I am a good parent. • Spending time with the family is more rewarding than work. • Children need siblings. • To have children is a confirmation of a good partner relationship.	
	What is your view of the following statements? Answers range from 1 'don't agree at all' to 5 'agree completely'. • To have children is part of what gives life meaning. • Something is missing if a couple never has children.	

Table A4: Continued. Items identified in the factor analysis and Cronbach's Alpha of the respective scales. YAPS data.[2] Sweden.

being successful at work	*People have different opinions about what is important in life. Can you tell us how important it is to you to achieve the following? Answers range from 1 'unimportant' to 5 'very important'.* • To do well economically. • To be successful in my work.	α=0.70
	What does a good job mean to you? Answers range from 1 'unimportant' to 5 'very important'. • That I can think and act independently. • That it offers good possibilities to advance. • That I can be proud of my work. • That I get a high salary and/or other benefits.	
gender equity	*What is your view of the following statements? Answers range from 1 'don't agree at all' to 5 'agree completely'.* • It is important for a woman as for a man to support herself. • A society where men and women are equal is a good society. • Men can do as well as women in caring jobs. • Women can do as well as men in technical jobs.	α=0.67

Source: wave 1, YAPS. Author's own calculations.

---

2   Moors and Bernhardt (2009), who created similar scales using the YAPS da-
    taset, followed an imputation strategy to overcome problems related to missing
    values. Creating the mean from the variables (at least including 3 of the identi-
    fied variables), produced very similar values compared to the imputation results.

Appendix D: Regional enrollment rates in Sweden

Table A5: Regional childcare provision and aggregated attitudes for Swedish regions. Children between 1 and 2 years enrolled in childcare as percent of this age group.

	childcare 2001	childcare 2002	childcare 2003
Stockholms län	64.7	67.9	68.5
Uppsala län	59.7	64.6	63.1
Södermanlands län	64.3	67.4	68.1
Östergötlands län	62.7	67.2	67.9
Jönköpings län	59.9	62.4	64.7
Kronobergs län	62.5	66.9	67.1
Kalmar län	62.7	64.5	64.9
Gotlands län	66.8	67.9	70.1
Blekinge län	66.8	70.2	70.4
Skåne län	61.0	64.7	65.7
Hallands län	60.4	62.5	62.9
Västra Götalands län	56.8	61.6	63.0
Värmlands län	64.0	66.7	67.8
Örebro län	57.9	63.4	62.2
Västmanlands län	63.7	66.2	67.4
Dalarnas län	57.3	60.7	58.8
Gävleborgs län	62.2	63.7	64.1
Västernorrlands län	59.0	64.5	65.0
Jämtlands län	58.1	61.9	63.7
Västerbottens län	63.3	65.9	68.3
Norrbottens län	57.7	61.2	62.0

Notes: Includes public and private childcare & pre-school and family daycare.
Source: Statistics Sweden (SCB). Author's own calculations.

Appendix E: Discrete-time hazard models

Table A6: Transition to first birth. Relative risks. Interaction between woman's attitudes and regional childcare provision. Sweden.

	childcare level (1- and 2-year-olds)		
	low level (<63% enrolled)	medium level (63 to <65.7% enrolled)	high level (65.7% or more)
Model 7:			
importance of family			
low	1.09	1.31	1
medium	2.46*	1.71	3.04***
high	4.11***	3.72***	3.10***
Model 8:			
importance of career goals			
lower	1.27	0.62	1.81
high	1.29	1.23	1
Model 9:			
gender role ideology			
non-egalitarian	1.44	0.67	1.85
egalitarian	1.12	1.02	1

Notes: *$p = 0.10$; **$p = 0.05$; ***$p = 0.01$. Source: YAPS data. Female respondents. Author's own calculations.

Table A7: Transition to first birth. Relative risks. Interaction between woman's education and regional childcare provision. Sweden.

	childcare level (1- and 2-year-olds)		
	low level (<63% enrolled)	medium level (63 to <65.7% enrolled)	high level (65.7% or more)
Model 10:			
educational attainment			
low	0.38*	0.64	0.34*
medium	0.94	0.98	1.28
high	1.07	0.42*	1

Notes: *$p = 0.10$; **$p = 0.05$; ***$p = 0.01$. Source: YAPS data. Female respondents. Author's own calculations.

9 References

Aaberge, R., U. Colombino, D. Del Boca, J. Ermisch, M. Francesconi, S. Pasqua and S. Strøm (2005). Women's Participation in the Labor Market and Fertility: The Effects of Social Policies. *Women at Work. An Economic Perspective.* T. Boeri, D. Del Boca and C. Pissarides (eds.). Oxford, Oxford University Press: 121-239.

Aassve, A. and T. Lappegård (2009). "Childcare Cash Benefits and Fertility Timing in Norway." *European Journal of Population* 25(1): 67-88.

Aassve, A., E. Meroni and C. Pronzato (2012). "Grandparenting and Childbearing in the Extended Family." *European Journal of Population* 28(4): 499-518.

Adserà, A. (2004). "Changing fertility rates in developed countries. The impact of labor market institutions." *Journal of Population Economics* 17(1): 17-43.

Ahlberg, J., C. Roman and S. Duncan (2008). "Actualizing the 'Democratic Family'? Swedish Policy Rhetoric versus Family Practices." *Social Politics* 15(1): 79-100.

Ahn, N. and P. Mira (2002). "A note on the changing relationship between fertility and female employment rates in developed countries." *Journal of Population Economics* 15(4): 667-682.

Aisenbrey, S., M. Evertsson and D. Grunow (2009). "Is There a Career Penalty for Mothers' Time Out? A Comparison of Germany, Sweden and the United States." *Social Forces* 88(2): 573-605.

Ajzen, I. (1991). "The Theory of Planned Behavior." *Organizational Behavior and Human Decision Processes* 50(2): 179-211.

Ajzen, I. (2011). "Reflections on Morgan and Bachrach's critique." *Vienna Yearbook of Population Research* 9: 63-69.

Ajzen, I. and M. Fishbein (2005). The Influence of Attitudes on Behavior. *The Handbook of Attitudes.* D. Albarracín, B. T. Johnson and M. P. Zanna (eds.). Mahwah/New Jersey, Lawrence Erlbaum Associates, Inc.: 173-221.

Ajzen, I. and J. Klobas (2013). Fertility intentions: An approach based on the theory of planned behavior. *Demographic Research* 29(8): 203-232.

Allison, P. D. (1982). "Discrete-Time Methods for the Analysis of Event Histories." *Sociological Methodology* 13: 61-98.

Alwin, D. F. (2005). Attitudes, Beliefs, and Childbearing. *The New Population Problem: Why Families in Developing Countries Are Shrinking and What It Means.* A. Booth and A. C. Crouter (eds.). Mahwah/NJ, Lawrence Erlbaum Associates: 115-126.

Alwin, D. F., M. Braun and J. Scott (1992). "The separation of work and family: Attitudes toward women's labour-force participation in Germany, Great Britain, and United States." *European Sociological Review* 8(1): 13-37.

Andersson, G. (2000). "The Impact of Labour-Force Participation on Childbearing Behaviour: Pro-Cyclical Fertility in Sweden during the 1980s and the 1990s." *European Journal of Population* 16(4): 293-333.

Andersson, G. (2008). "A review of policies and practices related to the 'highest-low' fertility of Sweden." *Vienna Yearbook of Population Research* 6: 89-102.

Andersson, G., A.-Z. Duvander and K. Hank (2004). "Do child-care characteristics influence continued child bearing in Sweden? An investigation of the quantity, quality, and price dimension." *Journal of European Social Policy* 14(4): 407-418.

Andersson, G., M. Rønsen, L. B. Knudsen, T. Lappegård, G. Neyer, K. Skrede, K. Teschner and A. Vikat (2009). "Cohort fertility patterns in the Nordic countries." *Demographic Research* 20(14): 313-352.

Andersson, G. and K. Scott (2005). "Labour-Market Status and First-Time Parenthood: The Experience of Immigrant Women in Sweden, 1981-97." *Population Studies* 59(1): 21-38.

Andrén, T. (2003). "The choice of paid childcare, welfare, and labor supply of single mothers." *Labour Economics* 10(2): 133-147.

Anttonen, A. and J. Sipilä (1996). "European Social Care Services: Is it Possible to Identify Models?" *Journal of European Social Policy* 6(2): 87-100.

Armitage, C. J. and M. Conner (2001). "Efficacy of the Theory of Planned Behavior: A meta-analytic review." *British Journal of Social Psychology* 40(Part 4): 471-499.

Arpino, B., C. Pronzato and L. Tavares (2010). All in the Family: Informal Childcare and Mothers' Labour Market Participation. *ISER Working Paper Series* No. 2010-24, Institute For Social & Economic Research.

Arts, W. and J. Gelissen (2002). "Three worlds of welfare capitalism or more? A state-of-the-art report." *Journal of European Social Policy* 12(2): 137-158.

Autorengruppe Bildungsberichterstattung (2010). *Bildung in Deutschland 2010. Ein indikatorengestützter Bericht mit einer Analyse zu Perspektiven des Bildungswesens im demografischen Wandel.* Bielefeld, W. Bertelsmann Verlag.

Bagozzi, R. P. and F. van Loom (1978). "Fertility as Consumption: Theories from the Behavioral Sciences." *Journal of Consumer Research* 4(4): 199-228.

Baizán, P. (2009). "Regional child care availability and fertility decisions in Spain." *Demographic Research* 21(27): 803-842.

Barber, J. (2001). "Ideational Influences on the Transition to Parenthood: Attitudes Toward Childbearing and Competing Alternatives." *Social Psychology Quarterly* 64(2): 101-127.

Barber, J. and W. G. Axinn (2005). How Do Attitudes Shape Childbearing in the United States? *The New Population Problem: Why Families in Developing Countries Are Shrinking and What It Means.* A. Booth and A. C. Crouter (eds.). Mahwah/NJ, Lawrence Erlbaum Associates: 59-91.

Barber, J., W. G. Axinn and A. Thornton (2002). The Influence of Attitudes on Family Formation Processes. *Meaning and Choice: Value Orientation and Life Course Decisions*. R. Lesthaeghe (ed.). The Hague/Brussels, NIDI/CBGS: 45-95.

Barber, J., S. A. Murphy, W. G. Axinn and J. Malples (2000). "Discrete-Time Multilevel Hazard Analysis." *Sociological Methodology* 30(1): 201-235.

Barnett, W. S. (2011). "Effectiveness of Early Educational Intervention." *Science* 333(6045): 975-978.

Bauernschuster, S. and H. Rainer (2012). "Political regimes and the family: how sex-role attitudes continue to differ in reunified Germany." *Journal of Population Economics* 25(1): 5-27.

Baxter, J., B. Hewitt and M. Haynes (2008). "Life Course Transitions and Housework: Marriage, Parenthood, and Time on Housework." *Journal of Marriage and Family* 70(2): 259-272.

Becker, B. (2007). Bedingungen der Wahl vorschulischer Einrichtungen unter besonderer Berücksichtigung ethnischer Unterschiede. MZES Working Paper Nr. 101, 2007.

Becker, G. S. (1965). "A Theory of the Allocation of Time." *The Economic Journal* 75(299): 493-517.

Becker, G. S. (1981). *A Treatise on the family*. Camridge/Massachusetts, Harvard University Press.

Bennett, J. (2008). Early Childhood Services in the OECD Countries: Review of the Literature and Current Policy in the Early Childhood Field. *Innocenti Working Paper* IWP-2008-01. Florence, UNICEF Innocenti Research Centre.

Bernardi, L. (2003). "Channels of social influence on reproduction." *Population Research and Policy Review* 22(5-6): 527-555.

Bernhardt, E. (1993). "Fertility and Employment." *European Sociological Review* 9(1): 25-42.

Bernhardt, E. and F. Goldscheider (2006). "Gender Equality, Parenthood Attitudes, and First Births in Sweden." *Vienna Yearbook of Population Research* 4: 19-39.

Bertrand, M. and S. Mullainathan (2001). "Do People Mean What They Say? Implications for Subjective Survey Data." *The American Economic Review* 91(2): 67-72.

Bettio, F. and J. Plantenga (2004). "Comparing Care Regimes in Europe." *Feminist Economics* 10(1): 85-113.

Biddle, B. J. (1986). "Recent Developments in Role Theory." *Annual Review of Sociology* 12: 67-92.

Biedinger, N. and B. Becker (2006). Der Einfluss des Vorschulbesuchs auf die Entwicklung und den langfristigen Bildungserfolg von Kindern. Ein Überblick über internationale Studien im Vorschulbereich. *Working Paper*

Nr. 97, 2006. Mannheim, Mannheimer Zentrum für Europäische Sozialforschung.

Billari, F. C., D. Philipov and M. R. Testa (2009). "Attitudes, Norms and Perceived Behavioural Control: Explaining Fertility Intentions in Bulgaria." *European Journal of Population* 25(4): 439-465.

Billingsley, S. and T. Ferrarini (2011). Family Policies and Fertility Intentions across New and Old Welfare Democracies. *Stockholm Research Reports in Demography* 2011: 15, Stockholm University.

Björnberg, U. (2002). "Ideology and choice between work and care: Swedish family policy for working parents." *Critical Social Policy* 22(1): 33-52.

Blau, D. M. (2001). *The Child Care Problem. An Econometric Analysis.* New York, Russell Sage Foundation.

Blau, D. M. and P. K. Robins (1988). "Child-Care Costs and Family Labor Supply." *The Review of Economics and Statistics* 70(3): 374-381.

Blau, D. M. and P. K. Robins (1989). "Fertility, Employment, and Child-Care Costs." *Demography* 26(2): 287-299.

Blau, F. D., M. A. Ferber and A. E. Winkler (2002). *The economics of women, men, and work. Fourth edition.* Upper Saddle River/New Jersey, Prentice Hall.

Blossfeld, H.-P. (1995). Changes in the Process of Family Formation and Women's Growing Economic Independence: A Comparison of Nine Countries. *The New Role of Women. Family Formation in Modern Societies.* H.-P. Blossfeld (ed.). Boulder/Oxford, Westview Press: 3-32.

Blossfeld, H.-P. (1996). "Macro-Sociology, Rational Choice Theory, and Time: A Theoretical Perspective on the Empirical Analysis of Social Processes." *European Sociological Review* 12(2): 181-206.

Blossfeld, H.-P. and J. Huinink (1991). "Human capital investments or norms of role transition? How women's schooling and career affect the process of family formation." *American Journal of Sociology* 97(1): 143-168.

Blum, S. and D. Erler (2012). Germany. *International Review of Leave Policies and Related Research 2012.* P. Moss (ed.). London, Institute of Education, University of London: 129-135.

BMFSFJ (2012). *Familienreport 2012. Leistungen, Wirkungen, Trends.* Berlin, Bundesministerium für Familie, Senioren, Frauen und Jugend.

Böttcher, A., S. Krieger and F.-J. Kolvenbach (2010). Kinder mit Migrationshintergrund in Kindertagesbetreuung. *Wirtschaft und Statistik* 2/2010. DESTATIS. Wiesbaden, Statistisches Bundesamt.

Brandon, P. (2004). "The Child Care Arrangements of Pre-School-Age Children in Immigrant Families in the United States." *International Migration* 42(1): 65-87.

Breunig, R., A. Weiss, C. Yamauchi, X. Gong and J. Mercante (2011). "Child Care Availability, Quality and Affordability: Are Local Problems Related to Labour Supply?" *Economic Record* 87(276): 109-124.

Brewster, K. L. and R. R. Rindfuss (2000). "Fertility and Women's Employment in Industrialized Nations." *Annual Review of Sociology* 26: 271-296.

Brodmann, S., G. Esping-Andersen and M. Güell (2007). "When Fertility is Bargained: Second Births in Denmark." *European Sociological Review* 23(5): 599-613.

Brüderl, J., K. Hajek, B. Huyer-May, V. Ludwig, B. Müller, U. Müller, J. Passet, K. Pforr, M. Scholten, P. Schütze and N. Schumann (2012). pairfam Data Manual. Release 3.1, University of Munich.

Budig, M. J. (2003). "Are women's employment and fertility histories interdependent? An examination of causal order using event history analysis." *Social Science Research* 32(3): 376-401.

Budig, M. and P. England (2001). "The Wage Penalty for Motherhood." *American Sociological Review* 66(2): 204-225.

Bulatao, R. A. (1981). "Values and Disvalues of Children in Successive Childbearing Decisions." *Demography* 18(1): 1-25.

Burkart, G. (1994). *Die Entscheidung zur Elternschaft. Eine empirische Kritik von Individualisierungs- und Rational-Choice-Theorien.* Stuttgart, Enke.

Castles, F. G. (2003). "The world turned upside down: below replacement fertility, changing preferences and family-friendly public policy in 21 OECD countries." *Journal of European Social Policy* 13(3): 209-227.

Chesnais, J.-C. (2000). Determinants of below replacement fertility. *Population Bulletin of the United Nations* No.40/41(Special Issue 1999 "Below replacement fertility"): 126-136.

Chronholm, A. (2009). Sweden: individualisation or free choice in parental leave? *The politics of parental leave policies. Children, parenting, gender and the labour market.* S. B. Kamerman and P. Moss (eds.). Bristol, The Policy Press: 227-241.

Colberg-Schrader, H. (1994). Einrichtungen für Kinder als unverzichtbarer Teil der sozialen Infrastruktur. *Kind, Beruf Soziale Sicherung. Zukunftsaufgabe des Sozialstaats.* G. Bäcker and B. Stolz-Willig (eds.). Köln: . Bund-Verlag: 155-176.

Coleman, J. S. (1986). "Social Theory, Social Research, and a Theory of Action." *American Journal of Sociology* 91(6): 1309-1335.

Coneus, K., K. Goeggel and G. Muehler (2008). "Maternal employment and child care decision." *Oxford Economic Papers* 61(suppl 1): i172-i188.

Connelly, R. (1992). "The Effect of Child Care Costs on Married Women's Labor Force Participation." *The Review of Economics and Statistics* 74(1): 83-90.

Cook, T. D. and D. T. Campbell (1979). *Quasi-Experimentation. Design & Anylasis Issues for Field Studies.* Boston/Dallas/Geneva, Ill./Hopewell, N.J./Palo Alto/London, Houghton Mifflin Company.

Cooke, L. P. (2006). "Policy, Preferences, and Patriarchy: The Division of Domestic Labor in East Germany, West Germany, and the United States." *Social Politics: International Studies in Gender, State & Society* 13(1): 117-143.

Corrigall, E. and A. Konrad (2007). "Gender Role Attitudes and Careers: A Longitudinal Study." *Sex Roles* 56(11): 847-855.

Craig, L. and K. Mullan (2010). "Parenthood, Gender and Work-Family Time in the United States, Australia, Italy, France, and Denmark." *Journal of Marriage and Family* 72(5): 1344-1361.

Creighton, C. (1996). "The Rise of the Male Breadwinner Family: A Reappraisal." *Comparative Studies in Society and History* 38(2): 310-337.

Davis, E. E. and R. Connelly (2005). "The influence of local price and availability on parents' choice of child care." *Population Research and Policy Review* 24(4): 301-334.

de Bruijn, B. J. (1999). *Foundations of Demographic Theory. Choice, Process, Context.* Amsterdam, Thela Thesis.

De Henau, J., D. Meulders and S. O'Dorchai (2006). "The Childcare Triad? Indicators Assessing Three Fields of Child Policies for Working Mothers in the EU-15." *Journal of Comparative Policy Analysis* 8(2): 129-148.

De Henau, J., D. Meulders and S. O'Dorchai (2007). Parents' care and career: comparing parental leave policies. *Social Policies, Labour Markets and Motherhood. A Comparative Analysis of European Countries.* D. Del Boca and C. Wetzels (eds.). Cambridge, Cambridge University Press: 63-106.

De Henau, J., D. Meulders and S. O'Dorchai (2010). "Maybe Baby: Comparing Partnered Women's employment and Child Policies in the EU-15." *Feminist Economics* 16(1): 43-77.

de Vaus, D. A. (2002). *Surveys in Social Research. 5th Edition.* New York: Routledge.

Del Boca, D. (2002). "The effect of child care and part time opportunities on particiaption and fertility decisions in Italy." *Journal of Population Economics* 15(3): 549-573.

Del Boca, D., M. Locatelli and D. Vuri (2005). "Child-Care Choices by Working Mothers: The Case of Italy." *Review of Economics of the Household* 3(4): 453-477.

Del Boca, D., S. Pasqua and C. Pronzato (2009). "Motherhood and market work decisions in institutional context: a European perspective." *Oxford Economic Papers* 61(supplement 1): i147-i171.

Del Boca, D. and D. Vuri (2007). "The mismatch between employment and child care in Italy: the impact of rationing." *Journal of Population Economics* 20(4): 805-832.

DESTATIS (2008). Geburten und Kinderlosigkeit in Deutschland. Bericht über die Sondererhebung 2006 "Geburten in Deutschland". Wiesbaden, Statistisches Bundesamt.

DESTATIS (2009a). Statistik der Kinder und tätigen Personen in Tageseinrichtungen 2008. Wiesbaden, Statistisches Bundesamt.

DESTATIS (2009b). Mikrozensus 2008. Neue Daten zur Kinderlosigkeit in Deutschland. Begleitmaterial zur Pressekonferenz am 29. Juli 2009 in Berlin. Wiesbaden, Statistisches Bundesamt.

DESTATIS (2010a). Alles beim Alten: Mütter stellen Erwerbsbeteiligung hinten an. Wiesbaden, Statistisches Bundesamt.

DESTATIS (2010b). Community statistics on income and living conditions. EU-SILC (LEBEN IN EUROPA), 2007. Quality Report. Wiesbaden, German Federal Statistical Office.

DESTATIS (2011a). Bevölkerung und Erwerbstätigkeit. Natürliche Bevölkerungsbewegung 2009. Fachserie 1, Reihe 1.1. Wiesbaden, Statistisches Bundesamt.

DESTATIS (2011b). Statistik der Kinder und tätigen Personen in Tageseinrichtungen 2006 bis 2010. Altersjahre. Wiesbaden, Statistisches Bundesamt.

DESTATIS (2012a). Geburten in Deutschland. Ausgabe 2012. Wiesbaden, Statistisches Bundesamt.

DESTATIS (2012b). Elterngeld – wer, wie lange und wie viel? Begleitmaterial zur Pressekonferent am 27. Juni 2012 in Berlin. Wiesbaden, Statistisches Bundesamt.

DESTATIS (2012c). Kindertagesbetreuung in Deutschland 2012. Begleitmaterial zur Pressekonferenz am 6. November 2012 in Berlin. Wiesbaden, Statistisches Bundesamt.

DESTATIS (2012d). Kindertagesbetreuung regional 2012. Ein Vergleich aller 402 Kreise in Deutschland. Wiesbaden, Statistisches Bundesamt.

DESTATIS (2012e). Statistiken der Kinder- und Jugendhilfe. Kinder und tätige Personen in Tageseinrichtungen und in öffentlich geförderter Kindertagespflege am 01.03.2011. Wiesbaden, Statistisches Bundesamt.

Deutscher Bundestag. (2008). Entwurf eines Gesetzes zur Förderung von Kindern unter drei Jahren in Tageseinrichtungen und in der Kindertagespflege (Kinderförderungsgesetz – KiföG). Retrieved April 7 2013 from

http://www.bmfsfj.de/RedaktionBMFSFJ/Abteilung5/Pdf-Anlagen/kifoeg-entwurf,property=pdf,bereich=,sprache=de,rwb=true.pdf.

Diez-Roux, A. V. (2002). "A Glossary for Multilevel Analysis." *Journal of Epidemiology and Community Health* 56(8): 588-594.

Dingeldey, I. (2001). "European Tax Systems and their Impact on Family Employment Patterns." *Journal of Social Policy* 30(4): 653-672.

Dommermuth, L., J. Klobas and T. Lappegård (2011). "Now or later? The Theory of Planned Behavior and timing of fertility intentions." *Advances in Life Course Research* 16(1): 42-53.

Doorewaard, H., J. Hendrickx and P. Verschuren (2004). "Work orientations of female returners." *Work, employment and society* 18(1): 7-27.

Dorbritz, J. (2008). "Germany: Family diversity with low actual and desired fertility." *Demographic Research* 19(17): 557-598.

Dorius, S. F. and D. F. Alwin (2010). The Global Development of Egalitarian Beliefs – A Decomposition of Trends in the Nature and Structure of Gender Ideology. *Population Studies Center Research Report* 10-723. Ann Arbour, University of Michigan.

Duncan, S., R. Edwards, T. Reynolds and P. Allred (2004). "Mothers and Child Care: Policies, Values and Theories." *Children & Society* 18(4): 254-265.

Duncan, S. and S. Irwin (2004). "The Social Patterning of Values and Rationalities: Mothers' Choices in Combining Caring and Employment." *Social Policy and Society* 3(04): 391-399.

Durfee, A. and M. K. Meyers (2006). "Who Gets What From Government? Distributional Consequences of Child-Care Assistance Policies." *Journal of Marriage and Family* 68(3): 733-748.

Duvander, A.-Z. (2006). När är det dags för dagis? En studie om vid vilken ålder barn börjar förskola och föräldrars åsikt om detta. [Time for daycare? A study on when children start daycare and parents' opinions]. *Arbetsrapport. Institute for Future Studies* 2006: 2.

Duvander, A.-Z., T. Ferrarini and S. Thalberg (2005). Swedish parental leave and gender equality. Achievements and reform challenges in a European perspective, *Arbetsrapport, Institutet för Framtidsstudier* 2005:11.

Duvander, A.-Z. and M. Johansson (2010). "What are the Effects of Reforms Promoting Fathers' Parental Leave Use?" *Stockholm Research Reports in Demography* 2010: 14.

Duvander, A.-Z., T. Lappegård and G. Andersson (2010). "Family policy and fertility: fathers' and mothers' use of parental leave and continued childbearing in Norway and Sweden." *Journal of European Social Policy* 20(1): 45-57.

Eagly, A. H. and W. Wood (1999). "The Origins of Sex Differences in Human Behavior. Evolved Dispositions Versus Social Roles." *American Psychologist* 54(6): 408-423.

Ehlert, N. (2010). Die Familienpolitik der Großen Koalition. *Die Große Koalition. Regierung-Politik-Parteien 2005-2009.* S. Bukow and W. Seemann (eds.). Wiesbaden, VS Verlag für Sozialwissenschaften: 142-158.

Ellingsæter, A. L. (2009). "Leave policy in the Nordic welfare states: a ‘recipe’ for high employment/high fertility?" *Community, Work & Family* 12(1): 1-19.

Ellingsæter, A. L. (2012). *Cash for Childcare. Experiences from Finland, Norway and Sweden. International Policy Analysis.* Berlin, Friedrich-Ebert-Stiftung.

Ellingsæter, A. L. and L. Gulbrandsen (2007). "Closing the Childcare Gap: The Interaction of Childcare Provision and Mothers' Agency in Norway." *Journal of Social Policy* 36(4): 649-669.

Ellingsæter, A. L. and A. Leira, eds. (2006). *Politising Parenthood in Scandinavia. Gender Relations in welfare states.* Bristol, Policy Press.

Ellingsæter, A. L. and M. Ronsen (1996). "The dual strategy: Motherhood and the work contract in Scandinavia." *European Journal of Population* 12(3): 239-260.

Erickson, B. H. (1988). The relational basis of attitudes. *Social Structures: A Network Approach.* B. Wellman and S. D. Berkowitz (eds.). New York, Cambridge University Press: 99-121.

Erler, D. (2009). Germany: taking a Nordic turn? *The politics of parental leave policies. Children, parenting, gender and the labour market.* S. B. Kamerman and P. Moss (eds.). Bristol, The Policy Press: 119-134.

Ermisch, J. F. (1989). "Purchased Child Care, Optimal Family Size and Mother's Employment: Theory and Econometric Analysis." *Journal of Population Economics* 2(2): 79-102.

Ermisch, J. F. (2003). *An Economic Analysis of the Family.* Princeton, Princeton University Press.

Esping-Andersen, G. (1990). *The Three Worlds of Welfare Capitalism.* Cambridge, Polity Press.

Esping-Andersen, G. (2000). *Social Foundations of Postindustrial Economies.* Oxford, Oxford University Press.

Esping-Andersen, G. (2002). A Child-Centred Social Investment Strategy. *Why We need a New Welfare State.* G. Esping-Andersen, D. Gallie, A. Hemerijck and J. Myles (eds.). Oxford University Press: 26-67.

Esping-Andersen, G. (2009). *The Incomplete Revolution. Adapting to Women's New Roles.* Cambridge, Polity Press.

Ette, A. and K. Ruckdeschel (2007). "Die Oma macht den Unterschied! Der Einfluss institutioneller und informeller Unterstützung für Eltern auf ihre weiteren Kinderwünsche." *Zeitschrift für Bevölkerungswissenschaft* 32(1-2): 51-72.

Eurofound (2010): European Employment Strategy. Retrieved April 7 2013 from http://www.eurofound.europa.eu/areas/industrialrelations/dictionary/definitions/europeanemploymentstrategy.htm

European Commission's Expert Group on Gender and Employment (2009). The provision of childcare services. A comparative review of 30 European countries. Belgium, European Commission's Directorate-General for Employment, Social Affaires and Equal Opportunities.

European Council (2002). Presidency Conclusions. Barcelona European Council 15 and 16 March 2002. Retrieved April 7 2013 from http://www.consilium.europa.eu/ueDocs/cms_Data/docs/pressData/en/ec/71025.pdf

European Parliament (2011). Resolution of 12 May 2011 on Early Years Learning in the European Union. Reference number T7-0231/2011. Strasbourg, European Parliament.

Eurostat (2008). Comparative Final EU Quality Report 2005 (Version 2 – September 2008), Eurostat.

Eurostat (2009a). Comparative Final EU Quality Report 2006 (Version 3 – October 2009), Eurostat.

Eurostat (2009b). Description of SILC User Database Variables: Cross-Sectional and Longitutional. Version 2007.1 from 01-03-09, Eurostat.

Eurostat (2010a). 2007 Comparative EU Final Quality Report. Version 2 – June 2010. Luxembourg, Eurostat.

Eurostat (2010b). 2008 Comparative EU Intermediate Quality Report. Version 2 – June 2010. Luxembourg, Eurostat.

Eurostat (2013a). Activity rates by sex, age and highest level of education attained, Eurostat statistics (variable "lfsa_argaed"). Retrieved April 7 2013 from
http://epp.eurostat.ec.europa.eu/portal/page/portal/statistics/search_database

Eurostat (2013b). Total fertility rate, Eurostat statistics (variable "tsdde220"). Retrieved April 7 2013 from
http://epp.eurostat.ec.europa.eu/portal/page/portal/statistics/search_database

Eurostat (2013c). Part-time employment as a percentage of the total employment for a given sex and age group. Eurostat statistics (variable "lfsa_eppga") Retrieved April 7 2013, from
http://epp.eurostat.ec.europa.eu/portal/page/portal/statistics/search_database

Evertsson, M. and A.-Z. Duvander (2011). "Parental Leave – Possibility or Trap? Does Family Leave Length Effect Swedish Women's Labour Market Opportunities?" *European Sociological Review* 27(4): 435-450.

Evertsson, M. and M. Nermo (2007). "Changing Resources and the Division of Housework: A Longitudinal Study of Swedish Couples." *European Sociological Review* 23(4): 455-470.

Eydal, G. B. and T. Rostgaard (2011). "Gender Equality Revisited – Changes in Nordic Childcare Policies in the 2000s." *Social Policy & Administration* 45(2): 161-179.

Fagan, C. (2001). "Gender, Money and the Gender Order: Work Orientations and Working-Time Preferences in Britain." *Gender, Work and Organization* 8(3): 239-266.

Fagnani, J. (2002). "Why do French women have more children than German women? Family policies and attitudes towards child care outside the home." *Community, Work & Family* 5(1): 103-120.

Ferrarini, T. (2006). *Families, States and Labour Markets. Institutions, Causes and Consequences of Family Policy in Post-War Welfare States*. Cheltenham/Northampton, Edward Elgar.

Ferrarini, T. and A.-Z. Duvander (2010). Conflicting Directions? Outcomes and New Orientations of Sweden's Family Policy. *Stockholm University Linnaeus Center on Social Policy and Family Dynamics in Europe (SPaDE), Working Paper* 2010: 4.

Fishbein, M. and I. Ajzen (1975). *Belief, Attitude, Intention and Behavior: An Introduction to Theory and Research*. Reading, Massachusetts, Addison-Wesley.

Fishbein, M. and I. Ajzen (2010). *Predicting and Changing Behavior. The Reasoned Action Approach*. New York, Taylor & Francis.

Fleckenstein, T. (2010). "Party Policies and Childcare: Comparing the Expansion of Service Provision in England and Germany." *Social Policy and Administration* 44(7): 789-807.

Folbre, N. (1997). "The Future of the Elephant-Bird." *Population and Development Review* 23(3): 647-654.

Ford, J. K., R. C. MacCallum and M. Tait (1986). "The application of exploratory factor analysis in applied psychology: a critical review and analysis." *Personnel Psychology* 39(2): 291-314.

Fram, M. S. and J. Kim (2008). "Race/ethnicity and the start of child care: A multi-level analysis of factors influencing first child care experiences." *Early Childhood Research Quarterly* 23(4): 575-590.

Fraser, N. (1994). "After the Family Wage. Gender Equity and the Welfare State." *Political Theory* 22(4): 591-618.

Frerich, J. and M. Frey (1996). *Handbuch der Geschichte der Sozialpolitik in Deutschland. Band 2. Sozialpolitik in der Deutschen Demokratischen Republik*. München/Wien, Oldenbourg.

Frone, M. R., M. Russell and M. L. Cooper (1997). "Relation of work-fmaily conflict to health outcomes: A four-year longitudinal study of employed parentsq." *Journal of Occupational an Organizational Psychology* 70(4): 325-335.

Fuller, B., S. D. Holloway and X. Liang (1996). "Family Selection of Child-Care Centers: The Influence of Household Support, Ethnicity, and Parental Practices." *Child Development* 67(6): 3320-3337.

Gash, V. (2008). "Preference or constraint? Part-time workders' transitions in Denmark, France and the United Kingdom." *Work, employment and society* 22(4): 655-674.

Gauthier, A. H. (2007). "The impact of family policies on fertility in industrialized countries: a review of the literature." *Population Research and Policy Review* 26(3): 323-346.

Gauthier, A. H. and B. DeGusti (2012). "The time allocation to children by parents in Europe." *International Sociology* (published online 17 May 2012).

Gauthier, A. H. and J. Hatzius (1997). "Family benefits and fertility: An econometric analysis." *Population Studies* 51(3): 295-306.

Gauthier, A. H. and D. Philipov (2008). "Can policies enhance fertility in Europe?" *Vienna Yearbook of Population Research* 6: 1-16.

Geier, B. and B. Riedel (2008). Ungleichheiten der Inanspruchnahme öffentlicher frühpädagogischer Angebote. Einflussfaktoren und Restriktionen elterlicher Betreuungsentscheidungen. *Zeitschrift für Erziehungswissenschaft* 10(Sonderheft 11): 11-28.

Geisler, E. and M. Kreyenfeld (2012). How Policy Matters: Germany's Parental Leave Benefit Reform and Fathers' Behavior 1999-2009. *MPIDR Working Paper* 2012-021. Rostock, Max Planck Institute for Demographic Research.

Gerhard, U., T. Knijn and A. Weckwert, Eds. (2003). *Erwerbstätige Mütter. Ein europäischer Vergleich.* München, C.H. Beck.

Gerson, K. (1985). *Hard Choices. How Women Decide about Work, Career, and Motherhood* Berkeley/Los Angeles/London, University of California Press.

Goerres, A. and M. Tepe (2012). "Doing it for the Kids? The Determinants of Attitudes towards Public Childcare in Unified Germany." *Journal of Social Policy* 41(2): 349-372.

Goffman, E. (1959). *The presentation of self in everyday life.* New York, Doubleday Anchor.

Goldin, C. (1997). Career and Family: College Women Look to the Past. *Gender and Family Issues in the Workplace.* F. D. Blau and R. G. Ehrenberg (eds.). New York, Russell Sage Foundation: 20-58.

Goldin, C. (2006). "The Quiet Revolution That Transformed Women's Employment, Education, and Family." *American Economic Review* 96(2): 1-21.

Goldscheider, F. K. and E. Bernhardt (2011). Domestic Gender Equality and Childbearing in Sweden. *Domestic Gender Equality and Modern Family Patterns. Working Paper Series: EQUAL WP* 01. Stockholm, Stockholm University.

Goldstein, J. and M. Kreyenfeld (2011). "Has East Germany Overtaken West Germany? Recent Trends in Order-Specific Fertility." *Population and Development Review* 37(3): 453-472.

Goode, W. J. (1960). "A Theory of Role Strain." *American Sociological Review* 25(4): 483-496.

Gornick, J. C. and M. K. Meyers (2003). *Families That Work. Policies for Reconciling Parenthood and Employment.* New York, Russell Sage Foundation.

Gornick, J. C., M. K. Meyers and K. E. Ross (1997). "Supporting the Employment of Mothers: Policy Variation Across Fourteen Welfare States." *Journal of European Social Policy* 7(1): 45-70.

Gornick, J. C., M. K. Meyers and K. E. Ross (1998). "Public Policies and the Employment of Mothers: A Cross-National Study." *Social Science Quarterly* 79(1): 35-54.

Greenberg, J. P. (2011). "The impact of maternal education on children's enrollment in early childhood education and care." *Children and Youth Services Review* 33(7): 1049-1057.

Greenhaus, J. H. and N. J. Beutell (1985). "Sources of Confilct Between Work and Family Roles." *The Academy of Management Review* 10(1): 76-88.

Grossbard-Shechtman, S. (2001). "The New Home Economic at Columbia and Chicago." *Feminist Economics* 7(3): 103-130.

Grzywacz, J. and B. L. Bass (2003). "Work, Family, and Mental Health: Testing Different Models of Work-Family Fit." *Journal of Mariiage and Family* 65(1): 248-261.

Gustafsson, S. (2001). "Optimal Age at Motherhood. Theoretical and Empirical Considerations on Postponement of Maternity in Europe." *Journal of Population Economics* 14(2): 225-247.

Gustafsson, S. and M. Bruyn-Hundt (1991). "Incentives for Women to Work: A Comparison between The Netherlands, Sweden and West Germany." *Journal of Economic Studies* 18(5/6): 30-65.

Gustafsson, S. and F. Stafford (1992). "Child Care Subsidies and Labor Supply in Sweden." *The Journal of Human Ressources* 27(1, Special Issue on Child Care): 204-230.

Haas, L. (2003). "Parental Leave and Gender Equality: Lessons from the European Union." *Review of Policy Research* 20(1): 89-114.

Hagemann, K. (2006). "Between Ideology and Economy: The 'Time Politics' of Child Care and Public Education in the Two Germanys." *Social Politics* 13(2): 217-260.

Hakim, C. (2000). *Work-Lifestyle Choices in the 21st Century: Preference Theory*. Oxford, Oxford University Press.

Hakim, C. (2002). "Lifestyle Preferences as Determinants of Women's Differentiated Labor Market Careers." *Work and Occupations* 29(4): 428-459.

Hakim, C. (2003). "A New Approach to Explaining Fertility Patterns: Preference Theory." *Population and Development Review* 29(3): 349-374.

Han, W. and J. Waldfogel (2001). "Child care costs and women's employment: A comparison of single and married mothers with pre-school-aged children." *Social Science Quarterly* 82(3): 552-568.

Hank, K. (2002). "Regional Social Contexts and Individual Fertility Decisions: A Multilevel Analysis of First and Second Births in Western Germany." *European Journal of Population* 18(3): 281-299.

Hank, K. and I. Buber (2009). "Grandparents Caring for Their Grandchildren. Findings From the 2004 Survey of Health, Ageing, and Retirement in Europe." *Journal of Family Issues* 30(1): 53-73.

Hank, K. and M. Kreyenfeld (2003). "A Multilevel Analysis of Child Care and Women's Fertility Decisions in Western Germany." *Journal of Marriage and Family* 65(3): 584-596.

Hank, K., K. Tillmann and G. Wagner (2001). "Außerhäusliche Kinderbetreuung in Ostdeutschland vor und nach der Wiedervereinigung. Ein Vergleich mit Westdeutschland in den Jahren 1990-1999." *MPIDR Working Paper* 2001-003. Rostock, Max Planck Institute for Demographic Research.

Hantrais, L. (1994). "Comparing Family Policy in Britain, France and Germany." *Journal of Social Policy* 23(2): 135-160.

Hantrais, L. (2004). *Family policy matters. Responding to family change in Europe.* Bristol, Policy Press.

Hauser, R. (2008). "Problems of the German Contribution to EU-SILC – A research perspective, comparing EU-SILC, Microcensus and SOEP." *SOEPpapers on Multidisciplinary Panel Data Research No. 86. Berlin: DIW.*

Heckman, J. J. (1974). "Effects of Child-Care Programs on Women's Work Effort." *Journal of Political Economy* 82(No 2, Part 2: Marriage, Family Human Capital and Fertility): S136-S163.

Heimer, A., T. Knittel and H. Steidle (2009). *Vereinbarkeit von Familie und Beruf für Alleinerziehende.* Berlin, Bundesministerium für Familie, Senioren, Frauen und Jugend.

Henninger, A., C. Wimbauer and R. Dombrowski (2008). "Demography as a Push toward Gender Equality? Current Reforms of German Family Policy." *Social Politics* 15(3): 287-314.

Hiilamo, H. and O. Kangas (2009). "Trap for Women or Freedom to Choose? The Struggle over Cash for Child Care Schemes in Finland and Sweden." *Journal of Social Policy* 38(3): 457-475.

Hilgeman, C. and C. T. Butts (2009). "Women's employment and fertiliy: A welfare regime paradox." *Social Science Research* 38(1): 103-117

Hillmann, J. and A.-K. Kuhnt (2011). Der Kinderwunsch im Kontext von Partnerschaft und Partnerschaftsqualität: eine Analyse übereinstimmender Elternschaftsabsichten von Eltern und kinderlosen Paaren. *MPIDR Working Paper* 2011-019. Rostock, Max-Planck-Institut für demografische Forschung.

Himmelweit, S. and M. Sigala (2004). "Choice and the Relationship between Identities and Behaviour for Mothers with Pre-School Children: Some Implications for Policy from a UK Study." *Journal of Social Policy* 33(3): 455-478.

Hirshberg, D., D. S.-C. Huang and B. Fuller (2005). "Which low-income parents select child-care? Family demand and neighborhood organization." *Children and Youth Services Review* 27(10): 1119-1148.

Hobcraft, J. and K. Kiernan (1995). Becoming a parent in Europe *EAPS-IUSSP European population conference, Vol. 1*. Milan, Franco Angeli: 27-65.

Hochschild, A. R. (1989). *The Second Shift. Working Parents and the Revolution at Home*. New York, Viking.

Hochschild, A. R. (1995). "The Culture of Politics: Traditional, Postmodern, Cold-modern, and Warm-modern Idals of Care." *Social Politics* 2(3): 331-346.

Hoem, B. (2000). "Entry into motherhood in Sweden: the influence of economic factors on the rise and fall in fertility, 1986-1997." *Demographic Research* 2(4).

Hoem, B. and J. Hoem (1996). "Sweden's family policies and roller-coaster fertility." *Jinko mondai kenkyu. [Journal of population problems]* 52(3-4): 1-22.

Hoem, J. (2005). "Why does Sweden have such high fertility?" *Demographic Research* 13(22): 559-572.

Hoem, J. (2008). "The impact of public policies on European fertility." *Demographic Research* 19(10): 249-260.

Hoem, J., A. Prskawetz and G. Neyer (2001). "Autonomy or conservative adjustment? The effect of public policies and educational attainment on third births in Austria, 1975-96." *Population Studies* 55(3): 249-261.

Hoffman, L. W. and M. L. Hoffman (1973). The value of children to parents. *Psychological perspectives on population*. J. T. Fawcett (ed.). New York, Basis Books: 19-76.

Hook, J. L. (2006). "Care in Context: Men's Unpaid Work in 20 countries, 1965-2003." *American Sociological Review* 71(4): 639-660.

Hosmer, D. W. and S. Lemeshow (2000). *Applied logistic regression. 2nd edition.* New York, Wiley.

Hotz, V. J., J. A. Klerman and R. J. Willis (1997). The Economics of Fertility in Developed Countries. *Handbook of Population and Family Economics*. M. R. Rosenzweig and O. Stark (eds.). Amsterdam, Elsevier: 275-347.

Huinink, J. (2012). "Book Review: Jennifer A. Johnson-Hanks, Christine A. Bachrach, S. Philip Morgan, Hans-Peter Kohler: Understanding Family Change and Variation. Toward a Theory of Conjunctural Action." *European Journal of Population* 28(2): 235-237.

Huinink, J., J. Brüderl, B. Nauck, S. Walper, L. Castiglioni and M. Feldhaus (2011). "Panal Analysis of Intimate Relationships and Family Dynamics (*pairfam*): Conceptual framework and design." *Zeitschrift für Familienforschung* 23(1): 77-100.

Huinink, J. and D. Konietzka (2007). *Familiensoziologie. Eine Einführung*. Frankfurt, Campus.

Human Fertility Database 2013. Max Planck Institute for Demographic Research (Germany) and Vienna Institute of Demography (Austria). Retrieved April 7 2013 from www.humanfertility.org

Huston, A. C., Y. E. Chang and L. Gennetian (2002). "Family and individual predictors of child care use by low-income families in different policy contexts." *Early Childhood Research Quarterly* 17(4): 441-469.

Hynes, K. and M. Clarkberg (2005). "Women's Employment Patterns During Early Parenthood: A Group-Based Trajectory Analysis." *Journal of Marriage and Family* 67(1): 222-239.

Iacovou, M. and L. P. Tavares (2011). "Yearning, Learning, and Conceding: Reasons Men and Women Change Their Childbearing Intentions." *Population and Development Review* 37(1): 89-123.

Immervoll, H. and D. Barber (2006). Can Parents Afford to Work? Childcare Costs, Tax-Benefit Policies and Work Incentives. *IZA Discussion Paper* 1932.

Jaffee, S. R., C. Van Hulle and J. L. Rodgers (2011). "Effects of Nonmaternal Care in the First 3 Years on Children's Academic Skills and Behavioral Functioning in Childhoode and Early Adolescence: A Sibling Comparison Study." *Child Development* 82(4): 1076-1091.

Jansen, M. and A. C. Liefbroer (2006). "Couples' Attitudes, Childbirth, and the Division of Labor." *Journal of Family Issues* 27(11): 1487-1511.

Jaumotte, F. (2004). "Labour Force Participation of Women: Empirical Evidence on the Role of Policy and other Determinants in OECD countries." *OECD Economic Studies* 37(2003/2): 51-108.

Johansen, A. S., A. Leibowitz and L. J. Waite (1996). "The Importance of Child-Care Characteristics to Choice of Care." *Journal of Marriage and Family* 58(3): 759-772.

Johnson-Hanks, J., C. A. Bachrach, S. P. Morgan and H.-P. Kohler (2011). *Understanding Family Change and Variation. Toward a Theory of Conjunctural Action.* Dordrecht/Heidelberg/London/New York, Springer.

Joshi, H. (1998). "The Opportunity Costs of Childbearing: More than Mothers' Business." *Journal of Population Economics* 11(2): 161-183.

Kagitcibasi, C. and B. Ataca (2005). "Value of Children and Family Change: A Three-Decade Portrait From Turkey." *Applied Psychology* 54(3): 317-337.

Kahn, J. M. and J. P. Greenberg (2010). "Factors predicting early childhood education and care use by immigrant families." *Social Science Research* 39(4): 642-651.

Kangas, O. and T. Rostgaard (2007). "Preferences or institutions? Work-family life opportunities in seven European countries." *Journal of European Social Policy* 17(3): 240-256.

Kaptijn, R., F. Thomese, T. Tilburg and A. Liefbroer (2010). "How Grandparents Matter." *Human Nature* 21(4): 393-405.

Kaufman, G. (2000). "Do Gender Role Attitudes Matter?: Family Formation and Dissolution Among Traditional and Egalitarian Men and Women." *Journal of Family Issues* 21(1): 128-144.

214

Kaufmann, F.-X. (2002). Politics and Policies towards the Family in Europe: A Framework and an Inquiry into their Differences and Convergences. *Family Life and Family Policies in Europe. Volume 2. Problems and Issues in Comparative Perspective*. F.-X. Kaufmann, A. Kuijsten, H.-J. Schulze and K. P. Strohmeier (eds.). Oxford, Oxford University Press: 419-490.

Keck, W. and C. Saraceno (2011). Comparative childcare statistics in Europe. Conceptual and methodolgical fallacies. *Multilinks Insights* No. 1. Berlin, WZB – Social Science Research Center.

Kim, J.-O. and C. W. Mueller (1978a). *Factor Analysis. Statistical Methods and Practical Issues*. Newbury Park, Sage Publications.

Kim, J.-O. and C. W. Mueller (1978b). *Introduction To Factor Analysis. What It Is and How To Do It*. Newbury Park, Sage Publications.

Kim, J. and M. S. Fram (2009). "Profiles of choice: Parents' patterns of priority in child care decision-making." *Early Childhood Research Quarterly* 24(1): 77-91.

Klement, C., G. Müller and G. Prein (2007). Vereinbarkeit muss man sich leisten können. Zur Erklärung von Betreuungs- und Erwerbsarrangements in Familien mit Kindern unter drei Jahren. *Wer betreut Deutschlands Kinder? DJI-Kinderbetreuungsstudie. 2. Auflage* W. Bien, T. Rauschenbach and B. Riedel (eds.). Berlin/Düsseldorf/Mannheim, Cornelsen Scriptor: 237-253.

Klevmarken, N. A. and A. C. Tasiran (1996). "Is the decision 'to work' endogenous to the fertility process?" *Paper presented at the 10th annual meeting of ESPE,* June 13-15 1996, Uppsala.

Klobas, J. (2011). "The Theory of Planned Behavior as a model of reasoning about fertility decisions." *Vienna Yearbook of Population Research* 9: 47-54.

Kolvenbach, F.-J. and D. Taubmann (2006). Neue Statistiken zur Kindertagesbetreuung. *Wirtschaft und Statistik* 2/2006. Wiesbaden, Statistisches Bundesamt: 166-171.

Konietzka, D. and M. Kreyenfeld, eds. (2007). *Ein Leben ohne Kinder. Kinderlosigkeit in Deutschland*. Wiesbaden, VS Verlag für Sozialwissenschaften.

Konietzka, D. and M. Kreyenfeld (2010). "The growing educational divide in mothers' employment: an investigation based on the German micro-census 1976-2004." *Work, Employment & Society* 24(2): 260-278.

Kornstad, T. and T. O. Thoresen (2007). "A discrete choice model for labour supply and childcare." *Journal of Population Economics* 20(4): 781-803.

Korpi, W. (2000). "Faces of Inequality: Gender, Class, and Patterns of Inequalities in Different Types of Welfare States." *Social Politics* 7(2): 127-191.

Kotowska, I., A. Matysiak, M. Styrc, A. Pailhé, A. Solaz and D. Vignoli (2010). Second European Quality of Life Survey. Family life and work. Dublin, European Foundation for the Improvement of Living and Working Conditions.

Krapf, S. (forthcoming). "Who uses public childcare for 2-year-old children? Coherent family policies and usage patterns in Sweden, Finland and Western Germany." *International Journal of Social Welfare.*

Krapf, S. and M. Kreyenfeld (2011). *Soziale Unterschiede in der Nutzung externer Kinderbetreuung für Ein- bis Sechsjährige: Gibt es Veränderungen im Zeitraum 1984-2009? Expertise im Rahmen des 14. Kinder- und Jugendberichts.* München, Deutsches Jugendinstitut.

Kravdal, O. (1996). "How the local supply of day-care centers influences fertility in Norway: A parity-specific approach." *Population Research and Policy Review* 15(3): 201-218.

Kravdal, O. and R. R. Rindfuss (2008). "Changing Relationships between Education and Fertility: A Study of Women and Men Born 1940 to 1964." *American Sociology Review* 73(5): 854-873.

Kremer, M. (2007). *How Welfare States Care: Culture, Gender and Parenting in Europe.* Amsterdam, Amsterdam University Press.

Kreyenfeld, M. (2000). Educational attainment and first births: East Germany before and after unification. *MPIDR Working Paper* 2000-011. Rostock, Max Planck Institute for Demographic Research.

Kreyenfeld, M. (2001). *Employment and Fertility – East Germany in the 1990s.* Rostock, University of Rostock.

Kreyenfeld, M. (2002). "Time Squeeze, Partner Effect or Self-Selection?: An Investigation into the Positive Effect of Women's Education on Second Birth Risks in West Germany." *Demographic Research* 7(2): 15-48.

Kreyenfeld, M. (2004). Sozialstruktur und Kinderbetreuung. *MPIDR Working Paper* 2004-009. Rostock, Max Planck Institute for Demographic Research.

Kreyenfeld, M. (2010). "Uncertainties in Female Employment Careers and the Postponement of Parenthood in Germany." *European Sociological Review* 26(3): 351-366.

Kreyenfeld, M. and K. Hank (2000). "Does the availability of child care influence the employment of mothers? Findings from western Germany." *Population Research and Policy Review* 19(4): 317-337.

Kreyenfeld, M. and D. Konietzka (2008). Education and fertility in Germany. *Demographic Change in Germany. The Economic and Fiscal Consequences.* I. Hamm, H. Seitz and M. Werding (eds.). Berlin, Springer: 165-187.

Kreyenfeld, M. and S. Krapf (2010). Soziale Ungleichheit und Kinderbetreuung. Eine Analyse der sozialen und ökonomischen Determinanten der Nutzung von Kindertageseinrichtungen. *Bildung als Privileg. Erklärungen und Befunde zu den Ursachen der Bildungsungleichheit.* R. Becker and W. Lauterbach (eds.). Wiesbaden, VS Verlag: 107-128.

Kreyenfeld, M., R. Scholz, F. Peters and I. Wlosnewski (2011a). "Order-Specific Fertility Rates for Germany Estimates from Perinatal Statistics for the Period 2001-2008." *Comparative Population Studies* 35(2): 207-224.

Kreyenfeld, M., R. Walke, V. Salzburger, C. Schnor, S. Bastin and A.-K. Kuhnt (2011b). DemoDiff – Wave 1. Supplement to the pairfam Data Manual. *MPIDR Technical Report* 2011-004. Rostock, Max Planck Institute for Demographic Research.

Kreyenfeld, M., H. Trappe and J. Huinink (2012a). "DemoDiff: a dataset for the Study of Family Change in Eastern (and Western) Germany." *Zeitschrift für Wirtschafts- und Sozialwissenschaften/Schmollers Jahrbuch* 132(4): 653-660.

Kreyenfeld, M., R. Walke, T. Hensel, R. Lenke and B. M. Mousavi (2012b). DemoDiff. Supplement to the pairfam Data Manual. Release 2.0. Rostock, Max Planck Institute for Demographic Research.

Kulu, H., A. Vikat and G. Andersson (2007). "Settlement size and fertility in the Nordic countries." *Population Studies* 61(3): 265-285.

Lang, C. (2007). Institutionelle Kinderbetreuung. Erschwinglich für alle? *wer betreut Deutschlands Kinder? DJI Kinderbetreuungsstudie.* W. Bien, T. Rauschenbach and B. Riedel (eds.). Mannheim, Cornelsen Scriptor: 105-121.

Lange, J. (2008). Rechtliche Entwicklung im Bereich der Kindertagesbetreuung. *Zahlenspiegel 2007. Kindertagesbetreuung im Spiegel der Statistik.* München, Deutsches Jugendinstitut: 233-246.

Lappegård, T. (2010). "Family Policies and Fertility in Norway." *European Journal of Population* 26(1): 99-116.

Lappegård, T. and M. Rønsen (2005). "The Multifaceted Impact of Education on Entry into Motherhood." *European Journal of Population* 21(1): 31-49.

Lehrer, E. L. and S. Kawasaki (1985). "Child Care Arrangements and Fertility: An Analysis of Two-Earner Households." *Demography* 22(4): 499-513.

Leibowitz, A. (1994). Child Care: Private Cost or Public Responsibility? *Individual and Social Responsibility: Child Care, Education, Medical Care, and Long-Term Care in America.* V. R. Fuchs (ed.). Chicago, University of Chicago Press: 31-58.

Leira, A. (2002). *Working Parents and the Welfare State. Family Changes and Policy Reform in Scandinavia.* Cambridge, University Press.

Leitner, S. (2005). Kind und Karriere für alle? Geschlechts- und schichtspezifische Effekte rot-grüner Familienpolitik. *Blätter für deutsche und internationale Politik* 50(8): 958-964.

Leitner, S. (2010). "Germany outpaces Austria in childcare policy: the historical contingencies of a 'conservative' childcare policy." *Journal of European Social Policy* 20(5): 456-467.

Lesthaeghe, R., Ed. (2002). *Meaning and choice: Value orientations and life course decisions.* The Hague/Brussels, NIDI/CBGS Publications.

Lesthaeghe, R. and G. Moors (2002). Life Course Transitions and Value Orientations: Selection and Adaptation. *Meaning and Choice: Value*

Orientations and Life Course Decisions. R. Lesthaeghe. The Hague/Brussels, NIDI/CBGS Publications.

Letablier, M.-T., A. Luci, A. Math and O. Thévenon (2009). The costs of raising children and the effectiveness of policies to support parenthood in European countries: a Literature Review. Brussels, European Commision.

Leu, H. R. (2002). Außerfamiliale Formen der Betreuung, Bildung und Erziehung von Kindern in der Diskussion. *Zahlenspiegel. Daten zu Tageseinrichtungen für Kinder. Kindertageseinrichtungen in Stadtteilen mit besonderem Entwicklungsbedarf*. München, Deutsches Jugendinstitut.

Lewis, J. (1992). "Gender and the Development of Welfare Regimes." *Journal of European Social Policy* 2(3): 159-173

Lewis, J. (2001). "The Decline of the Male Breadwinner Model: Implications for Work and Care." *Social Politics* 8(2): 152-169.

Lewis, J. and I. Ostner (1994). Gender and the Evolution of European Social Policies. *ZeS-Arbeitspapiere* Nr. 4/94. Centre for Social Policy Research, University of Bremen.

Liefbroer, A. C. (2005). "The Impact of Perceived Costs and Rewards of Childbearing on Entry into Parenthood: Evidence from a Panel Study." *European Journal of Population* 21(4): 367-391.

Liefbroer, A. C. (2011). "On the usefulness of the Theory of Planned Behavior for fertility research." *Vienna Yearbook of Population Research* 9: 55-62.

Liefbroer, A. C. and M. Corijn (1999). "Who, What, Where, and When? Specifying the Impact of Educational Attainment and Labour Force Participation on Family Formation." *European Journal of Population* 15(1): 45-75.

Linton, R. (1936). *The Study of Man. An Introduction*. New York, Appleton-Century-Crofts.

Mamolo, M., L. Coppola and M. Di Cesare (2011). "Formal Childcare Use and Household Socio-economic Profile in France, Italy, Spain and UK." *Population Review* 50(1): 170-194.

Mandel, H. and M. Shalev (2009). "How Welfare States Shape the Gender Pay Gap: A Theoretical and Comparative Analysis." *Social Forces* 87(4): 1873-1912.

Manow, P. and E. Seils (2000). Adjusting Badly The German Wlefare State, Structural Change and the Open Economy. *Welfare and Work in the Open Economy. Volume II. Diverse Responses to Common Changes*. F. W. Scharpf and V. A. Schmidt (eds.). New York, Oxford University Press: 264-307.

Mason, K. O. and K. Kuhlthau (1989). "Determinants of Child Care Ideals among Mothers of Preschool-Aged Children." *Journal of Marriage and Family* 51(3): 593-603.

Mason, K. O. and K. Kuhlthau (1992). "The Perceived Impact of Child Care Costs on Women's Labor Supply and Fertility." *Demography* 29(4): 523-543.

Matysiak, A. (2011). *Interdependencies Between Fertility and Women's Labour Supply.* Dordrecht/Heidelberg/London/New York, Springer.

Matysiak, A. and S. Steinmetz (2008). "Finding Their Way? Female Employment Patterns in West Germany, East Germany, and Poland." *European Sociological Review* 24(3): 331-345.

May, P. J., J. Sapotichne and S. Workman (2006). "Policy Coherence and Policy Domains." *The Policy Studies Journal* 34(3): 381-403.

McDonald, P. (2000a). "Gender Equity, Social Insitutions and the Future of Fertility." *Journal of Population Research* 17(1): 1-16.

McDonald, P. (2000b). "Gender Equity in Theories of Fertility Transition." *Population and Development Review* 26(3): 427-439.

McDonald, P. (2002). "Sustaining Fertility through Public Policy: The Range of Options." *Population* 57(3): 417-446.

McDonald, P. (2006). "Low Fertility and the State: The Efficacy of Policy." *Population and Development Review* 32(3): 485-510.

McDonald, P., K. Brown and L. Bradley (2005). "Explanations for the provision-utilisation gap in work-life policy." *Women In Management Review* 20(1): 37-55.

McLaughlin, E. and C. Glendinning (1994). Paying for care in Europe: is there a feminist approach? . *Family policy and the welfare of women.* L. Hantrais and S. Mangen (eds.). Loughborough, University of Loughborough: 52-69.

Merz, E.-M. and A. C. Liefbroer (2012). "The Attitude Toward Voluntary Childlessness in Europe: Cultural and Institutional Explanations." *Journal of Marriage and Family* 74(3): 587-600.

Meulders, D. and S. O'Dorchai (2007). The position of mothers in a comparative welfare state perspective. *Social Policies, Labour Markets and Motherhood. A Comparative Analysis of European Countries.* D. Del Boca and C. Wetzels (eds.). Cambridge, Campridge University Press: 3-27.

Michalopoulos, C. and P. K. Robins (2002). "Employment and child-care choices of single-parent families in Canada and the United States." *Journal of Population Economics* 15(3): 465-493.

Milewski, N. (2007). "First child of immigrant workers and their descendants in West Germany: Interrelation of events, disruption, or adaptation?" *Demographic Research* 17(29): 859-896.

Miller, W. and D. J. Pasta (1993). "Motivational and Nonmotivational Determinants of Child-Number Desires." *Population and Environment* 15(2): 113-138.

Miller, W. and D. J. Pasta (1994). "The psychology of child timing: A measurement instrument and a model." *Journal of Applied Social Psychology* 24(3): 221-250.

Miller, W. and D. J. Pasta (1995). "Behavioral intentions: Which ones predict fertility behavior in married couples?" *Journal of Applied Social Psychology* 25(6): 530-555.

Miller, W., L. Severy and D. J. Pasta (2004). "A framework for modelling fertility motivation in couples." *Population Studies* 58(2): 193-205.

Mills, M., L. Mencarini, M. L. Tanturri and K. Begall (2008). "Gender equity and fertility intentions in Italy and the Netherlands." *Demographic Research* 18(1): 1-26.

Mills, M., R. R. Rindfuss, P. McDonald and E. te Velde (2011). "Why do people postpone parenthood? Reasons and social policy incentives." *Human Reproduction Update* 17(6): 848-860.

Mincer, J. (1962). Labor Force Participation of Married Women: A Study of Labor Supply. *Aspects of Labor Economics*. National Bureau of Economic Research (ed.). Princeton/New Jersey, Princeton University Press: 63-106.

Mincer, J. (1963). Market Price, Opportunity Costs, and Income Effects. *Measurement in Economics*. C. Christ (ed.). Stanford/California, Stanford University Press: 66-82.

Ministry of Health and Social Affairs (2007). Financial support for families with children. Stockholm, Ministry of Health and Social Affairs Sweden.

Mischke, M. (2011). "Types of Public Family Support: A Cluster Analysis of 15 European Countries." *Journal of Comparative Policy Analysis* 13(4): 443-456.

Misra, J., M. Budig and S. Moller (2007). "Reconciliation Policies and the Effects of Motherhood on Employment, Earnings and Poverty." *Journal of Comparative Policy Analysis* 9(2): 135-155.

Moen, P. (2003). *It's about Time. Couples and Careers*. Ithaca, Cornell University Press.

Moen, P., M. A. Erickson and D. Dempster-McClain (1997). "Their Mother's Daughters? The Intergenerational Transmission of Gender Attitudes in a World of Changing Roles." *Journal of Marriage and Family* 59(2): 281-293.

Moors, G. (2003). "Estimating the reciprocal effect of gender role attitudes and family formation: A log-linear path model with latent variables." *European Journal of Population* 19(2): 199-221.

Moors, G. (2008). "The Valued Child. In Search of a Latent Attitude Profile that Influences the Transition to Motherhood." *European Journal of Population* 24(1): 33-57.

Moors, G. and E. Bernhardt (2009). "Splitting Up or Getting Married?: Competing Risk Analysis of Transition Among Cohabiting Couples in Sweden." *Acta Sociologica* 52(3): 227-247.

Morgan, K. J. and K. Zippel (2003). "Paid to Care: The Origins and Effects of Care Leave Policies in Western Europe." *Social Politics* 10(1): 49-85.

Morgan, S. P. and C. A. Bachrach (2011). "Is the Theory of Planned Behaviour an appropriate model for human fertility?" *Vienna Yearbook of Population Research* 9: 11-18.

Moscovici, S. (1985). Social Influence and Conformity. *The Handbook of Social Psychology Volume II*. G. Lindzey and E. Aronson (eds.). New York, Random House: 347-412.

Moss, P. (2010). *International Review of Leave Policies and Related Research 2010*. London, Department for Business, Innovation and Skills.

Multilinks (2011). *Multilinks Database on Intergenerational Policy Indicators. Version 2.0*. Multilinks and Wissenschaftszentrum Berlin für Sozialforschung (WZB). Retrieved April 7 2013 from http://multilinks-database.wzb.eu/

Nauck, B. (1989). "Intergenerational relationships in families from Turkey and Germany." *European Sociological Review* 5(3): 251-274.

Nauck, B. (2001). "Der Wert von Kindern für ihre Eltern. "Value of Children" als spezielle Handlungstheorie des generativen Verhaltens und von Generationenbeziehungen im interkulturellen Vergleich." *Kölner Zeitschrift für Soziologie und Sozialpsychologie* 53(3): 407-435.

Nauck, B. (2007). "Value of Children and the Framing of Fertility: Results from a Cross-cultural Comparative Survey in 10 Societies." *European Sociological Review* 23(5): 615-629.

Nauck, B., J. Brüderl, J. Huinink and S. Walper (2012). *Beziehungs- und Familienpanel (pairfam)*. GESIS Datenarchiv, Köln. ZA5678 Datenfile Version 3.0.0, doi:10.4232/pairfam.5678.3.0.0

Naumann, I. K. (2005). "Child care and feminism in West Germany and Sweden in the 1960s and 1970s." *Journal of European Social Policy* 15(1): 47-63.

Neumann, M. J. (2009). The Politics of (De)centralisation: Early Care and Education in France and Sweden. *Child Care and Preschool Development in Europe. Institutional Perspectives*. K. Scheiwe and H. Willekens (eds). Hounmills, Palgrave Macmillan: 157-179.

Neyer, G. (2003a). Family Policies and Low Fertility in Western Europe. *MPIDR Working Paper* 2003-021. Rostock, Max Planck Institute for Demographic Research.

Neyer, G. (2003b). Gender and Generations Dimensions in Welfare-State Policies. *MPIDR Working Paper* 2003-022. Rostock, Max Planck Institute for Demographic Research.

Neyer, G. (2006). Family policies and fertility in Europe: Fertility policies at the intersection of gender policies, employment policies and care policies. *MPIDR Working Paper* 2006-010. Rostock, Max Planck Institute for Demographic Research.

Neyer, G. and G. Andersson (2008). "Consequences of Family Policies on Childbearing Behavior: Effects or Artifacts?" *Population and Development Review* 34(4): 699-724.

Neyer, G. and D. Rieck (2009). Moving Towards Gender Equality. *How Generations and Gender Shape Demographic Change. Towards Policies Based on Better Knowledge.* UNECE (ed.). Geneva, United Nations: 139-154.

Nyberg, A. (2004). "Parental Leave, Childcare and the Dual Earner/Dual Carer-Model in Sweden." *Swedish National Institute of Working Life, Discussion Paper* April 2004.

Nyberg, A. (2010). Cash-for-childcare schemes in Sweden: history, political contradictions and recent developments. *Cash-for-Childcare. The Consequences for Caring Mothers.* J. Sipilä, K. Repo and T. Rissanen (eds.). Cheltenham, UK/Northampton, MA, USA, Edward Elgar: 65-88.

O'Connor, J. (1993). "Gender, Class and Citizenship in the Comparative Analysis of Welfare State Regimes: Theoretical and Methodological Issues." *The British Journal of Sociology* 44(3): 501-518.

OECD (2007). *Babies and Bosses: Reconciling Work and Family Life. A Synthesis of Findings for OECD Countries.* Paris, OECD.

OECD (2011a). *Education at a Glance 2011: OECD Indicators.* Paris, OECD Publishing.

OECD (2011b). *Doing Better for Families.* Paris, OECD Publishing.

Oláh, L. S. and E. M. Bernhardt (2008). "Sweden: Combining childbearing and gender equality." *Demographic Research* 19(28): 1105-1143.

Orloff, A. S. (1993). "Gender and the Social Rights of Citizenship: The Comparative Analysis of Gender Relations and Welfare States." *American Sociological Review* 58(3): 303-328.

Östberg, V. (2000). "Children's living conditions in Sweden. Social patterns and trends in parental accessibility, child care and economic resources." *International Journal of Social Welfare* 9(1): 64-75.

Ostner, I. (2010). "Farewell to the Family as We Know it: Family Policy Change in Germany." *German Policy Studies* 6(1): 211-244.

Pampel, F. (2011). "Cohort change, diffusion, and support for gender egalitarianism in cross-national perspective." *Demographic Research* 25(21): 667-694.

Parsons, T. (1959). The social structure of the family. *The family: its function and destiny. Revised edition.* R. Nanda (ed.). Ney York, Harper and Brothers: 241-274.

Pestoff, V. and P. Strandbrink (2004). TSFEPS Project: Changing Family Structures and Social Policy: Child Care Services in Europe and Social Cohesion. Case Study Sweden, EMES. European Research Network.

Pettit, B. and J. L. Hook (2005). "The Structure of Women's Employment in Comparative Perspective." *Social Forces* 84(2): 779-801.

Petty, R. E., D. T. Wegener and L. R. Fabrigar (1997). "Attitudes and Attitude Change." *Annual Review of Psychology* 48: 609-647.

Pfau-Effinger, B. (1999). "Change of Family Policies in the Socio-Cultural Context of European Societies." *Comparative Social Research* 18: 135-159.

Philipov, D. (2009). "The Effect of Competing Intentions and Behaviour on Short-Term Childbearing Intentions and Subsequent Childbearing." *European Journal of Population* 25(4): 525-548.

Philipov, D. (2011). "Theories on fertility intentions: a demographer's perspective." *Vienna Yearbook of Population Research* 9: 37-45.

Philipov, D. and L. Bernardi (2011). "Concepts and Operationalisation of Reproductive Decisions Implementation in Austria, Germany and Switzerland." *Comparative Population Studies* 36(2-3): 495-530.

Philipov, D., O. Thévenon, J. Klobas, L. Bernardi and A. C. Liefbroer (2009). Reproductive Decision-Making in a Macro-Micro Perspective (REPRO). State-of-the-Art Review. *European Demographic Research Papers* 1. Vienna, Vienna Institute of Demography of the Austrian Academy of Sciences.

Plantenga, J., C. Remery, M. Siegel and L. Sementini (2008). "Childcare Services in 25 European Union Member States: the Barcelona Targets Revisited." *Comparative Social Research* 25: 27-53.

Polachek, S. W. (1981). "Occupational Self-Selection: A Human Capital Approach to Sex Differences in Opccupationl Structures." *The Review of Economics and Statistics* 63(1): 60-69.

Pollak, R. A. and S. C. Watkins (1993). "Cultural and Economic Approaches to Fertility: Proper Marriage or Mesalliance?" *Population and Development Review* 19(3): 467-496.

Presser, H. B. and W. Baldwin (1980). "Child Care as a Constraint on Employment: Prevalence, Correlates, and Bearing on the Work and Fertility Nexus." *American Journal of Sociology* 85(5): 1202-1213.

Puur, A., L. S. Oláh, M. I. Tazi-Preve and J. Dorbritz (2008). "Men's childbearing desires and views of the male role in Europe at the dawn of the 21st century." *Demographic Research* 19(56): 1883-1912.

Rabe-Hesketh, S. and A. Skrondal (2008). *Multilevel and Longitudinal Modeling Using Stata. Second Edition.* College Station, Texas, Stata Press.

Radey, M. and K. L. Brewster (2007). "The influence of race/ethnicity on disadvantaged mothers' child care arrangements." *Early Childhood Research Quarterly* 22(3): 379-393.

Raudenbusch, S. W. and A. S. Bryk (2002). *Hierarchical Linear Models.* Newbury Park, CA, Sage.

Rauhala, P.-L. (2009). Child Care as an Issue of Equality and Equity: The Example of the Nordic countries. *Child Care and Preschool Development in Europe.* K. Scheiwe and H. Willekens (eds.). New York, Palgrave Macmillan: 142-156.

Rauschenbach, T. (2007). Wer betreut Deutschlands Kinder? Eine einleitende Skizze. *Wer betreut Deutschlands Kinder? DJI-Kinderbetreuungsstudie.* W. Bien, T. Rauschenbach and B. Riedel (eds.). Mannheim, Cornelsen Skriptor: 9-24.

Repo, K. (2003). On the Nordic Social Care Model: Finland as an Example. *SARE meeting,* October 13-14 2003. Donostia-San Sabastian.

Rindfuss, R. R. and K. L. Brewster (1996). "Childrearing and Fertility." *Population and Development Review* 22(Supplement: Fertility in the United States: New Patterns, New Theories): 258-289.

Rindfuss, R. R., D. Guilkey, S. P. Morgan, O. Kravdal and K. B. Guzzo (2007). "Child Care Availability and First-Birth Timing in Norway." *Demography* 44(2): 345-372.

Rindfuss, R. R., D. K. Guilkey, S. P. Morgan and O. Kravdal (2010). "Child-Care Availability and Fertility in Norway." *Population and Development Review* 36(4): 725-748.

Rindfuss, R. R., K. B. Guzzo and S. P. Morgan (2003). "The changing institutional context of low fertility." *Population Research and Policy Review* 22(5-6): 411-438.

Ronsen, M. (2004). "Fertility and Public Policies – Evidence from Norway and Finland." *Demographic Research* 10(6): 143-170.

Ronsen, M. and K. Skrede (2010). "Can public policies sustain fertility in the Nordic countries? Lessons from the past and questions for the future." *Demographic Research* 22(13): 321-346.

Rosenfeld, R. A., H. Trappe and J. C. Gornick (2004). "Gender and Work in Germany: Before and after Reunification." *Annual Review of Sociology* 30: 103-124.

Rosina, A. and M. R. Testa (2009). "Couples' First Child Intentions and Disagreement: An Analysis of the Italian Case." *European Journal of Population* 25(4): 487-502.

Rossier, C., S. Brachet and A. Salles (2011). "Family policies, norms about gender roles and fertility decisions in France and Germany." *Vienna Yearbook of Population Research* 9: 259-282.

Rovny, A. E. (2011). "Welfare state policy determinants of fertility level: A comparative analysis." *Journal of European Social Policy* 21(4): 335-347.

Ruckdeschel, K. (2008). Gender and Fertility. Attitudes Towards Gender Roles and Fertility Behaviour. *People, Population Change and Policies. Lessons from the Population Policy Acceptance Study Volume 2: Demographic Knowledge – Gender – Ageing.* C. Höhn, D. Avramov and I. Kotowska (eds.). Dordrecht, Springer: 175-192

Ruhm, C. J. (2011). "Policies to Assist Parents with Young Children." *The Future of Children* 21(2; Work and Family): 37-68.

Sainsbury, D., Ed. (1994). *Gendering Welfare States.* London, Sage.

Sainsbury, D. (1996). *Gender, Equality and Welfare States*. Cambridge, Cambridge University Press.

Salmi, M. (2006). Parental choice and the passion for gender equality in Finland. *Politicising parenthood in Scandinavia. Gender relations in welfare states*. A. L. Ellingsæter and A. Leira (eds.). Bristol, The Policy Press: 145-168.

Samuelsson, I. and S. Sheridan (2004). "Recent Issues in the Swedish Preschool." *International Journal of Early Childhood* 36(1): 7-22.

Sanchez, L. and E. Thomson (1997). "Becoming Mothers and Fathers. Parenthood, Gender, and the Division of Labor." *Gender & Society* 11(6): 747-772.

Saraceno, C. (1984). "The Social Construction of Childhood: Child Care and Education Policies in Italy and theUnited States." *Social Problems* 31(3): 351-363.

Saraceno, C. (2011). "Childcare needs and childcare policies: A multidimensional issue." *Current Sociology* 59(1): 78-96.

Saraceno, C. and W. Keck (2008). The institutional framework of intergenerational family obligations in Europe: A conceptual and methodological overview. Berlin, WZB/Multilinks.

Saraceno, C., & Keck, W. (2011). Towards an integrated approach for the analysis of gender equity in policies supporting paid work and care responsibilities. *Demographic Research, 25*(11), 371-406.

Sayer, L. (2005). "Gender, Time and Inequality: Trends in Women's and Men's Paid Work, Unpaid Work and Free Time." *Social Forces* 84(1): 285-303.

SCB (2010a). Tabell 2.3 in Utbildningsstatistisk årsbok 2010. Tabeller. [Table 2.3 in Yearbook of Educational Statistics 2010. Tables.]. Örebro, SCB.

SCB (2010b). Women and Men in Sweden. Facts and figures 2010. Örebro, Statistics Sweden.

SCB (2013). Tabell 2.3 in Utbildningsstatistisk årsbok 2013. Tabeller. [Table 2.3 in Yearbook of Educational Statistics 2013. Tables.]. Örebro, SCB.

Schmitt, C. and H. Trappe (2010). "Gender relations in Central and Eastern Europe – Change or continuity?" *Zeitschrift für Familienforschung* 22(3): 261-265.

Schneider, S. and W. Müller (2009). Measurement of Education in EU-SILC – Preliminiary Evaluation of Measurement Quality. *Equalsoc Working Paper* 2009/5.

Schnell, R., P. B. Hill and E. Esser (1999). *Methoden der empirischen Sozialforschung. 6. Auflage*. München, Oldenbourg.

Schultz, T. P. (1969). "An Economic Model of Family Planning and Fertility." *Journal of Political Economy* 77(2): 153-180.

Scott, J. (2006). "Family and Gender Roles: How Attitudes Are Changing." *GeNet Working Paper* No. 21. Economic and Social Research Council.

Sheppard, B. H., J. Hartwick and P. R. Warshaw (1988). "The Theory of Reasoned Action: A Meta-Analysis of Past Research with Recommendations for Modifications and Future Research." *Journal of Consumer Research* 15(3): 325–343.

Singer, J. D. and J. B. Willett (1993). "It's about Time: Using Discrete-Time Survival Analysis to Study Duration and the Timing of Events." *Journal of Educational Statistics* 18(2): 155-195.

Sjöberg, O. (2004). "The role of family policy institutions in explaining gender-role attitudes: a comparative multilevel analysis of thirteen industrialized countries." *Journal of European Social Policy* 14(2): 107-123.

Sjöberg, O. (2010). "Ambivalent Attitudes, Cotradicotry Institutions: Ambivalence in Gender-Role Attitudes in Comparative Perspective." *International Journal of Comparative* 51(1-2): 33-57.

Skolverket (2007). Five years with the maximum fee. English summary of report 294. Stockholm, Skolverket.

Sleebos, J. (2003). Low Fertility in OECD Countries: Facts and Policy Responses. *OECD Social, Employment and Migration Working Paper.* NO. 15.

Sobotka, T. (2004). "Is Lowest-Low Fertility in Europe Explained by the Postponement of Childbearing?" *Population and Development Review* 30(2): 195-220.

Sorensen, A. and H. Trappe (1995). Frauen und Männer: Gleichberechtigung – Gleichstellung – Gleichheit? *Kollektiv und Eigensinn. Lebensverläufe in der DDR und danach.* J. Huinink, K.-U. Mayer, M. Diewald, H. Solga, A. Sørensen, and H. Trappe (eds.). Berlin, Akademie Verlag: 189-222.

Stadelmann-Steffen (2011). "Dimensions of Family Policy and Female Labor Market Participation: Analyzing Group-Specific Policy Effects." *Governance: An International Journal of Policy, Administration and Institutions* 24(2): 331-357.

Stähli, M. E., J.-M. Le Goff, R. Levy and E. Widmer (2009). "Wishes or Constraints? Mothers' Labour Force Participation and its Motivation in Switzerland." *European Sociological Review* 25(3): 333-348.

Statistisches Bundesamt 2011a, Kinder- und Jugendhilfestatistiken, Tageseinrichtungen für Kinder. Verfügbare Plätze in Tageseinrichtungen für Kinder am 31.12.1990 nach Art der Plätze und Platz-Kind-Relation nach Ländern. Wiesbaden, Statistisches Bundesamt.

Statistisches Bundesamt 2011b, Kinder- und Jugendhilfestatistiken, Tageseinrichtungen für Kinder. Verfügbare Plätze in Tageseinrichtungen für Kinder am 31.12.1991 nach Art der Plätze und Platz-Kind-Relation nach Ländern. Wiesbaden, Statistisches Bundesamt.

Stefansen, K. and G. R. Farstad (2010). "Classed parental practices in a modern welfare state: Caring for the under threes in Norway." *Critical Social Policy* 30(1): 120-141.

Steiber, N. and B. Haas (2009). "Ideals or compromises? The attitude-behaviour relationship in mothers' employment." *Socio-Economic Review* 7(4): 639-668.

Sternitzky, A. and M. Putzing (1996). Kollabiert die Kinderversorgung? – Soziale Einrichtungen im Wandel. *Regionen im Vergleich: Gesellschaftlicher Wandel in Ostdeutschland am Beispiel ausgewählter Regionen.* H. Bertram (ed.). Opladen, Leske+Budrich: 17-39.

Streiner, D. L. (2003). "Starting at the Beginning: An Introduction to Coefficient Alpha and Internal Consistency." *Journal of Personality Assessment* 80(1): 99-103.

Strohmeier, K. P. (2002). Family Policy – How Does it Woork? *Family Life and Family Policies in Europe. Volume 2. Problems and Issues in Comparative Perspective.* F.-X. Kaufmann, A. Kuijsten, H.-J. Schulze and K. P. Strohmeier (eds.). Oxford, Oxford University Press: 321-362.

Surkyn, J. and R. Lesthaeghe (2004). "Value Orientation and the Second Demographic Transition (SDT) in Northern, Western and Southern Europe: An Update." *Demographic Research* Special Collection 3(3): 45-75.

Swedish National Agency for Education (2003). Descriptive data on childcare, schools and adult education in Sweden 2003. Stockholm, Swedish National Agency for Education.

Swedish National Agency for Education (2006). Descriptive data on pre-school activities, school-age childcare, schools and adult education in Sweden 2006. Stockholm, Swedish National Agency for Education.

Tesching, K. (2012). *Education and Fertility. Dynamic Interrelations between Women's Educational Level, Educational Field and Fertility in Sweden.* Stockholm, Stockholm University Demography Unit.

Thalberg, S. (2009). Money, Policy and Norms: Childbearing Behavior of Swedish Students in the 1980s and 1990s. *Stockholm Research Report in Demography,* SRRD-2009: 8.

Thévenon, O. (2011). Does Fertility Respond to Work and Family-life Reconciliation Policies in France? *Fertility and Public Policy. How to Reverse the Trend of Declining Birth Rates.* N. Takayama and M. Werding (eds.). Cambridge/Massachusetts, MIT Press: 219-259.

Thévenon, O. and K. Horko (2009). "Increased Women's Labour Force Participation in Europe: Progress in the Work-Life Balance or Polarization of Behaviour?" *Population* 64(2): 235-272.

Thomson, E. (1997). "Couple Childbearing Desires, Intentions, and Births." *Demography* 34(3): 343-354.

Thomson, E. (2002). Motherhood, Fatherhood and Family Values. *Meaning and Choice: Value Orientation and Life Course Decisions.* R. Lesthaeghe (ed.). The Hague/Brussels, NIDI/CBGS: 251-271.

Thomson, E. and J. Hoem (1998). "Couple Childbearing Plans and Births in Sweden." *Demography* 35(3): 315-322.

227

Tietze, W., H. G. Roßbach and K. Roitsch (1993). *Betreuungsangebote für Kinder im vorschulischen Alter. Ergebnisse einer Befragung von Jugendämtern in den alten Bundesländern.* Schriftenreihe des Bundesministeriums für Frauen und Jugend. Stuttgart, Kohlhammer.

Tomlinson, J. (2006). "Women's work-life balance trajectories in the UK: reformulating choice and constraint in transitions through part-time work across the life-course." *British Journal of Guidance & Counselling* 34(3): 365-382.

Tunberger, P. and W. Sigle-Rushton (2011). "Continuity and change in Swedish family policy reforms." *Journal of European Social Policy* 21(3): 225-237.

Turner, J. H. (2003). *The Structure of Sociological Theory. Seventh edition.* Belmont/USA, Wadsworth Publishing.

UNICEF (2008). The child care transition. A league table of early childhood education and care in economically advanced countries. Report Card 8. Florence, Innocenti Research Centre.

van Bavel, J. and J. Rózanska-Putek (2010). "Second birth rates across Europe: interactions between women's level of education and child care enrolment." *Vienna Yearbook of Population Research* 8: 107-138.

van der Lippe, T. and L. van Dijk (2002). "Comparative Research on Women's Employment." *Annual Review of Sociology* 28: 221-241.

van Gameren, E. and I. Ooms (2009). "Childcare and labor force participation in the Netherlands: the importance of attitudes and opinions." *Review of Economics of the Household.* 7(4): 395-421.

van Lancker, W. and J. Ghysels (2012). "Who benefits? The social distribution of subsidized childcare in Sweden and Flanders." *Acta Sociologica* 55(2): 125-142.

Vandenbroeck, M., S. De Visscher, K. Van Nuffel and J. Ferly (2008). "Mothers' search for infant child care: The dynamic relationship between availability and desirability in a continental European welfare state." *Early Childhood Research Quarterly* 23(2): 245-258.

Vatterrott, A. (2011). The fertility behaviour of East to West German migrants. *MPIDR Working Paper* 2011-013. Rostock, Max Planck Institute for Demographic Research.

Vikman, U. (2010). Does providing childcare to unemployed affect unemployment duration? *Working Paper* 2010: 5. Uppsala, IFAU Institute for Labour Market Policy Evaluation.

Vitali, A., F. C. Billari, A. Prskawetz and M. R. Testa (2009). "Preference Theory and Low Fertility: A Comparative Perspective." *European Journal of Population* 25(4): 413-438.

Wanders, F. (2012). Attrition in a Swedish Panel-study (YAPS). *YAPS Working Paper Series* 04/12. Stockholm, Stockholm University.

Wheelock, J. and K. Jones (2002). "Grandparents Are the Next Best Thing': Informal Childcare for Working Parents in Urban Britain." *Journal of Social Policy* 31(3): 441-463.

Willis, R. J. (1973). "A New Approach to the Economic Theory of Fertility Behavior." *Journal of Political Economy* 81(2): S14-S64.

Zuo, J. (2004). "Shifting the Breadwinning Boundary: The Role of Men's Breadwinner Status and Their Gender Ideologies." *Journal of Family Issues* 25(6): 811-832.

Index